THE PROVINCE OF STRATHNAVER

THE PROVINCE
OF
STRATHNAVER

Editor
John R. Baldwin

Associate Editor
William P.L. Thomson

SCOTTISH SOCIETY FOR NORTHERN STUDIES

Published in Scotland by:

The Scottish Society for Northern Studies
c/o School of Scottish Studies
University of Edinburgh
27 George Square
Edinburgh EH8 9LD

ISBN 0 9535226 0 1

Publication has been generously supported by:

Historic Scotland
National Museums of Scotland
Royal Commission on the Ancient and Historical
Monuments of Scotland

and

Iomairt Ghallaibh & Chataibh
Caithness & Sutherland
ENTERPRISE

Main text set in 10 on 11 Times

Printed by:
The Northern Times Ltd., Golspie, Sutherland, KW10 6RA, Scotland

CONTENTS

Editor's Preface   ix

The Medieval Province

Medieval Strathnaver
BARBARA E. CRAWFORD   1

A Scatter of Norse Names in Strathnaver
DOREEN WAUGH   13

A Viking Burial at Balnakeil, Sutherland
DOROTHY M. LOW, COLLEEN E. BATEY &
ROBERT GOURLAY   24

The Post-Medieval Province

From Clanship to Crofting: Landownership, Economy
and the Church in the Province of Strathnaver
MALCOLM BANGOR-JONES   35

Fearchar Lighiche and the Traditional Medicines
of the North
MARY BEITH   100

Working with Seaweed in North-West Sutherland
JOHN R. BALDWIN   116

Bighouse and Strath Halladale, Sutherland
ELIZABETH BEATON   143

The Excavation of a Turf Long-House at Lairg,
Sutherland
R.P.J. McCULLAGH   173

The Strathnaver Clearances in Modern Scottish Fiction:
History, Literary Perception and Memory
LAURENCE GOURIÉVIDIS   194

Pre-Medieval Times

Souterrains in Sutherland
ALEX. MORRISON   215

Palaeo-Environmental History of the Strathnaver
Area of Sutherland: 0 - 12,000 BP
JACQUELINE P. HUNTLEY   236

STRATH NAVERN

It toucheth at the East Catnes all alongst, upon the
west is Assyn at the south is Suthirland, and the great
green sea upon the north.

... This Province is devyded as followeth first Etyr a
Chewlis separat westward from Assyn, nixt to the
east therof is Durenish, more to the east followeth
West Moan then Kuntail, wherein is the Lord Chief
dwelling called Tung. Eastward from it is that part
which is cald Strath Naver therby understanding a part
of the countrey not the whole the last is Hallowdail
marching with Catnes.

from James Gordon of Rothiemay's mid 17th-century
Noates and Observations of dyvers parts of the
HIELANDS and ISLES of SCOTLAND
and most likely drawn from the
later 16th/early 17th-century papers of Timothy Pont.

(*Macfarlane's Geographical Collections.* Scottish History Society. 1907. vol II. 559)

PREFACE

Physical Background

West and south of lowland Caithness, the northern landmass is characterised by long winding valleys penetrating a core of mountains and moorland. The lower reaches of these straths generally terminate in substantial sea lochs or bays; middle and upper reaches frequently accommodate considerable expanses of freshwater; whilst relatively low land routes between the heads of the valleys have provided access and communication from earliest times.

Geologically, much of the area, particularly west of Loch Eriboll, is founded on unrelenting Lewisian gneiss, partly overlain with Torridonian sandstones, quartzite and sedimentary rocks laid down when a vast ocean covered what is now dry land. Folds, faults and granite intrusions interweave, with sedimentary strata further east overriding those to the west to give the Moine thrust – characterised by that bleak, eponymous expanse of moorland separating the Kyle of Tongue from Loch Eriboll. These low and boggy upland plateaux are punctuated by relatively isolated mountain massifs and have been heavily eroded by the force of wind, water and particularly glaciation. For it was glaciers that smoothed and striated the surface of the rocks and carved out the corries high up on such mountains as Ben Loyal, Ben Hope and Ben Klibreck; and it was glaciers that gouged out the deep troughs of lower Strath Naver, Loch Loyal and Loch Eriboll. It was the retreating glaciers, moreover, that deposited terminal moraines and large erratic boulders, and created moraine-dammed lochs; and it was meltwater that burst through to give the steep-sided gorges of the Armadale, Kirtomy and Swordly Burns. In addition, as the ice-caps melted, and their pressure on the landmass lessened, this landmass rose and one-time shorelines became the raised beaches and stranded sea cliffs around the mouths of the Borgie and the Naver rivers, at Bettyhill's Clachan Rock and elsewhere.

Heavy rainfall, generally low temperatures and but modest sunshine helped create extensive peat bogs and rough moorland that would provide good grazing. They also tended to restrict cultivation and settlement either to fluvio-glacial deposits and river-cut terraces in the lower valleys of such as Strath Halladale, Strath Naver, the Kyle of Tongue and Strath Dionard, or to a scatter of coastal locations often associated with fine sandy beaches or machair, or (in the case of Durness) a rare band of limestone.

Prehistoric Settlers

There is little to show for the earliest settlers beyond the occasional standing stone or cup-and-ring mark. The purpose of these monuments remains unclear: standing stones were possibly boundary or grave markers, whilst pecked circular hollows and rings such as those near Lochan Hakel, between

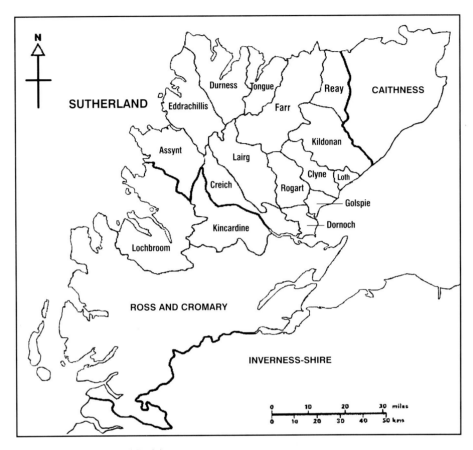

Map of Sutherland Parishes.

Ribigill and the Kyle of Tongue, may just conceivably have been some kind of decorative representation of a man-made landscape. By contrast, a considerable number of chambered burial cairns survive. These may be round, long or rectangular; they can also be oval, heel-shaped or with projecting corners or 'horns' suggesting forecourts. Re-used over considerable periods of time during the 4th/3rd millennia BC, there are significant examples at Skelpick, Skail and Coille na Borgie in Strathnaver.

Two or three thousands years separate these burial cairns from the fortified sites of the 1st millennium BC/1st millennium AD. Fortification is evidence of increasingly unsettled times, and hill-forts often betray several defensive 'rings'. In Strathnaver, such forts are commonly found on coastal headlands, where ditches and ramparts were engineered to cut off the landward side and provide protection for houses built within the enclosure –

Dun Mhairtein (Baligill), An Tornaidh Bhuidhe (Portskerra) and Seanachaisteal (Durness). Where such forts were small and built of stone, they are generally referred to as duns (Gaelic *dun*, a fort, fortified hill) – as at Durness, Loch Borralie and Borgie.

Brochs, however, were altogether more elaborate and sophisticated in their architecture, and probably constructed by specialist builders. Characteristically tall, and accessed by a single low narrow entrance, they comprised massively thick double walls – within which were stairs, galleries and chambers, including guard rooms flanking the entrance. Brochs, like duns, probably had thatched roofs to give shelter to activities taking place within the internal circular courtyard; they might also boast external buildings, abandoned when under attack. Examples survive beside the Armadale Burn, above Skelpick and at Grummore (Strath Naver), on Dun na Maigh (at the head of the Kyle of Tongue), at Dun Dornaigil/Dornadilla (south of Loch Hope) and at Clachtoll (Stoer).

Numerous hut circles or house sites, sometimes with nearby enclosures and field systems, can be of much the same date (although some may be much older, and others younger). So also are souterrains or earth-houses – slightly curved underground passages which were most likely used as storage chambers and approached from a house above. That so many hut circles and a number of souterrains have been found beyond the hill-dykes of later townships, suggests that at one time there were likely much greater numbers on lower land, swept away by subsequent ploughing. In other words, those surviving tend to confirm a one-time more attractive climate that encouraged settlement at a higher altitude. These were the ordinary, everyday farms and houses of those who, in times of trouble, would presumably retreat to their fortified duns and brochs.

In *The Province of Strathnaver*, '**Pre-Medieval Times**' offers two papers dealing with aspects of this prehistoric period. One traces environmental change through analyses of pollens and grains up to 12,000 years old; the other examines the underground earth-houses or souterrains in considerable detail, exploring their structure, functions and distribution across Sutherland.

Emerging Medieval Communities

It was the descendants and successors of these early peoples who were to become known as 'Picts' from around 300 AD – a name given them by others, rather than by themselves. Other than for a scatter of place-names and metalwork hoards, the main surviving evidence for the Picts lies in their carved stones. In general, Pictish stones are divided into three groups or classes – symbol stones without Christian symbols (probably later 7th - mid 8th century); stones with Pictish and Christian symbols (later 8th - 9th century); and cross-slabs with no Pictish symbols (maybe later 8th - 10th century). Though many have since been moved, the original locations of

Broch at Baile Mhargaite, west side of River Naver, Bettyhill. Sketches by
J. Horsburgh, 1867.

those in the first group, where known, are thought to correlate – at least in part – with the distribution of *pit* names and hill-forts: unsurprisingly, stones in the two later groups are often found in close association with ecclesiastical sites. Pictish stones from Sutherland and neighbouring Caithness include a symbol stone from Sandside and cross-slabs from Farr and Reay – as well as from Golspie, where there is a remarkable series of Class 1 stones. There is little agreement as to the significance of either the symbols or the stones' original locations, but they may have been territorial markers, or perhaps a permanent record of battles, marriages or other events or alliances. Then there are such as the Grumbeg cross-slabs from the shores of Loch Naver – one of which, albeit more roughly executed, shows similarities with the Isle Martin cross-slab, Clach Fear Eilean-Mhàirtein, in Lochbroom. For at some point following the union of the Picts and the Scots ca 843 AD, cross-slabs stop being 'Pictish' and become part of the legacy of the wider, Gaelic-speaking, early Celtic church in the north – part of a tradition that has left early monastic sites and place-names incorporating such elements as *annaid* and *cill*.

The Picts are referred to but obliquely in *The Province of Strathnaver*, as part of the search for **'The Medieval Province'**. In an attempt to help establish the area's extent and character, it is this section that opens the book. There are three interrelating contributions: a study of the origins and

Pictish symbol stones at Sandside, Caithness, 1991 (left) and Golspie, 1987.

Pictish cross-slabs at Reay (left) and Clachan, Bettyhill. 1991.

Cross-slabs from Grumbeg, Strathnaver, 1991. The carving on the right bears some resemblance to that on Isle Martin, Loch Broom.

evolution of the territory during Norse and immediately post-Norse times, an analysis of a Viking burial at Durness, and an exploration of Norse place-names along the north Sutherland coast and its straths. The Norse term for the Pentland Firth, *Pettalands-fjörðr*, helps confirm an indigenous tribal group prior to the arrival of both Norse and Gaelic speakers, whilst *Katanes*, initially applied to Duncansby Head, acknowledges this as the ness or promontory of the 'Catti'. This pre-Norse, pre-Gaelic-speaking people seems to have inhabited an area roughly similar to modern Caithness and Sutherland. The lands south of the Ord of Caithness were later designated *Suðrland* by the Norse (the southern part of *Katanes*), whilst that area west of lowland Caithness was referred to in the sagas as the 'Dales' of Caithness (*Dalir*). The contributors argue that the 'province' of Strathnaver likely equates with these 'dales', and should be seen as part of the earldom lands of Caithness. To the descendants of the incoming Gaelic speakers, however, Irish Scots who had penetrated north up the west coast and the Great Glen from their Dalriadic base, *Cataibh* continued to describe those one-time Pictish territories outwith the original *Katanes*. And it was only in much later times that the name 'Sutherland' spread to encompass the 'county' of the same name, following consolidation of their extended territories by the earls of Sutherland. The name, in other words, followed the family.

Post-Medieval Life and Society

As 'Strathnaver' emerges from the Norse and Celto-Norse periods, certain powerful interests came to the fore – notably the bishops of Caithness, the earls of Caithness, the earls of Sutherland and the Mackays. There is scant surviving evidence in the landscape for their early presence, however, particularly in the north and the west. Virtually nothing remains of modest castles, essentially tower houses, at Balnakeil and Borve – the latter a Mackay stronghold destroyed in 1556. And as for Caisteal Bharraich, overlooking Kirkiboll and the Kyle of Tongue, it has been associated variously with the 'Beruvik' of *Orkneyinga Saga*, with the bishops of Caithness (en route from their castle at Scrabster to their house and lands at Balnakeil), and with Angus Dubh Mackay – who may conceivably have built or rebuilt it ca 1420 following the Lordship charter of 1415.

The policies, influence and inter-relationships of these powerful interests, particularly the Mackays and the Sutherlands, dominate much of the ensuing centuries. With the help of written accounts by travellers and ministers, landowners and improvers, however, as well as an increasingly wide range of government, estate and other formal documents, it becomes possible to supplement the evidence of archaeology, place-names and early charters, and to explore not just the lives and lifestyles of these families, but those also of the ordinary people.

The underlying thread is of fundamental change. Particularly from the 18th century, there was increasingly less emphasis on a sense of mutual responsibility and inter-dependence. And no longer was the focus on working in harmony with the environment and living, as it were, through plants or animals – where domestic animals were nurtured for their multipurpose role as providers of energy, food and all manner of other useful things around the farm. Instead, animals and crops became end-products whose financial value was to be maximised by the increasingly intensive use of land and sea.

This was the philosophical framework within which sub-tenants, cottars, fishermen and kelpworkers came also to be seen primarily as wealth-creators for the landowners – resources to be maximised. If insufficient wealth were being created, then activities and practices had to be changed. In practical terms, this led to the removal of vast areas of hill-land and infield from community use and to the final disintegration of the old order. Local populations were evicted and relocated on marginal coastal lands; numbers of livestock were increased beyond any reasonable sustainable limit; new intensive sheep farms, once they became less profitable, were converted to sporting deer forests; new, mainly coastal holdings were established and further subdivided as population growth was encouraged; sub-tenants and cottars were obliged to neglect the seasonal work upon which their survival depended in order to maximise cash crops of fish and kelp. And when these new industries contracted or collapsed, emigration was used as a means of solving the problem of an expanded, impoverished and periodically starving population. For by the early 19th century, if not earlier, Highland communities in the north and west were no longer self-supporting in any balanced sense. The products of so much of their labour were exploited and exported by others; the modest income they received was returned in large part to landowners in the form of higher rents; and deprived of the multiple resources of their erstwhile lands, ordinary people became increasingly dependent upon basic subsistence strategies. Some landowners sought to stand by and help their tenants in times of want, and often suffered financially as a result, but they were increasingly a minority and most were eventually replaced by proprietors and factors whose backgrounds were more attuned to the maximisation of financial returns than to any obvious notion of mutual support.

Change of some kind had been inevitable. Economic systems were changing throughout Scotland, England and beyond, and the Highlands and Islands could not remain sheltered. Rather was it partly the nature of that change, but more particularly the way in which change was carried out, that gave rise to so much hardship, so much anger and so much bitterness.

The visible results of these changes remain scattered across the landscape – the fertile straths remain empty, punctuated by an occasional mains farm, shepherd's house or shooting lodge; the foundations of cleared townships are grazed by sheep or buried beneath forestry. Along with Patrick Sellar's early 19th-century house at Syre (Strath Naver), the likes of earlier Rossal or Grumbeg are ghostly reminders of landscapes once populated with thriving, broadly self-sufficient communities. Meantime, the once-congested, mainly coastal and linear post-clearance holdings (Laid is a good example, beside Loch Eriboll), are all-but abandoned nowadays as actively-crofted units, although they may well be grazed, ironically, by the crofters' sheep. The land was too poor, the holdings too small, and supplementary industries too precarious to encourage a dislocated population to survive there once more attractive opportunities had opened up in the towns, the Lowlands, England or further afield. Today's landscape is littered with the evidence of former croft houses, many now converted into second homes or holiday cottages; and the little harbours that were supposed to nurture the brave new fishing industries lie largely deserted – victims of uncertain or over-fished shoals, larger boats and the hazardous currents and seaways that were to be marked by lighthouses at Cape Wrath (1828), Stoer (1870) and Strathy Point (1958). Today, the likes of Port Vasgo and Talmine, Skullomie and Skerray, Portskerra and Strathy (along with such west coast jetties as Fanagmore or Tarbet) shelter at best a handful of small lobster, crab or prawn fishing boats. Nineteenth century ice-houses for salmon lie empty at Bettyhill and Bighouse, and new uses have been sought for fishery piers, houses and storehouses at Rispond (18th century) and Badcall Bay (19th-century). Meanwhile, long-abandoned ferry piers at Portnancon mark the most effective route to the other side of Loch Eriboll (to Heilam), prior to the building of a longer, tortuous, but more reliable road.

As for the more fertile agricultural land, improvements were pursued by landowners and their principal tenants after the manner of the Lowlands. The land was reorganised geometrically into large rectangular and enclosed fields, and drained; lime kilns (as at Ard Neackie and Baligill), along with increased amounts of dung and seaweed, provided the wherewithal to sweeten the soil and produce more luxuriant crops – not just barley and oats, but sown grasses and turnips better to keep and fatten cash-crop livestock. Substantial lairds' houses, sometimes successors to earlier castles, were either built, rebuilt or enlarged at Scourie, Balnakeil, Melness, Tongue and Bighouse; elaborate 19th-century steadings in lowland style (as at Tongue, Melness and Scourie) accommodated up-to-date agricultural machinery and in-wintered cattle; estate mills ground the grain (though small horizontal mills continued to be used by the small tenants in townships such as Kirtomy); and new roads and bridges helped improve communications both between individual valleys and with the south and east. By way of example, after the Earl of Sutherland acquired the Reay estate in 1829, he proceeded to link his old and new lands with a road over the Moine; and Moin House [sic] was built in 1830 as a refuge, approximately halfway across that bleak and inhospitable moor.

Finally, ecclesiastical evidence. Little survives from the medieval period, though at Crosskirk, a few miles east of Reay, the chancelled ruins of St Mary's Chapel, probably 12th century, echo the architecture of Northern Isles rather than Highland churches, and reflect the influence of the Orkney earldom. Otherwise, there had been medieval churches at Reay, Farr and Durness, with chapels in Strath Halladale, Strath Naver and at Kirkiboll.

Harbour at Port Skerra, 1974.

Lime kilns at Ard Neackie, Loch Eriboll, close by Heilam, the former ferry-point opposite Portnancon. 1983.

Steading at Tongue mains farm, 1974.

Late 18th century pulpit,
Farr Church, Bettyhill,
1985.

Post-Reformation churches include Balnakeil (Durness), built 1619, later extended, now roofless, but housing a fine 1619 armorial as well as the 1623 grave slab of Duncan MacMorrach. And a further 17th-century church, somewhat altered, survives at Tongue. A good, late 18th-century church survives at Bettyhill (now the Strathnaver Museum); there are 19th-century Parliamentary churches at Strathy (1828), Kinlochbervie (1829) and Stoer (1829), a post 1843 Disruption church at Strathy (ca 1845), and late 19th/ early 20th-century 'tin' (corrugated iron) churches at Syre and Torrisdale. This contrasting, and far from comprehensive array of church buildings betrays in part the growing need by the 19th-century to provide more conveniently situated places of worship for an increased population spread across a vast and inhospitable landmass; it also helps document the growing disenchantment with the established church and its ministers that accompanied the breakdown in relations between landowners and tenants as clearances intensified.

This then is the backdrop against which other contributors tease out a picture of everyday life in the later period. 'The Post-Medieval Province' continues the story of land-ownership, family feuding and the influence of the church. It also focuses on buildings, whether the excavation of an 18th/ 19th-century farmhouse near Lairg or architectural surveys of the 'big hooses' of Bighouse at the mouth of Strath Halladale; it explores 20th-century literary treatment of the clearances in the work of Neil Gunn, Fionn MacColla and Iain Crichton Smith; it delves into the collection and uses of seaweed around Loch Laxford and Badcall; and it takes a look at the survival of traditional healing following the collapse of the clans and the eclipse of such hereditary clan physicians as Fearchar Lighiche of Melness.

Acknowledgement

Several valuable collections about Sutherland have been published during the past 20 years. Donald Omand's *The Sutherland Book* (1982) gives a good general introduction to the natural and historical environment, and includes more specific studies of themes such as agriculture, fisheries, place-names and folklore. It was followed in 1987 by Alex. Morrison's *North Sutherland Studies* – a short collection of papers from the Scottish Vernacular Buildings Group, with a particular focus on domestic buildings and settlement history around Strathnaver and Skerray before and after the Clearances. Subsequently, Elizabeth Beaton's *Sutherland: An Illustrated Architectural Guide* (1995) provides a crisp introduction to the area's built environment.

The Scottish Society for Northern Studies' conference at Bettyhill in 1992 sought to complement rather than duplicate earlier studies. *The Province of Strathnaver*, therefore, concentrates mainly on new research, some of which was presented at the conference and some of which has been completed since. In line with earlier practice in the Society's monograph series, certain chapters also reflect more extensive and detailed studies. It is a wide-ranging, multi-disciplinary collection, frequently site- or area-specific, and the Society is pleased to record its gratitude to all contributors. In a climate of continually increasing pressures and restrictions, we well recognise how difficult it can be to find the time and resources to carry out new research and to prepare it for publication. We would also express particular thanks to Jim Johnston and Pat and Elliot Rudie (Bettyhill) for unstinting help before and during the Society's Conference, and for much friendly advice thereafter; and to Jim Johnston for so freely making available both geological material for inclusion in this Preface and a selection of illustrations. As always, warm thanks are due to Donald Omand (Scrabster) and colleagues in the Department of Continuing Education, University of Aberdeen; and it is a particular pleasure to record the contribution of Willie Thomson, Burray, Orkney, in reading and commenting on all of the papers.

For grants towards publication, the Society much appreciates the support of Historic Scotland and Caithness and Sutherland Enterprise. In addition, a number of institutions and individuals have provided assistance in kind or at significantly reduced cost: Joanna Close-Brookes, Tom Gray, John Hume, National Museums of Scotland (Scottish Life Archive), Royal Commission on the Ancient and Historical Monuments of Scotland, School of Scottish Studies (University of Edinburgh). On a point of information, the Scottish Record Office (SRO) has recently been renamed, albeit not in this volume, as the National Archives of Scotland (NAS).

The Province of Strathnaver follows *Caithness: A Cultural Crossroads* (1982), *Firthlands of Ross and Sutherland* (1986) and *Peoples and Settlement in North-West Ross* (1994). With *Scandinavian Shetland: An Ongoing Tradition?* (1978), *Shetland's Northern Links; History and Language* (1996) and a volume on Orkney to follow, the Society will soon have published studies covering all the most northerly districts of the Scottish mainland and the Northern Isles. We hope this achievement will prove a lasting contribution to our knowledge and understanding of life and settlement, historical and cultural inter-relationships in the north.

John R. Baldwin
Edinburgh 2000

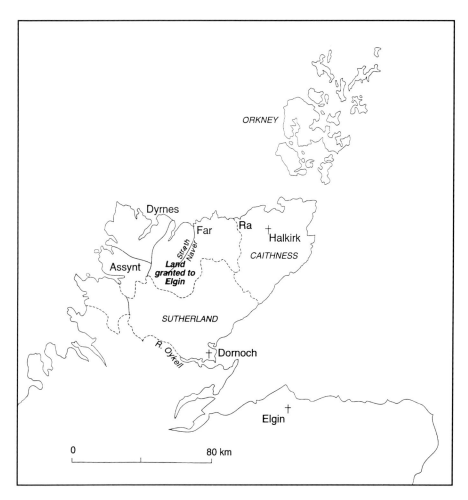

Fig. 1.1   The lands of Strathnaver are first mentioned in a charter of 1269 granting lands to Reginald Cheyne and Mary de Moravia. They had seemingly been given to the cathedral at Elgin by Joanna's mother.

MEDIEVAL STRATHNAVER

Barbara E. Crawford

The medieval history of Strathnaver is an impossible subject to talk or write about, as the subject barely exists! What information we have is fraught with difficulties, not least the problem of the origin of the Clan Mackay, which I will be avoiding as much as possible. In my studies of the Norse in Scotland I have tried to steer clear of clan history, which is for those who understand Gaelic culture, which I do not. However, when studying the history of the earldom of Caithness, I have been well aware of the significance of the province of Strathnaver, which appears as an already existing entity in the time of disruption of the old Norse earldom in the 13th century. This period of change in the north, from the Norwegian to the Scottish world, is of great interest: in my previous studies I have only referred marginally to Strathnaver (Crawford 1982. 65; 1985. 34). This paper is an attempt to get a little closer to understanding the significance of the territorial unit which was included in the term 'Strathnaver' when it appears in the 13th-century documentary sources.

THE NORTHERN 'PROVINCES': NESS, SUTHERLAND & STRATHNAVER

The first point to be made – and it needs making – is that we are going back to a time when this part of the north coast was not included in the later county of Sutherland. It is surprising how many maps of Norse Scotland, or of the Vikings in Scotland, will show Sutherland as it was after the creation of the regality of Sutherland in the 17th century. However, Strathnaver was never part of Norse Sutherland, and could never have been so in the way that Dornoch, Golspie and Skelbo are in the *Suðrland* of Caithness – the southern part of the Caithness province [Fig. 1.1].

Strathnaver only became part of Sutherland due to post-medieval political development, and as a by-product of the spread of power and authority to this area of the earls of Sutherland. When they got hold of estates in Strathnaver (Mackay estates), these were absorbed into the earldom domain. As the Sutherlands got increased political power, culminating in a Charter of Regality in 1601, all their estates became an administrative unit – a sheriffdom and then a county.[1]

In the Norse period Strathnaver acquired an identity of its own, which had nothing to do with Sutherland. It was, however, in a broad sense a part of Caithness, in that the whole area north of the Oykell was included in the province of Caithness, and this was the area that the earls of Orkney held as their Scottish earldom. When the Scottish bishopric of Caithness was founded in the 12th century, it was based on the area which lay under the control of the earls of Caithness (Crawford 1974. 20). By the time that the documentary sources appear, Strathnaver was not then a part of the Caithness earldom; but nonetheless I think it can be assumed that the earls must have controlled it at one time, because of the fact that it was within the bishopric. The extent of the bishopric simply mirrored the earls' secular holding at its most extensive.

This large bloc of the northern Mainland of Scotland (the old Pictish province of Cat) was sub-divided into separate provinces from time to time. The north-east corner was Ness, and the southern portion was Sutherland from the 11th century at least. Earl Thorfinn is said in the saga to have been given Caithness *and Sutherland* by his grandfather Malcolm II (*OS.* chap. 13). We have no knowledge of why Sutherland was considered to be a separate unit, but one supposes that this must reflect some tenurial separateness, perhaps indicating a holding given by a 10th-century earl to one of his warriors, to defend as a frontier region. Certainly the natural feature of the Ord divides Sutherland geographically from the lands of Ness to the north of the Ord, and Ausdale (which is a valley running to the east coast in the middle of the Ord) is said in the Saga to lie 'where Caithness and Sutherland meet' (*OS.* chap. 112). Fordun, in the 14th century, refers to 'both the provinces' of the Caithness men which were in revolt against the king in the late 12th century (*Scotichron.* 4.419). Sutherland continued to maintain its separate identity, and eventually eclipsed the earldom of Caithness as the most important power centre in the north.

The third part of Caithness, which also developed a separate identity, became known as the 'province' of Strathnaver; the river valleys running north into the Pentland Firth west from Strathhalladale as far as Durness [Fig. 1.1]. The name Strathnaver – unsurprisingly – never appears in the sagas, but perhaps is to be identified with the district referred to as the 'Dales' of Caithness. In the late 10th century Skuli and Liotr met in battle in the Dales of Caithness (*i Dǫlum á Katanesi: OS.* chap. x). In the 12th century the family of Moddan 'in Dale' in Caithness seem to have been resident in Thursodale (Cowan 1982. 30-33). Skene, however, thought that the Dale in question was Strathnaver (1837. 361), and our older historians of the area seem generally to think the term 'the Dales' (*Dalir*) is referring to the valleys west of Thurso: Strathalladale, the Strathy Water and Strathnaver.[2]

STRATHNAVER: NAME, EXTENT & STATUS

Whatever the name by which the district was known to the Norse, the ancient name for the Naver survived through the Norse period, and this fine river valley became the centre of a separate territorial unit. According to Watson (1926. 47), the name is the same as Ptolemy's *Nabaros* (one of the rivers on the west side of Albion, which, due to the 'turning' of Scotland, must be the north coast). It is said to be one of the few pre-Celtic names in Scotland, deriving from an Indo-European root meaning 'moist, cloud, water, mist' (Nicolaisen 1976. 188-9).

The survival of this ancient name through the Norse period does not mean that the strath was not settled by Vikings. Scandinavian place-names far up the valley such as Skaill, Longdale (= Langwall), Syre and Rossal, prove that Scandinavian speakers owned these farms in sufficient numbers, and for sufficiently long, to imprint the Old Norse names on the toponymic landscape. By the time that the name Strathnaver is recorded in the documentary sources (1269), however, we can be sure that Gaelic speech was dominant in the strath once again. The first recorded use of the name 'Strathnaver' is in a charter granting certain lands to Reginald Cheyne and Mary de Moravia. These lands in Strathnaver are said to have been given to the Church of Moray (ie the Cathedral at Elgin) by Mary's mother, *nobilis mulier domina Johanna* ('the noblewoman lady Joanna') (*Moray Reg.* no. 126) [Fig. 1.1]. Seventeen years later, Christian, Joanna's other daughter (and her husband) granted to the same Reginald Cheyne four davachs of land in Strathnaver, to be held 'as the original charter of the said land of Strathnaver contained' (*Moray Reg.* no. 263), and promising to give them all other lands they might come to have in the future *in tenemento de Strathnavyr*.

Before going into the relationship of all these people in detail, there are one or two points to make about the use of the territorial designation 'Strathnaver'. In neither of these two documents is Strathnaver said to be in any lordship, either in the earldom of Caithness or of Sutherland (both of which are in existence at that date), or of anywhere else. That is unusual.[3] Moreover, it is clearly a holding on its own as it is called *tenementum de Strathnaver*, and that holding has a charter which presumably defined it, but which has unfortunately not survived. To whom was this charter given and by whom? We do not know, but my guess would be that it was granted to Lady Joanna at the time when the whole of Caithness and Sutherland were reorganised by Alexander II in the 1230s; and when we know that the earldom of Caithness and the newly-created earldom of Sutherland were granted out with feudal charters (Crawford 1985. 32-3).

How large was this provincial unit? Strathnaver was the centre of a territory which at times stretched from Strathalladale to Edderachillis and down to Assynt. This is a point which the Revd. Angus Mackay very firmly stressed in his *Book of Mackay* (1906), although he admits that Sir Robert Gordon said in *The History of Sutherland* that Strathnaver was limited to the parish of Farr. But then, as he points out, Sir Robert's motive was to lessen the territorial designation 'MacKay of Strathnaver': 'It was ever so with Sir Robert but the facts ... are all against him' (Mackay 1906. 29). The facts quoted relate, however, to the period when the Mackays had built up their possessions into a wide territorial holding – which at that time was said to be 'in Strathnaver'. But Sir Robert Gordon's point that the territory of Strathnaver was co-terminous with the parish of Farr may be relevant to another, earlier period of time.

In the absence of the 'charter of Strathnaver' referred to in 1286, we are

3

never likely to know the extent of the *tenementum* of Strathnaver in the 13th century, but it seems likely that it would have consisted of the parish of Farr at the most at that time. There is no evidence that Joanna or her descendants held any land in Durness or further west. By the time of the first maps of north Scotland in the late 16th century, Strathnaver is of wide extent however. It is certainly a distinct unit and tenurially separate from both Caithness and Sutherland.[4] This reflects a medieval situation, and the question one needs to ask next is how and why did this provincial lordship develop in the Norse period?

DEVELOPMENT OF THE STRATHNAVER
LORDSHIP IN THE NORSE PERIOD

If we go back to the 1230s and examine the upheavals that took place at that time in the north, we first and foremost find there was a big break in the inheritance of the earldom with the ending of the old line of Norse earls. Their claim passed to a Scottish family who had to move north and adapt to the different world of joint Norse-Celtic authority in the Western Isles and in Caithness. This break in the traditional pattern of family inheritance coincided with the assertion of authority in the north by the Scottish kings, through expeditions and feudal grants of land to loyal vassals. There must have been big changes in Caithness as new families filled the power vacuum, and the old order gave way to a new one.

Secondly, the historical sources change just as dramatically, for the remarkable compilation known as the *Orkneyinga Saga* comes to an end at exactly the same time – symbolically signifying the breaking of links with the northern world. The Icelandic authors of the saga narrative must have known less and less of what was going on in north Scotland, as the main actors in the scenario changed and families moved in who had no contacts with the wider Scandinavian world. We do know something of the dramatic events attendant on the collapse of the old order, however, from other Norwegian sagas: but for information about changes in landholding in the north we are dependant on sparse documentary Scottish sources.

Earl John Haraldsson, the last of the Norse line of earls of Orkney and Caithness [Fig. 1.2], must have been an ill-fated man; but maybe he deserved his fate. Unlike his father, who was a survivor, John crossed all those with whom he had to learn to live and compromise, and he came out badly every time. For the first few years after the death of his father (the great Harald Maddadson), John ruled the two earldoms with his brother David (*OS*: chap. 112). During that period, in 1210, the two earls had to come to terms with their Norwegian overlord, Inge Bardsson, during a lull in the Civil Wars that dominated Norwegian history in the early 13th century. The terms were rather humiliating ones, which included the imposition of a royal bailiff (Sysselman) in Orkney, the payment of a heavy fine, the giving of security and hostages, and the swearing of oaths of loyalty and obedience. It is even

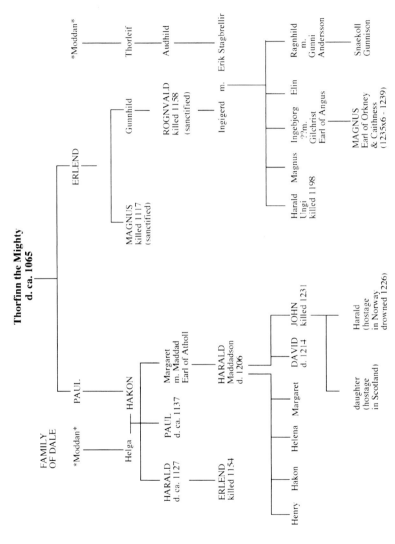

EARLDOMS OF ORKNEY AND CAITHNESS
Demise of Old Line

Thorfinn the Mighty
d. ca. 1065

FAMILY OF DALE

Moddan

Moddan

Thorleif

Audhild

PAUL

ERLEND

Helga — HAKON

PAUL d. ca. 1137

HARALD d. ca. 1127

ERLEND killed 1154

Margaret m. Maddad Earl of Atholl

Gunhild

MAGNUS killed 1117 (sanctified)

ROGNVALD killed 1158 (sanctified)

Ingigerd m. Erik Stagbrellir

HARALD Maddadson d. 1206

Henry   Hakon   Helena   Margaret

DAVID d. 1214

JOHN killed 1231

daughter (hostage in Scotland)

Harald (hostage in Norway drowned 1226)

Harald Ungi killed 1198

Magnus

Ingebjorg ??m. Gilchrist Earl of Angus

Elin

Ragnhild m. Gunni Andersson

MAGNUS Earl of Orkney & Caithness (1235x6 - 1239)

Snaekoll Gunnison

Fig. 1.2   The earldoms of Orkney and Caithness at the demise of the old Norse line of earls.

5

said in *Ingi Bardson's Saga* that David and John were made earls 'upon such terms as were adhered to until their death-day' (*ES*. ii. 381).

After the death of David in 1214 John ruled his earldoms alone. He was immediately in trouble with his Scottish overlord, however, and must have been considered untrustworthy, for he had to give his daughter as a hostage to the king when he made a treaty of peace with William who was in Moray for a campaign (according to Fordun; see *ES*. ii. 397n). In 1222 the earl was also considered blameworthy in the attack on Bishop Adam (which resulted in the bishop's death at Halkirk), and he had to buy back half of his confiscated earldom and King Alexander's good will with a heavy fine (Crawford 1985. 32).

The unfortunate Earl John also ended up on the wrong side of the powerful King Hakon Hakonsson, and was summoned to Norway in 1224 on suspicion of being involved in a conspiracy against the king and Jarl Skule. On that occasion he had to take his son Harald and leave him behind in the custody of the Norwegian king, as a hostage (*ES*. ii. 455). The attempts of both Scottish and Norwegian kings to enforce the good behaviour of this earl by the same means is some indication of his inability to conduct relationships with his overlords with any sensibility. It is quite remarkable that both a daughter and a son were handed over into the care of his two overlords! On the latter occasion the event resulted in tragedy, for Harald was killed two years later by drowning (*Icelandic Annals*) and this left the earldom without a direct heir and open to a wide range of claimants jockeying for control.

Finally, John got embroiled in a feud with the royal official in Orkney, Hanef Ungi, which is hardly surprising for the earls hated having royal officials sitting beside them, and there had been trouble over this in his father's time. This time, the rival dynasty to the earldom got involved, in the person of Snaekollr Gunnison, the grandson of Earl Rognvald, and Earl John met a humiliating end in the underground store of a house in Thurso where he tried to hide from attack. The comment in *Chronicle of Melrose*: 'John earl of Caithness was killed in his own house and burnt. He received deservedly from God vengeance of the same kind as the torture that the venerable Bishop Adam had suffered under him' (*ES*. ii. 479), shows the reputation that this last earl of the Norse line had earned, at least with the monastic chroniclers.

The next act in the saga is even more dramatic, and there is a fascinating account of it in *Hakon Hakonsson's Saga*, which shows how significant the contemporary writer thought the circumstances to be. Two rival factions, the earl's kin and Hanef and his companions, agreed to go before the King's Court in Bergen for Hakon to adjudge between them, presumably to decide who was responsible for the earl's death, and who should pay atonement. The result was that five members of Hanef's party were executed – but not Snaekollr who 'remained long with earl Skuli and king Hakon' (*ES*. ii. 483-4). Although *Hakon's Saga* does not tell us, presumably one of the earl's kin was appointed his successor and granted rights and title of earl by the king. The tragic climax was reached when the ship in which all the 'best men' of the Orkneys were returning west, was lost in the autumn of 1232. Even in the *Icelandic Annals* this was recorded as the loss of the Orkney *goeðingaskip* (Storm 1888. 129); the term *goeðingr* for chieftains was particularly used of the Orkney landholders. With the portentous comment 'and of this many men have been long in getting the atonement', the saga-writer rings down the curtain, and the earls of Orkney-Caithness appear very rarely in Norwegian sources thereafter.

SCOTTISH CLAIMANTS TO THE LORDSHIP

Time was not wasted by Scottish relatives of the last earl, and already on 7 October 1232 'M. comite de Anegus et Katanie' witnessed a charter (*Moray Reg.* no. 123). There must have been no male members of the *jarla-aett* left who were considered acceptable as claimants,[5] and the title passed through the female line to Scottish cousins of the house of Angus. The claimant must have received a grant of the earldom of Caithness from the Scottish king first, before venturing into unknown territory and being accepted by the Norwegian king as rightful heir to the Orkney earldom. This was a reversal of the long-established usual pattern, whereby the Orkney earldom was awarded first to the heir with the best claim, who then took up the Caithness earldom.

This situation provided Alexander II with an ideal opportunity for reorganising the far north of his kingdom, which was only just coming under his control after the final quelling of the MacWilliam rebels in Moray. Some aspects of his reorganising policy are clear, such as his rewarding of the faithful de Moravia family with the newly-created earldom of Sutherland. But exactly what happened to the rest of the Caithness earldom, is very confused.[6] There seems to have been a division into two halves, north and south Caithness (Grey 1922-3. 289); not many years later, probably with another blip in the inheritance, half of the earldom lands were granted to an important heiress, probably of the house of Angus, whom we have already come across, *nobilis mulier domina Johanna*. The fact that she was married to another de Moravia, Freskin, shows that whatever division of the earldom took place at that time was done in a very structured way, and with a marriage which was intended to ensure that her inheritance was firmly controlled by the main royalist family in the north of Scotland.

All this detail about the collapse of the powerful earldom of Caithness is of immediate importance for our understanding of the history of Strathnaver in the period. For Joanna inherited – or acquired – the *tenementum* of Strathnaver, as well as half the lands of the earldom. Her half of the earldom lands was divided between her two daughters and can then be traced coming back to Ranald Cheyne III, and then dividing again between *his* two daughters, and passing down the lines of Keith of Inverrugy and Sutherland of Duffus. A 16th-century record of the divided inheritance gives a list of all the estates (Crawford 1982. 65-6).

This inheritance was, however, quite distinct from Joanna's Strathnaver holding. As mentioned earlier, the latter is never described as being within the earldom of Caithness, but seems to have been acquired by Joanna as a separate entity. Where did it come from and why did she get hold of it? These are questions which have been puzzled over by many historians of the north. One suggestion has been made that Joanna got Strathnaver as the heiress of the Moddan in Dale family, and that she may have been the daughter of Snaekollr Gunnison who went to Bergen in 1232 to claim Earl John's inheritance (but never seems to have come home again) (Grey 1922. 110-11). All the hypotheses rest on unprovable assumptions, but my own belief is that Joanna was a member of the Angus family (Crawford 1985. 36). This does not, however, help to explain why she should have been awarded Strathnaver in the general carve-up by Alexander in the 1230s, for it seems to have been additional to her earldom property. The breaking-down of the old order, and the arrival of new families, created a new structure through which it is very hard to penetrate to the previous tenurial circumstances.

IMPACT OF CHANGE ON SOCIAL
& ECONOMIC STRUCTURES

What we similarly know nothing about is what effects these changes had on the social and economic situation in the north. How closely involved were these new families in the Norse-Celtic social structures? Instead of earls based across the Pentland Firth, within easy maritime reach, the landowners were now feudal lords with southern power bases, from which access to the north was across difficult Highland terrain.

Lady Joanna's links with Strathnaver cannot have been easy or very close. Her husband was of the de Moravia family which was firmly entrenched in Sutherland, although Freskin's own power base was Duffus in Moray. This was his main residence, although he and Joanna would probably have resided on their northern estates from time to time. Their relations with the tenants who farmed the estates can only have been as feudal overlords, and new tenurial arrangements were probably enforced to suit the new landowners' economic requirements.

It is only thanks to the piety of Lady Joanna that we know about her possession of Strathnaver at all. Sometime prior to 1269, she gave in 'free alms' a consolidated territorial bloc of lands in upper Strathnaver and around Loch Naver to the Cathedral Church of the diocese of Moray for the perpetual service of two chaplains, presumably in the Cathedral. Twelve marks sterling were to be rendered for this purpose, at two terms per year. This would have been granted for the benefit of the souls of deceased relatives, perhaps her husband, Freskin, who was dead by 1262. The lands given were Langwall and Rossal, Toftis, Dowyr, Achenedesse, Clybr' (Clibreck), Ardowyr and Carnferne (see Grey's discussion of these names: 1922. 110). Of all Joanna's lands, these estates in upper Strathnaver must

have been the nearest to the south and Moray, by way of Lairg[7] [Fig. 1.1].
We only know of this grant to Elgin Cathedral because, in 1269, it was granted back by Bishop Archibald to Reginald Cheyne junior and his wife Mary, one of Joanna's and Freskin's two daughters – a rather strange thing to happen. The Cheynes were, however, an exceedingly successful dynasty in acquiring the lands of the former earldom and reconsolidating them. Reginald managed to get hold of another portion of Joanna's Strathnaver holding from her other daughter Christian, although not until 1286 (*Moray Reg.* no. 263). As already noted, this amounted to four davachs of land (the estates are not named), and Christian and her husband also promised to hand over any other lands in Strathnaver which they might come to have in the future. Is there a hint here of some unresolved claims to territory? It is not clear how much of lower Strathnaver these four davachs represented. Did Mary also inherit land in lower Strathnaver? We can probably assume that their mother had most of Strathnaver from the reference to the 'charter of Strathnaver' and the use of the term *tenementum* which implies a consolidated holding.

STRATHNAVER AND THE MACKAYS

This is as far as one can go with respect to Lady Joanna's possession of Strathnaver and her daughters' inheritance of it. If her acquisition is shrouded in mystery, there is an even more mysterious change of landholding in Strathnaver to come.

By 1415 Strathnaver had become the domain of the MacKays, and there are precious few facts to explain how that had happened. The whole origin of Clan MacKay is obscure, although it is traditionally connected with the MacEths, the independent rulers of Moray who consistently caused trouble for the house of Canmore. One tradition, based on a comment by Fordun, asserts that they were moved to Strathnaver after the final defeat of Malcolm MacHeth in the 1160s. Skene thought, however, that they were native to the area and descended from the Moddan family (1837. 362). Another tradition suggests that Iye Mor MacKay came into possession of the Church lands of Durness (twelve davachs) by marrying the daughter of Bishop Walter (1263-70) (MacKay 1906. 37).

My interpretation that a witness to a charter of John, earl of Caithness called 'Ivor MacEothe'[8] was the same as Iye MacKay – if correct – suggests that the family were highly-placed in Caithness landowning politics by the late 13th century (Crawford 1982. 65). The fact that this charter is a grant of land by Earl John to Reginald Cheyne 'the elder' may hint at links between MacKays and Cheynes, although the more obvious deduction is that the witness was in the entourage of the earl (as clearly the other witnesses were). Taken in conjunction with the tradition that Iye Mor MacKay had control of the twelve davachs of episcopal land at Durness through marriage to Bishop Walter's daughter, this evidence of a MacKay being involved in a land-

9

holding transaction in Caithness is another clue to the position that the family had established in the north by the late 13th century. If Iye Mor and Ivor MacEothe were indeed the same person, he was clearly well-placed to move into Strathnaver when the opportunity offered itself.

That opportunity would not be there so long as the Cheynes were in control, but on the death of Rannald Cheyne III ca 1350, when his vast inheritance was divided between two heiresses, another period of instability must have opened up in the north. The new dynasties moving in this time were the Keiths of Inverrugy and a scion of the Sutherland family who married the two heiresses, and the pattern was set for the MacKay-Sutherland feud which was to last for centuries. By 1370 tensions were so high that a meeting was held at Dingwall by the earl of Ross to settle matters between MacKays and Sutherlands, one of whom, Nicholas, was married to Marjory, daughter of Reginald Cheyne III. The meeting ended with the murder of two MacKays. We can guess that the lands of Strathnaver were part of the dispute. Despite this setback, Clan MacKay became entrenched along the whole north coast province of Strathnaver. In the 1540s the Sutherlands and MacKays were disputing those very lands of the Church of Moray in Upper Strathnaver which had been donated by Lady Joanna three hundred years before (*OPS*. II. ii. 711).

CONCLUSION

This very limited survey of what is known about medieval Strathnaver has revolved around the lands in Upper Strathnaver which were granted to the Church of Moray by Lady Joanna. They clearly remained a valuable and desirable holding. The virtual lack of any other documentary evidence from the period concerning Strathnaver may mean that this upland territory has acquired an importance which is out of all balance to the land's economic value. On the other hand, the value of the area may have lain more in its strategic significance than in its productive capabilities.

This significance is probably connected to its location at a junction of routeways. As outlined in note 7, the holdings may have been important to the earls of Orkney and Caithness because of their military requirements at a date when Norse place-names were being given and becoming fixed in the north Scottish landscape (late 10th - 11th centuries).[7] After the diminution of the earls' power, and the division of their north mainland possessions (described above), Upper Strathnaver may have become desirable as a strategic centre for new territorial lordships which were based on inland routes and waterways rather than maritime ones. The territorialisation process in the post-Norse era has to be taken into account when interpreting the new political scenario created by the de Moravia family's rise to power in northern Scotland in the 12th and 13th centuries. Their northward-looking standpoint from Moray was diametrically different from the earls of Orkney's southern-looking viewpoint from islands across a waterway.

It is changed political and geographical circumstances such as these which help us to interpret the documents issued under this new family's control and reflecting its political priorities.

Notes

1. See Sir W Fraser, *The Sutherland Book* and *CP*, XII (i) p538, n. (d) for details. In the same way, the county of Cromarty was created out of the estates of the first earl of Cromarty in the late 17th century (Richards & Clough 1989. 6).
2. Mackay (1906. 28) even assumes that Edderachillis, Durness, Kintail of Tongue as well as Farr was 'the old *dolum Cathanensi'*.
3. Similarly in 1401, in a contract between Margaret Lady Ard and the Lord of the Isles, lands were transferred which lay 'in Strathnaver' (*OPS*. 2. ii. 709). Other lands were transferred at the same time which lay 'in the earldom of Sutherland' and other lands which lay 'in the earldom of Caithness'. Clearly Strathnaver was quite a distinct entity.
4. Blaue's maps define Strathnaver most distinctly where its western limit is shown to lie on the Kyle of Durness.
5. The *jarla-aett* were members of the earldom family who carried the right to claim the earldom of Orkney for themselves, or to pass it on to male descendants. The persisting lack of primogeniture in the Norwegian inheritance system, and the practice of dividing the earldom, naturally resulted in a very confusing inheritance structure. Although the saga gives plentiful information about the family relationships of those members of the *jarla-aett* who remained in the islands, it does not provide any details of marriages with Scottish families further south.
6. See my discussion of this problem (Crawford 1985. 33-7).
7. Since writing this paper, I have been pursuing a study of Langwell and Rossal names in North Scotland, of which these Strathnaver examples form an interesting pair. Such names appear to have some significance in terms of the transport requirements of earldom retinues needing to cross the mountainous terrain of Sutherland and Ross. The appearance of these two names (apparently linked together as there is no *de* before Rossal), heading the list of lands granted to the Church of Moray by Joanna, indicates an importance which is belied by the apparently insignificant nature of the names themselves. Langwell (ON *lang* + *vǫllr*, 'long field') and Rossal (ON *hross* + *vǫllr*, 'horse field') may have had some significance as pasturing places for horses required for crossing from Strathnaver to Ross. See 'Earldom Strategies in North Scotland and the Significance of Place-Names' in G. Williams (ed). forthcoming.
8. In 1982 I transcribed the name as 'Mac Goth'. However, I am now interpreting the capital letter as 'E' rather than 'G'. There is also a small 'e' at the end of the name, which may be the result of the medieval clerk attempting to render the Gaelic 'Aiodh' into acceptable Latin. The full documentary evidence relating to this charter was discussed by me in 1971 (St. Andrews Ph.D thesis).

References

Printed Sources:

ES	A.O. Anderson (ed). *Early Sources of Scottish History.* 1922. 2 vols.
OPS	*Origines Parochiales Scotiae* (Bannatyne Club. 1851-5)
OS	*Orkneyinga Saga.*
Moray Reg.	*Registrum Episcopatus Moraviensis* (Bannatyne Club. 1837)
Scotichron. 4	D.J. Corner et al (eds) *Scotichronicon* by Walter Bower. Books VII & VIII. (General Editor: D.E.R. Watt). 1994.
Storm, G. (ed)	*Islandske Annaler indtil 1578.* 1888. Christiania.

Secondary Sources:

CP: *The Complete Peerage.*
Cowan, E.J. 'Caithness in the Sagas', in J.R. Baldwin (ed) *Caithness: A Cultural Crossroads.* 1982.
Crawford, B.E. *The Earls of Orkney – Caithness and their Relationship with the Kings of Norway and Scotland, 1150 - 1470.* Ph.D thesis. University of St Andrews. 1971.
Crawford, B.E. 'Peter's Pence in Scotland', in G.W.S. Barrow (ed) *The Scottish Tradition.* 1974: 14-22.
Crawford, B.E. 'Scots and Scandinavians in Mediaeval Caithness: A study of the Period 1266-1375', in J.R. Baldwin (ed) *Caithness: A Cultural Crossroads.* 1982: 61-74.
Crawford, B.E. 'The Earldom of Caithness and the Kingdom of Scotland, 1150-1266', in K.J. Stringer (ed) *Essays on the Nobility of Medieval Scotland.* 1985: 25-43.
Crawford, B.E. 'Map of the reduction of the earldom of Orkney and Caithness', in P. MacNeill & H.L. MacQueen (eds) *Atlas of Scottish History to 1707.* 1996: 449.
Crawford, B.E. 'Earldom Strategies in North Scotland and the Significance of Place-Names', in G. Williams (ed) *Sagas, Saints and Sacrifices.* British Museum Press. forthcoming.
Gordon, Sir Robt. *The Genealogical History of the Earldom of Sutherland.* 1813.
Grey, J. *Boundaries of Estates in Caithness Diocese shortly after 1222.* SHR. 1922-3.
MacKay, Revd. A. *The Book of Mackay.* 1906.
Nicolaisen, W.F.H. *Scottish Place-Names.* 1976.
Richards, E. & Clough, M. *Cromartie: Highland Life, 1650-1914.* 1989.
Skene, W.F. *Highlanders of Scotland.* 1837.
Watson, W.J. *The Celtic Place Names of Scotland.* 1926.

A SCATTER OF NORSE NAMES
IN STRATHNAVER

Doreen Waugh

BACKGROUND

Strathnaver first came to my attention during my study of Caithness place-names, in particular those of the parish of Reay, which included the neighbouring valley of Strath Halladale prior to 1245, as indicated in the Caithness and Sutherland Records (*CSR*. 20). To the west of Strath Halladale, past Strathy and Armadale, the next major north/south valley or strath is Strathnaver, now part of Sutherland but not referred to as such during the Norse period when *suðrland* 'southern land' was the name used for the territory in the southern part of the province of Caithness. Neither Reay, Strath Halladale nor Strathnaver is mentioned in *Orkneyinga Saga*, which is unfortunate for the researcher, but which tends to confirm the view that these were not central territories in terms of the Norse in Caithness and their links with the Orkney earldom.

I favour a Norse interpretation of the place-name Reay (1995. 68-70), although a Gaelic-based interpretation has also been suggested (Watson 1926. 117-118) and, at this distance in time from the creation of the name, it is impossible to be certain which is closer to the truth. The place-names which occur in the area surrounding the village of Reay are of varied linguistic origin, with Norse, Gaelic, English and Scots all being represented to some extent. There is plenty of evidence in the naming to suggest that there was an active Norse farming community around the village of Reay.

If we go west from Reay to Strath Halladale, the proportion of Gaelic names becomes higher and that of Norse names lower; and the same is true, in turn, if we go further west to Strathnaver. The name Halladale itself, however, is of Norse origin (Macaulay 1982. 283), as is Armadale, and several of the habitative names in these valleys to the west of Reay confirm the presence of the Norse language and, therefore, of people who could use it in the naming of their farms.

I have defined Strathnaver as a valley, as indeed it is – the valley of the River *Naver* – a Celtic name which was in use prior to the arrival of the Norse and which outlasted their presence (Watson 1905-6. 233; 1926. 44, 47, 72). Sometimes we can surmise that Norse settlers heard existing Celtic names and 'translated' them in such a way as to make them meaningful in their own language (as may possibly have happened in the case of Reay, for instance), but sometimes the Celtic name was either so well established, or so different from Norse, that no attempt was made to translate it in this way, and Strathnaver is a case in point.

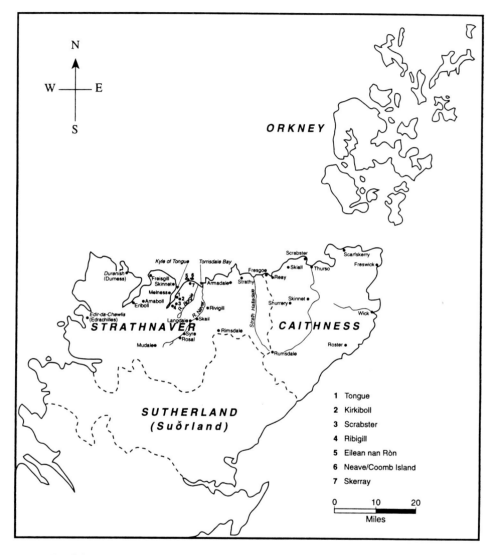

N

W ——— E

S

ORKNEY

Durenish
(Durness)
Kyle of Tongue   Torrisdale Bay   Scrabster   Scarfskerry
                                                          Freswick
Freisgill   Fresgoe   Skiall   Thurso
Skinnet   5   Strathy Reay
Melness   7   Armadale
Amaboll   2   3   Skinnet
Eriboll   Roope   Shurrery
Edir-da-Chewtis   Rivigill
(Edrachilles)   Langdale Skail   Wick
STRATHNAVER   Syre   CAITHNESS
Mudale   Rosal   Rimsdale
                                   Roster
                        Rumsdale

SUTHERLAND   1 Tongue
(Suðrland)   2 Kirkiboll
                    3 Scrabster
                    4 Ribigill
                    5 Eilean nan Ròn
                    6 Neave/Coomb Island
                    7 Skerray

0   10   20
         Miles

Fig. 2.1   Some key place-names in the 'province' of Strathnaver.

14

As well as being a reference to a valley, the name Strathnaver had a wider territorial application, as can be seen in the following 17th-century text cited in Macfarlane in translation (1907. II. 453-454):

> STRATHNAVER: This district derives its name from the River Naver, which intersects its centre. It begins where Caithness ends, at the River Hallowdail, and stretches right westwards. Separated from Edir-da-Chewlis by the bay and river of Durenish, it has the wide and open sea on the north, and no land, no island opposite, even in the extreme north. On the south ... Sutherland is next to it, and is separated from it by very high mountains.

It is from this wider land area that I shall select some place-names for discussion [Fig. 2.1], because I propose to concentrate on the Norse rather than the Gaelic names and to suggest that the Norse did settle along the north coast and into the river valleys where these offered scope for habitation, although the extent of the Norse presence is less than in Caithness which was more favoured for settlement. The flatness and fertility of the land in Caithness would have made it more attractive, but it may also have been more easily controlled by the Norse colonists because of its closeness to the centre of power in Orkney.

Many questions still have to be answered about the historical position of Strathnaver within or outwith the Caithness earldom. The linguistic situation in Strathnaver in the medieval period is much less open to argument than its territorial position. By the 13th century the Gaelic language was in the ascendancy, but the fact that Norse names have survived through centuries of Gaelic use suggests that, at some point – probably in the 10th to 12th centuries – Norse inhabitants were sufficient in number and length of stay to leave their place-names behind when they eventually departed – whether literally, through death, or metaphorically, through intermarriage and gradual language change and loss of distinctive Norse identity.

PLACE-NAMES INCORPORATING
ON *dalr, völlr*

When examining evidence for Norse settlement, it is traditional to look for those place-name generics which describe farms or other types of human habitation and, of course, they are the most reliable indicators of extensive and prolonged Norse presence. It is my opinion, however, that we should give more weight than we do to topographical naming as evidence of Norse presence in a settled capacity in north and north-west Scotland. I find it difficult to accept that, on the one hand we argue that topographical names are often the oldest names in a region of Norse settlement (eg Fellows-Jensen 1984. 154) and yet, on the other hand, we tend not to cite these as sound evidence of any form of permanent settlement if *bólstaðr, setr, sætr* and other primary elements indicative of habitation and farming are not to be found in place-names in the vicinity. It is difficult to believe that Norse terms could attach themselves with such tenacity to topographical features if the

15

Scandinavians were not present, on the land, in numbers large enough and permanent enough to perpetuate the names surrounding their dwellings.

The Norse names along the north coast and in the river valleys from Halladale to Durness are frequently topographical in reference, but I would argue that they should, nevertheless, be seen as indicators of settlement. Norse names are more numerous closer to the coast, as they are in Caithness, although there is a smattering of names at fairly regular intervals along the valleys which run south from the coast, such as Strathnaver itself. The Rivers Naver and Borgie reach the sea at Torrisdale Bay – Torrisdale containing the Norse element *dalr* 'a valley' – and it is certainly interesting that this eminently suitable Norse name did not compete successfully with Strathnaver as a description of the valley at the mouth of which it lies, although the issue is slightly complicated by the fact that the River Borgie also empties into the sea in the same bay. The River Borgie, however, already has a Norse name which applies to its valley.

In neighbouring Caithness, what appears to have happened is that the two Norse settlements at the mouths of the Thurso and Wick Rivers gave their names to the rivers, and if there were earlier Celtic river names, these have been forgotten along with the language in which they may have been coined. The River Borgie, to some extent, follows this pattern in that the generic in its name is ON *borg*, 'a broch' with reference to an earthwork at the side of the river in its lower reaches, although not at its confluence. The fact that something similar did not happen in Strathnaver again highlights the tenacity of this particular Celtic name vis-à-vis a potential Norse alternative As Watson says: 'It rises in *Loch Nabhair*, flows through *Srath Nabhair*, and enters the sea at *Inbhir Nabhair*' (Watson 1926. 47), and has been recorded in variants of this Celtic format since written records began.

There is no doubt that the Norse name Torrisdale, or *Thorisdaill* as it appears in 1565 (*RMS*. IV. 388), was seen to be closely related to the confluence of the River Naver because it is described in a list as follows: 'Invernaver, Thorisdaill, cum salmonum piscaria earundem'. Donald Macaulay suggests the interpretation 'Thor's dale' for Torrisdale and he could be right, although it is impossible to be certain (Macaulay 1982. 283). If he is right, the name forms an interesting parallel with Thurso in Caithness which, as has already been noted, is also situated at the mouth of a river and which appears on record in the form *Þórsá* in the 13th-century *Orkneyinga Saga*. Initial /þ/ was replaced by /t/ in Gaelic but, in the case of Thurso, the original pronunciation would have been preserved in a more lastingly Norse environment. There is some disagreement about the nature of the generic in the name Thurso, to which reference was made in the proceedings of an earlier Scottish Society for Northern Studies Conference (Nicolaisen 1982. 84-85), but all scholars who have discussed the matter are agreed that the specific in the name is Thor.

Other names containing the Norse element *dalr* 'a valley' are scattered along the north coast from Halladale to Armadale to Torrisdale; and in the innermost reaches of several of the valleys running south from the coast there are Norse names such as Rumsdale, Rimsdale and Mudale, which point to

Scandinavian penetration deep into these valleys in search of viable farms. There is also Langdale in Strathnaver itself, although it is deceptive, because it is earlier recorded as *Langwall*; Langdale appears to be the result of a 19th-century switch of generic, perhaps because 'dale' is a word which can fit readily into either Gaelic, Norse or English vocabulary. As such, it renders the modern name more comprehensible to users, which is an impulse that occasionally governs naming and, in particular, the replacement of generics by other, more easily understood generics appropriate to the situation of the name. This explanation, however, begs the question why other names in -*wall* or -*well* in the vicinity did not experience a switch of generic, and there is no ready answer. There are several written references to *Langwall*, dating from as early as 1269 when it is recorded as *Langeval* (*CSR*. 33) but the reference which most clearly identifies it as an alternative to Langdale is: 'There were chapels also ... at Langdale or Langwall on the Naver' (*OPS*. 708). The element which appears as -*wall* in this name is most probably the Norse word *völlr* 'a field', which is quite common in place-names in the Northern Isles.

Another neighbouring place-name, Rosal, is very similar in the early form of its final element, and it seems likely that it too derives from Norse *völlr*. The earliest recorded form of this name is from 1269, when it appears in the combination 'Langeval et Rossewal' (*CSR*. 33). It is also recorded with Langdale in 1542 as *Langewall* and *Rossewall* (*Sutherland Charters: OPS*. 711), and again in 1621 as *Longaveall* and *Roseveall* (*RMS*. VIII. 35). One possible source of the specific in *Rossewall/Roseveall* is ON *hross* 'a horse', which is also likely to be the specific in the name Roster in Latheron Parish, Caithness, which was recorded in 1541, and several times thereafter, as Rosbister (*RMS*. III. 561), but the -*bister* form of the original Norse generic *bólstaðr* has been further reduced in the modern name, as often happens in Caithness place-names. There may be other possibilities for the specific in *Rossewall/Roseveall*, but ON *völlr* does often occur in combination with reference to animals.

PLACE-NAMES INCORPORATING
ON *skáli, bólstaðr, ærgi, saurr*

Lying to the north of Langdale and Rosal in the valley of the River Naver we find Skail, which is a Norse name that also occurs in Reay Parish in Caithness. Skail (deriving from ON *skáli*) is a place-name which is common in Orkney but rare in Caithness, although it occurs in Reay Parish. Again, we can discern a link between the west side of Caithness and Strathnaver in its occurrence in the Naver valley. In its earliest sense, the term *skáli* referred to a hut or shed put up for temporary use, but the Orkney examples indicate that it refers to a much more permanent and important residence, and that seems to be true of the Caithness example and, I would argue, of the Strathnaver example. A name which survives so effectively in a predominantly Gaelic linguistic environment bespeaks the importance of the habitation to which it originally referred, and the fact that it appears in written records from the 16th-century in references such as: 'terras de Skaill et Regeboill (extenden. ad 6 lib.), Strathnaverne' (*RMS*. IV. 402), also argues its importance as a settlement. It was also the site of one of the chapels in the valley of the Naver (Pennant [1769] 1979. 326).

Another place-name clearly associated with a chapel, both in terms of the real building and the initial element in the name itself, is Kirkiboll, situated by the Kyle of Tongue: 'There was a chapel at Kirkboll or Kirkiboll, the burialplace of the family Macky, which was standing and was repaired about the year 1630' (*OPS*. 708). The final element of this name, along with many other -*bols*, was scrutinised in a very useful and thought-provoking article by Dr Richard Cox (Cox 1994. 53). I am sorry to have to disagree with him on the interpretation of this name, for which I would suggest ON *kirkja* + *bólstaðr* 'church farm', rather than the *kirkja* + *pollr* 'church (by the) pool or pond', which is favoured by Dr Cox. It is, however, a matter of opinion, because there are no definitive early written references to the name and the reader will, like the writer, have to weigh factors in the balance and reach his or her own conclusion.

Earliest written references to the Strathnaver name are 16th-century and take the forms *Kirkeboll* (1565) (*RMS*. IV. 388) and *Kirkboill* (1583, 1588) (*RMS*. V. 178, 1588). Other references are similar in displaying no hint of a final syllable which might derive from an earlier Norse *bólstaðr* 'a farm'. In the absence of written evidence, Dr Cox relies on the modern Gaelic pronunciation of the name for its etymology, but I would rather turn to parallel place-name evidence in the Northern Isles, which were also colonised by the Norse and where the original Norse names have been more fully preserved because the Norn language survived there for a much longer time and was replaced by another Germanic language, rather than a Celtic language such as Gaelic. *Kirkja* + *bólstaðr* is a common compound in the Northern Isles, particularly in Orkney where numerous examples are recorded (Marwick 1952. 2, 25, 32, 56, 72, 78, 105, 136, 163, 182), but also in Shetland (Jakobsen 1936. 10, 27, 93; MacGregor 1984. 10; Stewart 1987. 54, 55, 56, 58). There are, however, no known examples of *kirkja* + *pollr* 'a pool or pond' in the Northern Isles. The location of Kirkiboll also militates against *pollr* as generic. It is situated at the side of a sea-loch, the Kyle of Tongue, which does not have a particularly narrow neck to give rise to the description *pollr*. With *pollr* as generic one would expect a basin of water with only a narrow access passage to the sea but the Kyle is broad at its mouth, narrowing gradually inland and, in view of this and the other circumstantial evidence from the Northern Isles, I believe that the generic in the name is ON *bólstaðr*.

If that is true of Kirkiboll, the likelihood is that other names ending in -*boll* in the vicinity also derive from *bólstaðr*: ie Arnaboll and Eriboll. There is one puzzling name which I have not successfully identified and that is *Regeboill*, as recorded above, which also appears in the form *Rogeboll*,

1581 (*RMS*. V. 90), *Rigabold*, 1608 (*RMS*. VI. 762), *Regiboll*, 1608 (*RMS*. VI. 790). It is tempting to suggest that the final /d/ of *Rigabold* represents just a hint of a dental cluster following, as in *bólstaðr*, but that is perhaps to read too much into limited information (cf however, the final /d/ of *Kirkebold* in the same document, and of *Kirkebold* in Tiree (*RMS*. V. 510), which is also one of the names discussed by Dr Cox).

The origin of the generic in *Regeboill* is certainly puzzling, but what is even more puzzling is the location of the name. It clearly had territorial significance in the 16th and early 17th centuries and yet it seems to vanish thereafter, unlike Skail in Strathnaver with which it is often cited in legal documents. Has the name simply been lost along with the settlement to which it applied, or could it be that the name we are looking for is Ribigill at the side of the Kyle of Tongue? Another candidate could be Rivigill in the valley of the Naver, situated close by Skail, but we can probably discount the latter because it is recorded as *Rewigill* in a list of Naver valley names, which includes Skail, whereas *Regeboll* appears a little later in the same list among names of places lying at the side of the Kyle of Tongue, as follows (*OPS*. 710; *RSS*. VIII. 168-9):

> In 1530 King James V granted to William Sutherland of Duffois the nonentry and other dues of the lands of Galvell and Bellinaglis, with the fishing in the water of Halladal, the lands of Strathy with fishing of the same, the lands of Armadall and Far with the fishing, the lands of Rennewe, Skelpik, Rewigill, Syre, Skale, Skarray, Allanye, Dilrit, Catak, and the lands of Towng, Kirkkeboll, Scrabustir, Regeboll, Kennesett, Elyngiell, Kinloch, Mellenis, Latirlioll, Hop with the fishing of the same ... .

Rivigill in the valley of the Naver (or Rifa-gil as it is recorded on the Ordnance Survey 1:50,000 map) is now used with reference to a hill, a loch and a burn flowing down towards the River Naver and the generic is ON *gil* 'a deep narrow glen with a stream at the bottom' – although the deepness of the glen is not particularly important if the landscape is generally flat when, by contrast, a slight indentation can assume gigantic proportions, as in Caithness where the element *gil* occurs quite frequently. The specific may possibly be ON *rif* 'a rib, or ridge', but one cannot be certain. Various early forms of this name and others in Strathnaver are recorded in an interesting article by Alex Morrison (Morrison 1987. 14-15). I note that he records *Rigibald* as an early form of Ruigh na Sealbhaig (shieling or slope where sorrel grew) but that seems unlikely, not only because of the great difference between the written forms but also because the records suggest that *Rigibald/Regeboll* – wherever it was situated – was more significant than a shieling.

If Ribigill – the small farm beside the Kyle of Tongue with no clearly marked 'gill' in the vicinity – is what the map-makers now give us in lieu of the earlier *Regeboill*, it gives us pause to think about the pitfalls and traps awaiting the place-name researcher. Unfortunately, I have not heard a present-day pronunciation of the name and, therefore, cannot say whether or not the oral form differs from the written form. Whatever the history of its development, however, we can at least be reasonably certain that Ribigill is a name of Norse origin.

Another very debatable name is Syre, which now applies to a settlement and a loch in the Naver Valley, next to Norse Langdale and Skail. I have no firm suggestion to make for the etymology of this name but it brings me to a theme which I should like to explore further, and that is the marked similarity between Norse naming in the wider area of Strathnaver, and that in Reay and Thurso Parishes on the west side of Caithness, in particular. I have already mentioned that Skail is a name which occurs in both Reay and the valley of the Naver. I suspect that the specific in the name Syre may derive from the same source as that in Shurrery in Reay Parish and, if I am correct, then it is likely that both Syre and Shurrery, as well as Skail, are of Norse origin.

Shurrery is recorded frequently from the 16th-century onwards – e.g. Showrarne, 1558 (*RSS*); Schourari, 1619 (*RMS*. VII .725); Schurarie, 1640 (*Retours*). Because of the word order in the compound, we can assume that the final element is most probably ON *ærgi* 'a shieling' – itself a borrowing from Gaelic *airigh* – which is quite common in Gaelic-influenced parts of present-day Caithness. For the specific, I would tentatively suggest ON *saurr* 'mud', which is frequently used in place-names, with reference to the swampy nature of the soil in the vicinity of any name which contains it. In Iceland, for instance, the name *Saur-bær* is common. The reference would be to the swampy ground around Loch Shurrery and Loch Syre. The generic in Syre is problematic, but it could be that this name also contains *ærgi*, further abbreviated due to earlier and more long-lasting influence from the Gaelic language. The settlement at Syre appears in written records from the 16th-century onwards – e.g. Shyre, 1570 (*Sutherland Charters* : *OPS*. 713); Syr, 1583 (*RMS*. V. 178); Schyre, 1608 (*RMS*. VI. 762). Like Shurrery, it displays some of the palatalisation of the initial consonant which could result from Gaelic influence.

While the above suggestions regarding the etymology of Syre and Shurrery rely much too heavily upon supposition, there can be no question about the exact parallel between some of the other Norse names which occur in Strathnaver and names in Thurso and Reay parishes. Beside the Kyle of Tongue, for example, one finds the name Scrabster to parallel Scrabster beside Thurso. The Thurso name is well documented from the 13th-century *Orkneyinga Saga* onwards, where it is recorded as *Skarabólstaðr* (in which the specific is either ON *skári* 'a young sea-mew' or *Skári*, the related personal name). The Scrabster beside the Kyle of Tongue, on the other hand, has not been so prominent in the settlement history of the area and now refers to a deserted site, although it was more significant in the 16th and 17th centuries when it appears in the same form as its more well-known counterpart in Caithness – e.g. Scrabuster, 1583 (*RMS*. V. 178). I believe, in fact, that the Strathnaver name has retained the *-buster* ending in this instance because the people who applied it and used it were very familiar with the Thurso name and, therefore, the subsequent Gaelic influence was not strong enough to lead to an alteration in the name.

PLACE-NAMES INCORPORATING
ON *gil, vík, gjá, skínandi, sker*

Another place-name which is reminiscent of names further to the east is Fresgill (sometimes Freisgill), by the side of Loch Eriboll. There are parallels in Caithness in Reay Parish, where Fresgoe is a coastal name (although Sandside Harbour is now built where Fresgoe was), and in Canisbay Parish on the east coast where there is an attested Norse settlement at Freswick (Morris & Rackham 1992. 43-102). The specific in each of these names could be ON *fress* 'a tom-cat', with reference to a wildcat, or it could even be ON *fyrsa* 'to gush or stream in torrents', although the metathesis has then to be explained. As Dr Barbara Crawford has rightly pointed out in a personal comment, it is difficult to accept that *fyrsa* should develop into Fres-, when ON *fors* 'a waterfall' remains nearby, without metathesis, as Forss.

The etymology of Fresgoe and Freswick may be debatable but, whatever the nature of the specific, fresh water would have been an important prerequisite of permanent settlement – which there certainly was at Freswick and in the vicinity of Fresgoe. One could speculate that Fresgill, likewise, might be situated in an area which has something of interest to offer archaeologists. The cave of Fresgill, which one assumes is the eponymous *gil*, is described in hyperbolic terms in the *Old Statistical Account* (*OSA.* 475), and the Norse might well have been similarly drawn to it:

> ... *the Great Cave of Fraisgill* ... |which| is about 50 feet high, and 20 feet wide at the entrance, and grows narrow by degrees, till at last a man can scarcely creep in it. Its sides are variegated with a thousand colours, which are lost in each other with a delicacy and softness that no art can imitate. Upon entering the cave, the mind is impressed with a pleasing sort of awe ... .

Each of the names – Freswick, Fresgoe and Fresgill – is topographical in reference, deriving from ON *vík* 'a bay', *gjá* 'a geo or steep-sided inlet of the sea' and *gil* 'a gully'. It is, of course, to some extent, chance which has led to archaeological digs being undertaken and finds being made in or near two places in Caithness where the names are topographical in reference, rather than habitative; but these names with their attested settlements should be weighed in the balance when considering whether or not topographical names should be seen as indicators of settlement.

At the other side of the Kyle of Tongue – itself a Norse name deriving from *tangi* 'a spit of land' – one finds Skinnet which, like Scrabster, is a name which is much better known from the Thurso area where it is situated in the valley of the River Thurso. The Thurso valley name is recorded from the time of Bishop Gilbert: ' ... tres ecclesias parochiales, videlicet, Olrich, Donotf, Canenisbi, separatim, adjunximus ecclesiam de Scynend ... ' (*CSR.* 16). Further references to the name are made in 1500 (Skenand) (*RSS.* ii. fol. 23); in 1561, 1566 & 1567 (Skenand), and in 1620 (Skynand) (*OPS.* 756-757). W.F.H. Nicolaisen has suggested an interpretation which identifies the name as Norse and relates it to the river beside which it lies (ON *skínandi* 'the shining one') (Nicolaisen 1982. 84), and it seems a very good suggestion in the context of the Thurso valley name. But what of Skinnet at the head of the Kyle of Tongue? There are no neighbouring rivers which could be described as 'shining', and I have found no early references to the name in the sources used for other names in the area. One reasonable conclusion which could be drawn is that there is some direct connection between the two Skinnets, at least in terms of the people who named them and possibly in terms of land ownership or use.

We must also take into account the possibility that, in the absence of early forms to prove the contrary, the name is of Gaelic origin (the map now records Skinnet and Ard Skinid), but it is no easier to suggest a realistic etymology from Gaelic than it is from Norse. I would favour Norse origin, and would suggest that the Gaelic name Ard Skinid, which means 'height of Skinnet', is a later coinage which incorporates an earlier Norse habitative name in a hybrid compound in which Gaelic *àrd* becomes the new generic. That the Norse were present on the west side of the Kyle of Tongue is confirmed by the name Tongue itself, which has already been mentioned, and by the name Melness – ON *melr* + *nes* 'sandy headland' (*melr* usually relates to an area of bent-grass growing in sandy soil) – which occurs in several early documents from the 14th-century onwards. It is recorded in the *Caithness and Sutherland Records*, for example, in a Charter dated 1379, confirming the gift by King Robert II 'to Farquhar, our physician, of the lands of Melness ... ' (*CSR*. 168).

It is certainly true that, when the Norse were giving names to places, they were using an onomastic vocabulary which was simultaneously wide in its range of possibilities and yet narrow, in that elements – particularly generics – were used repeatedly if appropriate to the situation. For example, there are many instances of ON *sker* 'an isolated rock in the sea' being used both as the common dialect term 'skerry' and as the first element in a place-name in a situation where there is a neighbouring rock or island in the sea, just as there is at Scarfskerry (the specific is ON *skarfr* 'the green cormorant') in Dunnet Parish in Caithness, or at Skerray which is a settlement on the coast between Torrisdale Bay and the Kyle of Tongue, opposite the two islands which are now known as Eilean nan Ròn and Neave or Coomb Island.

CONCLUSION

Whether the similarities I have been pointing to between Strathnaver names and names from Caithness have to do with this general tendency towards replication in naming or, as I believe, to direct links between the Norse settlers along the north coast, may never be proven. Common sense argues that the latter is true, although it cannot tell us when the links occurred or how they functioned. For instance, were the Norse who settled in Strathnaver or by the Kyle of Tongue contemporary with the initial colonisation of Caithness from Norway or Orkney? Or were they the sons and daughters of people who had settled in the vicinity of Thurso and Reay in the first instance and who, therefore, looked with affection to their earlier homes for inspiration in naming new homes of their own? We shall perhaps never know, but I hope that archaeologists working in the area may provide at least some of the answers.

In the meantime, I believe that, rather than being influenced in our thinking by modern county divisions, it is useful to think of the whole of the north mainland of Scotland, from Caithness westwards, as an area which the Norse found attractive for settlement and which they could easily have penetrated from the Atlantic by boat, until their route was blocked by high mountains to the south. The evidence of the names suggests that, while settlement was undoubtedly more concentrated in the east, for reasons already cited, it also extended westwards into the wide area known as Strathnaver; and it does seem reasonable to propose that the Strathnaver settlement occurred in or very shortly after the period when colonisation was taking place in Caithness, immediately opposite Orkney. I am conscious of straying into the domain of the historian, but I see no good reason to assume that Strathnaver was not part of the Caithness earldom.

References

Cleasby, Vigfusson & Craigie, *An Icelandic-English Dictionary*. 1874 (reprinted 1982).
Cox, R. 'Descendants of Norse *Bólstaðr*': A Re-Examination of the Lineage of *Bost* & Co.', in J.R. Baldwin (ed) *Peoples and Settlement in North-West Ross*. 1994: 43-67.
CSR : A.W. & A. Johnston (eds) *Caithness and Sutherland Records*. 1909.
Fellows-Jensen, G. 'Viking Settlement in the Northern and Western Isles – the Place-Name Evidence as seen from Denmark and the Danelaw', in A. Fenton & H. Pálsson (eds) *The Northern and Western Isles in the Viking World*. 1984.
Jakobsen, J. *The Place-Names of Shetland*. 1936 (reprinted 1993).
Macaulay, D. 'Place Names', in D. Omand (ed) *The Sutherland Book*. 1982: 278-292.
Macfarlane, W. *Geographical Collections*. 1907. vols I-III.
MacGregor, L.J. 'Sources for a Study of Norse Settlement in Shetland and Faroe', in B.E. Crawford (ed) *Essays in Shetland History*. 1984: 1-17.
Marwick, H. *Orkney Farm-Names*. 1952.
Morris, C.D. & Rackham, D.J. *Norse and Later Settlement and Subsistence in the North Atlantic*. 1992.
Morrison, A. 'Strathnaver – Some Notes on Settlement History', in *North Sutherland Studies*. (Scottish Vernacular Buildings Working Group). 1987: 7-22.
Nicolaisen, W.H. 'Scandinavians and Celts in Caithness: The Place-Name Evidence', in J.R. Baldwin (ed) *Caithness; A Cultural Crossroads*. 1982: 75-85.
ON: Old Norse
OPS : *Origines Parochiales Scotiae*. Bannatyne Club. vol II. 1855.
OS : *Orkneyinga Saga*.
OSA : J. Sinclair (ed) *Old Statistical Account of Scotland*. XXI vols. 1791-99.
Pennant, T. *A Tour of Scotland in 1769*. 3rd edition. 1979.
Retours: T. Thomson (ed) *Inquisitionum ad Capellam Domini Regis Retornatarum, quae in publicis archivis Scotiae adhuc servantur, Abbreviatio*. 1811-16.
RMS : *Registrum Magni Sigilli Regum Scotorum*. vols I-XI. Reprinted 1984.
RSS : *Registrum Secreti Sigilli Regum Scotorum*.
Stewart, J. *Shetland Place-Names*. 1987.
Watson, W.J. 'Some Sutherland Names of Places', in *The Celtic Review*. 1905-6. vol II: 232-242.
Watson, W.J. *Celtic Place-Names of Scotland*. 1926.
Waugh, D. 'Settlement names in Caithness with particular reference to Reay Parish', in B.E. Crawford (ed) *Scandinavian Settlement in Northern Britain*. 1995: 64-79.

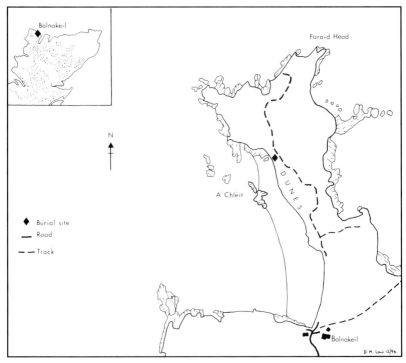

Fig. 3.1   Location of Balnakeil and burial site.

Fig. 3.2   The burial site lies approximately above the gateway to the church, on the far side of the bays.

24

A VIKING BURIAL
AT BALNAKEIL, SUTHERLAND

Dorothy M. Low, Colleen E. Batey & Robert Gourlay

The excavation of the Viking burial at Balnakeil was brought about by chance. Storms in May 1991 caused blowouts in the sand dunes which partially uncovered the remains of what appeared to be a human skeleton. These were noticed by Mr and Mrs Powell, who were holidaying in the area, and they promptly informed the local police of their discovery, handing in a pin which they had found lying on top of the skeleton. The police in turn alerted the Procurator Fiscal, and the site was visited with the local doctor who confirmed that the remains were human and of some antiquity. The police carefully covered the remains without further disturbance, and contacted the Archaeology staff of Highland Regional Council, requesting that the remains be professionally examined as soon as possible.

THE EXCAVATION

Excavation, undertaken by Dorothy Low and Robert Gourlay, commenced the following day. The remains were situated in the most northerly dune of the northernmost of the two bays [Fig. 3.1; 3.2]. The bones protruded from the edge of the dune, approximately 4 m above the high water mark, and some 5 m to 6 m below the dune top.

The visible remains initially consisted of most of the vertebrae, rib cage, pelvic bones and the left elbow joint. Some of the leg bones were found to be lying in loose and disturbed sand below the *in situ* remains, and it is presumed that they had fallen from their original position as the sand had blown away. There was no visible evidence at this stage of the skull or bones of the right arm. Examination of the position and angle of the skeleton led to the conclusion that the body had been placed on its right side, so that the rib cage and remaining sand overburden were obscuring the rest of the skeleton. The angle of the body in relation to the sand dune further indicated that the skull probably survived within the main dune, close to where a piece of corroded metal was protruding.

The wind erosion of the dunes had led to a highly unstable situation, with the strong possibility of an imminent collapse of the dune face. This would have led to the burial being covered with a large weight of sand which would have destroyed many of the more fragile remains. This threat also meant that working conditions were somewhat precarious, with small sand falls occurring regularly. For these reasons, the excavation was conducted with the utmost speed!

A number of objects were found lying in association with the skeleton, mainly concentrated around the pelvic area in a close group. The first stage of the excavation involved careful excavation of the visible remains, and the making of a full record through photographs and drawings [Fig. 3.3]. The next stage involved clearance of the sand overburden before it collapsed and destroyed the burial. During this process, the corroded remains of an iron object were found projecting upwards from the skeleton. This was later identified as a spearhead with part of the shaft still attached. Once all of the overlying sand had been removed, the skull could be seen lying on its right side, with the corroded remains of a shield boss lying on the back of the skull. The position of this, in conjunction with the remains of the spear, gave rise to the conclusion that they had been so placed to rest against one another, forming a kind of canopy over the head. In the area of the neck, two amber and one blue and white glass beads were found, representing a small necklace.

The group of finds in the pelvic area was seen to be considerably larger, while the closeness of the finds suggested that all had been held together in one container – perhaps a leather bag. These finds are identified and located in Figure 3.4 and listed below in the Appendix. Once all of these finds had been recovered, the bones were lifted and labelled with much assistance from the local doctor. One of the most interesting finds was left until last. Underlying the skeleton were the well-preserved remains of a sword, with wooden and other organic remains of the scabbard attached. The body had obviously been placed overlying the sword, thus concealing it from view.

Fig. 3.3   Excavation of the burial.

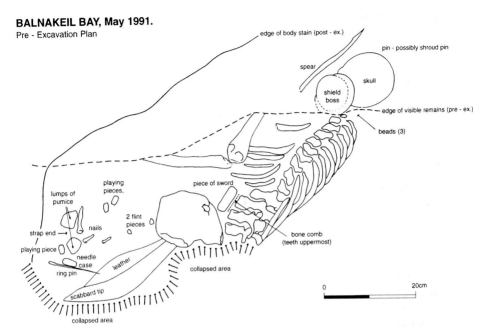

BALNAKEIL BAY, May 1991.
Pre - Excavation Plan

edge of body stain (post - ex.)

pin - possibly shroud pin

spear

skull

shield
boss

edge of visible remains (pre - ex.)

beads (3)

playing
pieces,

lumps of
pumice

piece of sword

2 flint
pieces

strap end →

nails

playing piece

needle
case

ring pin

leather

scabbard tip

collapsed area

bone comb
(teeth uppermost)

collapsed area

0   20cm

Fig. 3.4   Plan of the burial deposit.

The difficult problem of how to lift the sword and scabbard with the minimum of disturbance was solved with a slat from a lone fish box from the beach! The remains of the sword were isolated and slid onto the wooden slat, within a block of sand, and carefully secured prior to transportation.

THE SCALE OF THE PROBLEM: POST-EXCAVATION

The remains were initially taken to the Archaeology Office of Highland Regional Council, Inverness, where they were re-examined. Many of them proved to be in a relatively poor and fragile state. Some basic conservation work was carried out on the advice of the National Museums of Scotland, and the remains were removed the next day to their Conservation Laboratories in Edinburgh for specialist work. This material is still in the process of being conserved. The following discussion is based on information provided by the National Museums Conservation Section in late 1994, and some detailed work remains to be undertaken. However, much of the preliminary identification work has been undertaken at this stage and it is possible to present here a brief interim report on the skeleton and the grave goods from the site. A full report is being prepared for the *Proceedings of the Society of Antiquaries of Scotland.*

The Skeleton

A detailed report on the skeletal remains has been prepared by Yvonne Hallen and will appear in the final report on the burial. There are a number of interesting features about the remains which can be highlighted here. Although parts of the skeleton were missing at the time of excavation (such as the right fibula, sternum and pubis), and others had been damaged following burial (in particular the skull), the evidence is sufficient to suggest that the remains are those of a young person, probably male and aged between eight and thirteen years old.

Although it is difficult to sex a pre-pubescent skeleton precisely, the balance of evidence suggests it is male, and this coincides with the nature of the burial assemblage. He was approximately 4ft 9in to 5ft (1.48 m to 1.52 m) tall, and the right clavicle, humerus and ulna (ie right arm), seem enlarged in comparison to those on the left side. This assymetrical development is also seen in the skull, where the left eye orbit is higher than the right one. In addition, there are traces on the skeleton of a nonspecific infection which has caused pitting on both humeri and interior of the skull.

The Grave Goods

The burial was accompanied by a wide range of objects [Figs. 3.4; 3.5]. These comprised weapons including a sword, shield and spear; items related to his manner of dress, including a ringed-pin or brooch, beads and possible strap end; and accompanying grave goods of 14 gaming pieces which were probably originally in a bag. There was also a possible wooden gaming board (although these wood fragments could have originally formed part of the shield). The distinctive, but badly-preserved antler comb and needle case may be classed as grave goods rather than items related to dress, particularly the suggested needle case in view of the fact that the burial is that of a young male.

A pin-like item at the head may perhaps even be related to a head-dress although this is at present unclear, and could conceivably be related to a fastening for a shroud. The textile traces are still being examined, and the differences provisionally identified could indicate the remains of a cloak. The evidence of feathers incorporated into the corrosion products of the sword hilt seem to suggest the presence of a pillow placed beneath the body. However, the underside of the sword is also covered with a mass of straw-like material, suggesting a bed of straw. It is possible that a soft surface may have been created by a scatter of straw contaminated with feathers, although there is a concentration of feathers in the area of the hilt.

Fig. 3.5   Reconstruction drawing of the grave (Alan Braby, 1993).

The Weaponry

The fragmentary spear and domical shield boss were both recovered from the head area; the sword was lying under the body itself. A fragment of mineralised wood adhering to a finger bone may have been from the spear shaft or even the shield grip itself. The positioning of the spear, pointing upwards, in conjunction with the iron shield boss representing the remains of a wood and leather shield, placed as if to protect the head area, can be paralleled from other Viking graves in the British Isles.

At Westness in Orkney, a male burial within a boat was accompanied by several fine grave goods including a sword and a shield boss. In that case, the boss was located as if to suggest that the shield had been laid over the face, and was of specific interest because of the distinctive slash damage on the upper surface (Kaland 1993. 314). In the Balnakeil example, the corrosion on the shield boss has preserved straw, twig and leaf-like remains. A further parallel for the positioning of the spear can be noted from the Isle of Man, where the graves at Ballateare and Cronk Moar both showed evidence of a spear which was placed awkwardly in the grave, probably because the shaft was too long to fit within the coffin (Bersu & Wilson 1966. figs. 32, 40). In the Balnakeil example, it is most likely that the spearhead, its shaft and the shield had formed a canopy over the dead boy's head. The domical shield boss is a type which is commonly recorded from Viking graves (Type Rygh 562; Rygh 1885). Several examples were recorded from the graves at Birka in Sweden (Arbman 1940), and nearer examples can be cited from Reay on the north coast of Caithness (eg Batey 1993. fig 6.4, 154).

The sword itself is interesting, chiefly because of its condition. Although to the untrained eye, this fractured mass of rusting iron seems to be rather unprepossessing, in the hands of the conservator the story unfolds. The corrosion has preserved around the sword (and the spear head/shaft) large amounts of insect pellets which could represent woodworm! The sword was badly cracked by the pressure of the sand on the top of the burial, so it broke during lifting. However, on X-ray, the sword is shown to have an intact hilt, with domical pommel, possibly decorated cross bar and the remains of the padding on the handle section, secured with wires. The blade is virtually complete and housed within the remains of its organic scabbard. There are several questions which can be asked, which include detail of the decorative elements of the hilt concealed within the corrosion, and the nature of the scabbard and its lining. Detailed study can reveal leather, wood and textile traces forming the scabbard (op cit 1966. fig 33, 70-73, re Ballateare and Cronk Moar).

The sword is of further interest, however. Firstly, its position within the grave suggests that it lay beneath the body. This is a little unusual because, where the evidence survives, the sword is usually lain to the side of the individual. It will be necessary to examine whether the sword was wrapped within a shroud – if this can demonstrated – and next to the cloak, if one existed. Examination of the textile traces could help here. Preliminary examination certainly indicates the presence of textile on the underside of the sword, sandwiched between the scabbard and the straw-like material. It is conceivable that the body had been slightly displaced after burial, with the body falling onto the sword, but the supporting evidence for this is not strong. Some of the grave goods do, however, seem to suggest a slight post-burial disturbance, such as the brooch in the leg area.

Of further significance is the fact that the sword is clearly a full-sized example, buried here with a young boy. Whether he himself used the sword is a point to consider. The skeletal remains suggest a slight enlargement of the bones on the right side, supporting the idea that the young boy was forced to develop skills with full-sized weapons. Attractive as this idea might be, parallels are difficult to find, and it is possible that the enlargement may be due to other causes. Certainly, if enhanced muscle development was present, it should also be noticeable on the scapula bone.

There are stories in the saga sources of young boys being taken into battle with their fathers, and presumably fighting with a weapon which was, after all, a major status symbol and potential heirloom. Orkneyinga Saga records the death in battle of Ivarr, son of Earl Rognvald, during a campaign in the North of Scotland and Western Isles (ironically to subdue the 'vikings' who were harrying others from the Scandinavian homelands!). As compensation for this death, Rognvald was given the lands of Orkney and Shetland (Pálsson & Edwards 1978. chap 4. 30). The same story is recalled in Heimskringla (Smith 1932. chap 22. 58-9), and clearly the Icelandic tradition of saga-telling accepted the role of young boys in battle, if not always as heroes. In the absence of historical evidence, it can only be suggested that Ivarr may have been no older than 14 years at his death, possibly slightly younger. (We are grateful to Mrs Bridget MacKenzie for researching this information.) The type of sword is commonly found in other Viking contexts dating to the late 9th - 10th centuries, such as at Birka in Sweden (Arbman 1940. taf 4, 5) and elsewhere. The hilt of a similar fine example from Sties, Sanday in Orkney, can be seen at the Hunterian Museum, Glasgow.

Items Related to Dress

Although it is most likely that the body was buried fully-clothed, the remains of items in this category are few. A possible strap end, found in the lower body area, could indicate the former presence of a belt. However, this cannot be corroborated on the available evidence.

The three beads, two of amber and the third of glass with applied decoration, probably formed part of a simple necklace. The bead types can be readily-paralleled, particularly the 'eyed' glass example (cf Birka, Arbman 1940. taf 121, 122, 123). The small assemblage may perhaps be mirrored in the single find from the burial of a young child discovered at Kneep (Cnip), Lewis (Cowie et al 1993. fig 6A. 4, 169). Where bead necklaces have been identified to date, they are usually from female graves and most commonly there are many beads eg Kneep (Welander, Batey & Cowie 1987. illus 6, 156), presumably because the individual had been collecting rather longer! The token beads may perhaps be paralleled also at Birka (Arbman 1940. 40 grave 91).

The simple copper alloy ring pin or brooch with circular terminals, however, is rather more diagnostic. Parallels can be cited from Lagore in Ireland of a pre-Viking date (Hencken 1951. 73, Fig. 15 no. 1531). The inclusion of an artefact of greater antiquity than the rest of the burial can be seen at several sites throughout the Viking World. In Orkney the situation is similar – compare Westness (Stevenson 1989) and Pierowall (Grieg 1940. 93). The use of heirlooms in burials, pagan or Christian, is not so uncommon as one might think. In the case of a child, it is appropriate to think in terms of such a token link with the past – a cherished gift, perhaps, from a grieving parent? The location of the brooch in the pelvic region seems to suggest that it has become misplaced after burial. It should be a cloak fastening, but in this case could it be securing a shroud or similar item? There is a fragment of textile remaining in the ring of the pin, and further work is required to enable comparison between this and other textile material in the grave.

Other Grave Goods

This category includes the remaining items which do not fall into the above two categories, but which can be described as gifts to the dead for use in the after-life.

A bag of 14 conical gaming pieces made of antler, each with traces of a bone peg for affixing to a board, was located in the area of the legs. There may also be traces of a gaming board, in the form of wooden fragments (although see above).

Several graves have produced sets of simple gaming pieces, in carved horses' teeth, glass or antler – eg Westness and Scar in Orkney, and two beautiful sets from Birka in Sweden made of coloured glass (Arbman 1940. taf 148, 1 & 2, from graves 523 & 644). Gaming boards are rather more difficult to identify because they are usually organic and have decayed beyond recognition in the grave. An exception to this is from Ireland, where the site of Ballinderry produced a fine complete example of an incised board with decorative features (Graham-Campbell 1980. 23 no. 92). Elsewhere in Scotland, examples of simple incised stones have been recorded commonly, but not exclusively in pre-Viking contexts (Sterckx 1973; Ritchie 1977. 187, 198-9; Batey 1989. 215 no. 280). It has to be presumed that a board game such as *hnefatafl* or Nine Mens Morris was played. In the Balnakeil grave, a single piece of flint may have originally been in the same bag, but it is not known whether this was actually associated with the playing of the game itself.

Other grave goods include a fragmentary antler comb and a probable needle case (cf Birka, Arbman 1940. taf 167 no. 7, grave 1081), which were both found in the mid-body area. It is conceivable that they were originally attached to the belt suggested above. The comb is a single-sided composite example, and although fragmentary, it is likely that it would originally have had five iron rivets and three or four tooth plates in all. The presence of a comb is not surprising, as both male and female, young and old would have had one. However, if indeed the other item is a needle case, it certainly does suggest an enlightened approach to the education of a young Viking! The needle case is badly corroded, comprising thread preserved in the corrosion products, wound around up to three iron needles. It is not of the type most commonly found, which is made of a bird bone tube, although metal examples are known form Scandinavia (Arbman 1940. taf 168).

CONCLUSION: THE LOCAL SITUATION

At this stage, the evidence from Balnakeil suggests a single burial of a young boy, interred with a wide range of accompanying items. It cannot be known how he died, because the surviving skeletal remains do not show any signs of fatal wounds. A drowning accident is a possible but unprovable cause. The circumstances of the excavation were not conducive to detailed study of the immediate area, which might hold additional burials. It is increasingly common to discover that an apparent single burial is, in fact, part of a larger group or a cemetery, as at Scar in Orkney (O. Owen, pers. comm.), or as at Reay near Thurso in Caithness (Batey 1993. 152-154). There is a suggestion that at Keoldale on the Durness peninsula, remains of a grave were disturbed in the last century and recorded briefly by Lethbridge (1950. 96), although its Scandinavian character is fugitive.

The recovery of Norse remains on the North-West coast is exciting, but not unexpected. Cape Wrath was a crucial landmark for the Viking seafarers on their route towards the Western Isles and Ireland. Place-names such as Durness and Tongue prove that the Norse were familiar with the coastline, if not to the same extent with the northern interior (see Crawford & Waugh, this volume). It is even possible that the Balnakeil boy may have had links with Ireland, either himself or through his parents, as suggested by the origins of the ringed brooch in the grave.

There is, however, one certainty – with the increase in coastal erosion more remains of the period will be uncovered along exposed coastal stretches. With careful monitoring this can be used greatly to increase the amount of information available for the period in Northern Scotland.

Acknowledgement

The level of evidence amassed was possible only through the prompt reporting of their find by Mr & Mrs Powell. Thanks are also extended to the local GP, Dr George Sanders for assisting with the skeletal identification during excavations.

Colleen Batey would like to thank Theo Skinner of the National Museums of Scotland Conservation Section for his help in the preliminary statements about the conserved pieces; also the assistance of the Artefact Research Unit of NMS for the resources made available during the study of the artefacts. Alison Sheridan (National Museums of Scotland) has helped to clarify several points of discussion within the paper, whilst the contribution of Mrs Bridget MacKenzie in relation to the Saga sources is also gratefully acknowledged.

Figure 3.2 is Crown copyright, courtesy of the Royal Commission on the Ancient and Historical Monuments of Scotland; Figure 3.3 is Highland Region copyright; Figure 3.4 was provided by Dorothy Low. The reconstruction drawing (Figure 3.5) was commissioned from Alan Braby by the National Museums of Scotland, on behalf of the then Highland Regional Council.

Appendix

List of Artefactual Material (provided by T Skinner, National Museums of Scotland Conservation Section). NMS Accession Numbers IL 921-963.

Sword and fragmentary scabbard
Shield boss
Spearhead and part of shaft
Ringed pin
Possible strap end
Small copper alloy ?pin
12 miscellaneous iron nails
2 indeterminate iron objects
Antler comb
14 complete and fragmentary gaming pieces of antler
Fragment of mineralised wood with finger bone attached (?shield grip or spear shaft)
Fragment of mineralised wood (?possibly a fragment of gaming board)
2 amber beads, 1 blue and white glass bead
Needle case with possible needles inside
Small lump of pumice
Small flint flake

References

Arbman, H. *Birka I: Die Graber.* Stockholm. 1940. 2 vols.

Batey, C.E. *Excavations beside the Brough Road, Birsay: The Artefact Assemblage*, in Morris 1989: 191-229.

Batey, C.E. *Viking and Late Norse Graves of Caithness and Sutherland*, in CE Batey *et al* (eds), 1993: 148-164.

Batey, C.E., Jesch, J. & Morris C.D. (eds). *The Viking Age in Caithness, Orkney and the North Atlantic.* Select Papers from the Proceedings of the Eleventh Viking Congress. Edinburgh. 1993.

Bersu, G. & Wilson, D.M. *Three Viking Graves in the Isle of Man.* Soc. Medieval Archaeol. Monog. Ser. No. 1. London. 1966.

Cowie, T., Bruce, M. & Kerr, N. *The Discovery of a Child Burial of Probable Viking-Age Date on Kneep Headland, Uig, Lewis, 1991: Interim Report*, in C.E. Batey et al. 1993: 165-172.

Graham-Campbell, J. *Viking Artefacts, A Select Catalogue.* London. 1980.

Grieg, S. 'Viking Antiquities in Scotland', in H. Shetelig (ed) *Viking Antiquities in Great Britain and Ireland.* vol II. Oslo. 1940.

Hencken, H.O'N. 'Lagore Crannog: an Irish royal residence of the 7th to 10th centuries AD', in *Proc Royal Irish Acad.* C. 53. 1950-1: 1-247.

Kaland, S. *The Settlement of Westness, Rousay*, in C.E. Batey *et al.* 1993: 308-317.

Lethbridge, T.C. *Herdsmen and Hermits.* Cambridge. 1950.

Morris, C.D. *The Birsay Bay Project. Volume 1. Brough Road Excavations 1976-1982*, University of Durham, Department of Archaeology Monograph Series No 1. 1989.

Pálsson, H. & Edwards, P. *Orkneyinga Saga. The History of the Earls of Orkney.* London. 1978.

Ritchie, A. 'Excavation of Pictish and Viking-age farmsteads at Buckquoy, Orkney', in *Proc Soc Antiq Scot.* 108. 1976-7: 174-227.

Rygh, O. *Norske Oldsager, Ordnede og Forklarede.* Christiania. 1885.

Smith, A.H. (trans) & Monsen E.(ed). *Heimskringla or the Lives of the Norse Kings by Snorre Sturleson.* Cambridge. 1932.

Sterckx, C. 'Les trois damiers de Buckquoy (Orcades)', in *Annales de Bretagne.* 80. 1973: 675-89.

Stevenson, R.B.K. 'The Celtic brooch from Westness, Orkney, and hinged-pins', in *Proc Soc Antiq Scot.* 119. 1989: 239-269.

Welander, R.D.E., Batey, C.E. &Cowie, T.G. 'A Viking Burial from Kneep, Uig, Isle of Lewis', in *Proc Soc Antiq Scot.* 117. 1987: 149-174.

FROM CLANSHIP TO CROFTING: LANDOWNERSHIP, ECONOMY AND THE CHURCH IN THE PROVINCE OF STRATHNAVER

Malcolm Bangor-Jones

INTRODUCTION

The history of Strathnaver from the period of the clans to the Clearances is the subject of the late Ian Grimble's well-known trilogy, *Chief of Mackay*, *The World of Rob Donn*, and *The Trial of Patrick Sellar*.[1] This study, which is intended to supplement Grimble's work, explores a number of topics grouped under the broad headings of:
  * landownership
  * economy
  * the church.

The process whereby, over a period of two hundred years, the house of Mackay was supplanted by the Sutherland interest, is central to the history of landownership in the north. However, the landed families were also deeply concerned with their status, standard of living and frequently their financial survival. Landlords were pivotal to the functioning of the Highland economy, although important roles were also played by the middlemen, the tacksmen, and the small but significant numbers of merchants. The central section of this essay deals with the main elements of the economy and aspects of landholding including the establishment of crofting and the impact of the clearances. The final section, a brief history of the church, examines the impact of the Reformation, the evolution of the parish structure, education, the role of the ministers in the clearances and the rise of evangelical presbyterianism.

The study is intended to be read in conjunction not only with Grimble's works but also with the Rev Angus Mackay's *The Book of Mackay*, which contains a good deal of basic genealogical information and valuable material on the general historical background.[2] As will be apparent, there is considerable scope for more detailed research on the various Mackay families and subjects such as kelp manufacture, fishing and the clearances.

There is a distinction to be made between the province of Strathnaver (which, at its widest extent, reached from the border with Caithness to the bounds of Assynt on the west), and the valley of the Naver. As befits modern usage, the former is referred to as the province of Strathnaver, while the latter is Strathnaver.

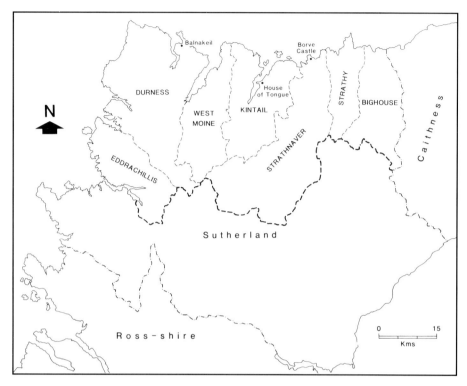

Fig. 4.1   Territorial divisions of the province of Strathnaver.

LANDOWNERSHIP

Origins of the Mackays and the Province of Strathnaver

The name Mackay derives from the Gaelic *Mac Aoidh* meaning son of Aodh. However the identity of Aodh, the eponymous ancestor of the Mackays is not known. It is generally stated that the clan came from Moray and was descended from the royal house of Moray which was driven out by the Scottish kings in the 12th century.[3] The Mackays may have found protection in the north because of links between Moray and the Norse earldom of Caithness which included Caithness, Sutherland and the province of Strathnaver (see Crawford, this volume), although tradition asserts that the Mackays forcibly took possession from the Norse.[4] The Moray origin is plausible although it is not supported by any documentation or early clan genealogy.

The first possible appearance of the Mackays in the documentary record is a reference to one 'Iver MacEothe' who witnessed a charter of the Earl of Caithness in the late 13th century.[5] Laying this aside, the first unequivocal reference is to Angus Mackay of Strathnaver in 1415. It is unclear, however, what the geographical extent of this 'Strathnaver' was; it may well have been limited to the area around Tongue and the valley of the Naver, and thus have been equivalent to the later parishes of Tongue and Farr. The wider province of Strathnaver which was to become associated with the clan was made up of a number of territories, Strathnaver, Kintail and West Moine, Durness, Eddrachillis and Strath Halladale [Fig. 4.1], each of which had its own history of landownership.

Strathnaver

In the 13th century, Strathnaver was in the possession of Lady Joanna, who also held half of the earldom of Caithness and was the wife of Freskin de Moravia, the nephew of William, the first earl of Sutherland. Joanna gifted upper Strathnaver to the Church of Moray which took the sensible course of feuing the lands while retaining the superiority.[6] In the mid-14th century the lands of upper Strathnaver formed part of the holdings of the great Reginald Cheyne, or *Morar na Schein*.[7] It is not known who owned Strathnaver between Cheyne and Angus Mackay in 1415.[8] The Mackay stronghold was at Castle Borve (also known as Castle Farr) [Fig. 4.2].

Kintail and West Moine

Nothing is known of the landholding history of the districts of Kintail, the area on both sides of the Kyle of Tongue, and of West Moine (the lands on the east shore of Loch Eriboll). It may be assumed that they were among the earliest possessions of the Mackays. The stronghold at Tongue is first recorded in the late 16th century.

Durness

The district of Durness, between Loch Eriboll and Loch Laxford, belonged to the bishops of Caithness. There is no record as to when these lands were acquired by the church although the 17th-century historian of the house of Sutherland, Sir Robert Gordon, asserted that they were granted by Alexander III (1249-86) to Bishop Gilbert.[9] The possibility that the lands were attached to an earlier Celtic monastery cannot be ruled out.[10] It is likely that most of the district was let to tenants, probably Mackays. The castle at Balnakeil is traditionally held to have been a summer residence of the bishops of Caithness who may also have owned Castle Varrich [Fig. 4.3], which has no definite association with the Mackays and was situated on the churchlands of Ribigill.[11] At the time of the Reformation, Durness passed to the earls of Sutherland, and the Mackays were eventually confirmed as their feudal vassals.

Fig. 4.2   Castle Borve, near Farr.

Fig. 4.3   Castle Bharraich, a late medieval stronghold on the churchlands of Ribigill.

Eddrachillis

The lands of Eddrachillis reached from the River Laxford to Loch Glencoul on the borders of Assynt and appear to have formed part of the barony of Skelbo, owned by the Kinnairds as vassals of the earls of Sutherland. Whether Eddrachillis was part of the grant of Skelbo, Ferenbeuthlin in Creich and other unspecified lands to the west made by Hugh Freskin to Gilbert archdeacon of Moray in 1212 x 1214, is not clear.[12] Certainly Sir Robert Gordon and 19th-century historians friendly to the house of Sutherland were prepared to assert that Eddrachillis was formerly part of the parish of Lairg.[13]

In 1515 Kinnaird granted the lands to Mackay; a transfer which may have recognised Mackay claims to Eddrachillis. During the 16th century the lands were possessed by the MacLeods of Eddrachillis, a branch of the MacLeods of Lewis. Kinnaird's grant to the Mackays may, therefore, have been to further their claims against the MacLeods whom they were eventually able to oust (there were, however, MacLeod wadsetters in the province of Strathnaver until the late 17th century).[14] Mackay ownership of Eddrachillis became absolute: a claim to the superiority of Eddrachillis by Sir Robert Gordon was unsuccessful.

Strath Halladale

Strath Halladale appears to have been held by the earls of Caithness and was probably acquired by the earls of Ross when they took control of Caithness in the mid-14th century. Through whatever route, Donald Lord of the Isles appears to have inherited rights to Strath Halladale because in 1415 he granted a charter of Strath Halladale and part of Creich to his brother-in-law, Angus Mackay of Strathnaver, and Neil his eldest son. The lands were possessed by Angus's cousin, Thomas Neilson Mackay, but were forfeited after he killed Mowat of Freswick in the chapel of St Duthac in Tain. Thomas Neilson was captured by his brothers, Morgan and Niel, at the instigation of their father-in-law, Angus Moray of Culbin. In 1430, as a reward for their service, James I granted the lands of 'Galvale and Balehegliss' (Golval and what is now Kirkton) to Morgan Mackay, and Spinningdale (in the parish of Creich), 'Byghosse', the two 'Tronculis' and the two 'Forssis' (Forsinain and Forsinard) to Angus Moray.[15] Lower Strath Halladale was thus in the hands of the Mackays, while upper Strath Halladale was owned by the Morays.

However, in 1467 John earl of Ross and Lord of the Isles granted Strath Halladale to his brother, Celestine of Lochalsh. With presumably this in mind, it has been suggested that Strath Halladale became part of the Mackay lands at the turn of the 16th century. The grant appears, though, to have been ineffective as the Murrays of Spinningdale, who were descended from Angus Moray of Culbin, continued to possess their share of the lands and in 1579 obtained a decreet against Donald McAngus McAlester of Glengarry as nearest heir to the family of Lochalsh. Disputes arose between the Murrays and the Mackays which eventually led to the Mackay take-over of the whole of Strath Halladale and the establishment of the Mackays of Bighouse (see below; also Beaton, this volume).[16]

The Possessions of the Beatons of Melness

Mention must also be made of the landholdings of the Beatons of Melness, a branch of the renowned Gaelic kindred of physicians, who were given lands in Strathnaver as a reward for their faithful service to the Crown.[17]

In 1379, Robert II confirmed a grant of the lands of Melness and Hope by his son Alexander Stewart, Lord of Badenoch, to Fearchar 'Leich'; and in 1386, Fearchar received a grant from the king himself of the Little Isles of Strathnaver[18] [Figs. 4.4; 4.5]. By the end of the 15th century the islands were apparently in the hands of the Mackays, and in 1511 Donald, son of Duncan of Melness, granted the lands of Melness and Hope to Aodh Mackay.[19] Sir Donald Mackay of Strathnaver formally purchased the Little Isles from William Macallan in Tongue in 1624.[20] Traditions relating to Fearchar may still be heard around Melness[21] (see Beith, this volume).

Mackays of Strathnaver

In 1539, Donald Mackay of Strathnaver received from James V a charter of his lands in Sutherland including of the lands between Eriboll and Strathy: all were included within the barony of Farr.[22] The following year, Bishop Andrew of Caithness granted a charter to Donald of the churchlands of Durness, Ribigill and Skail, giving ownership of lands which the Mackays may well have possessed as the bishop's tenants.[23] The Mackays now had rights to lands from Dirlot in Caithness to the borders of Assynt on the west coast. However, the grant of Durness was to bring the clan into the extraordinary feuds between the Earls of Sutherland and Caithness in which they were to be a lesser but by no means an insignificant power. In 1544, when Bishop Andrew's successor, Robert Stewart, was absent, Donald and the Earl of Caithness seized the lands and rents of the bishopric. However, the Earls of Sutherland and Huntly intervened and restored the lands to Bishop Robert.[24] In 1559, Durness was included in the disposition of church lands in Caithness and Sutherland made by the bishop to the Earl of Sutherland on the eve of the Reformation.

The death of Donald in 1550 was the cause of further trouble. Despite the fact that he had been legitimated many years previously there apparently remained room for doubt and, on the grounds that he died without lawful heirs, Queen Mary granted the lands of Strathnaver to Robert Reid, the reforming bishop of Orkney.[25] Reid, who gave Donald's son, Aodh a title to his lands, may have wished to protect Strathnaver from the Gordon interest. However, the disputes between Sutherland and the Mackays continued, and when Aodh failed to appear before the Queen Regent, the Earl of Sutherland

Fig. 4.4   Eilean nan Ròn, from Farr, across Torrisdale Bay.

Fig. 4.5   Melness across the Kyle of Tongue.

was given a commission to proceed against him. In 1555, the Earl led a major expedition into Strathnaver, during which he besieged, captured and destroyed Castle Borve [Fig. 4.2]. Four years later, the Queen gave Strathnaver to the Earl of Huntly to whom Aodh submitted as his feudal vassal in 1570.[26]

Hugh or Uisdean Mackay [Fig. 4.6] was faced with a difficult situation when he succeeded his father, Aodh in 1572: not only was he a minor but his elder brothers were the offspring of an irregular marriage. Furthermore the Abrach Mackays had effectively deserted their chief and fought for the Earl of Sutherland against the Gunns, their neighbours in the heights of Sutherland with whom they may well have had march disputes. In 1583, the Earl of Sutherland was given the superiority of Farr by Earl of Huntly. The Earl was thus feudal superior of both the former church lands of Durness and the remainder of Hugh's possessions. In 1588, Hugh, faced with an alliance between the Earls of Caithness and Sutherland, and as yet without a title to his lands, made his feudal submission to the Earl of Sutherland. The terms were complex and were significantly amended by a further agreement made the following year, when Hugh recognised the Earl as his feudal superior and was given the Earl's daughter in marriage. The Earl, on the other hand, remained entitled to pursue for substantial arrears of feu duty for which Hugh appears to have granted security over the lands of West Moine.[27]

The Earl of Sutherland had indeed acquired a 'private army of Gaels' to use against the Earl of Caithness.[28] On the other hand, the Mackays continued in possession of the churchlands of Durness (which had been included within the earldom of Sutherland in 1601) and eventually, in about 1613, the Earl of Sutherland feued the lands to Hugh in return for his service to the family of Sutherland. The Earls of Sutherland continued as feudal superiors of Durness, known as the 'barony of Ardurness', with the Mackays holding the lands as their feudal vassals. In the meantime, Hugh had, in 1605, granted a wadset of the lands between Kylesku and Kinlochbervie, and also Eriboll, to his elder half brother, Donald.[29] Hugh and his son Donald granted another wadset to Murdoch Neilson of the Abrach Mackays in 1613 for £1,000 over the lands of Lochnaver. Whether these grants were in recognition of past claims or in return for financial help is not known. However, the grant to Murdoch Neilson was the first of various agreements which Hugh and Donald made with the Abrach Mackays and appears to qualify the assertion that Hugh failed to accommodate this branch of the clan.[30]

Hugh was succeeded in 1614 by his son Donald, who had already married Barbara, daughter of Lord Mackenzie of Kintail and was thus related to two of the most powerful families in the north, the Mackenzies and the Gordons. Donald was knighted in 1616 through the influence of his uncle, Sir Robert Gordon, a very able man with access to the King. Sir Robert was tutor to the Earl of Sutherland and aimed to use his nephew as vassal to the house of Sutherland in its dealings with the Earl of Caithness. However, Sir Donald was, in Sir Robert's own words, 'a gentleman of a stirring spirit'. He had inherited something from his mother's family – as he said to his uncle,

The Mackays of Strathnaver

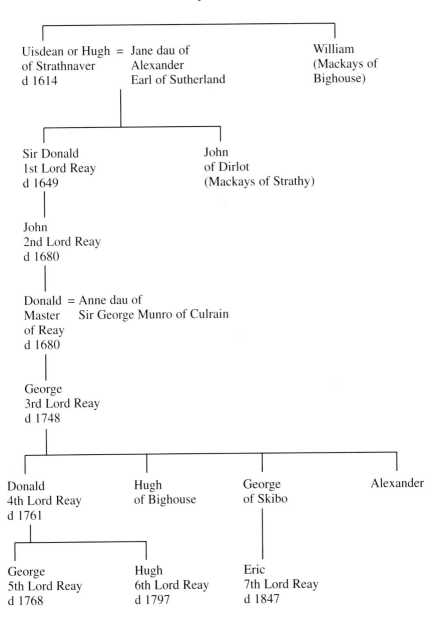

Fig. 4.6   The Mackays of Strathnaver.

he was 'an imp of that same stock' – and he grew to mistrust Sir Robert.

With rising expenditure and the burden of past claims on the estate, Sir Donald was soon hard put to meet his obligations. His wife's uncle, Sir Rorie Mackenzie of Coigach, was a cautioner in a bond of 5,000 merks granted in 1617 to Sir Robert Bruce of Clackmannan. Sir Rorie evidently settled the debt, but Sir Donald was unable to repay him and by the following year was trying to satisfy Sir Rorie by selling him Eddrachillis. However, although Sir Donald's nephew resigned his wadset of the lands, the sale did not go through.[31] Sir Donald may have been counselled against the loss of part of the Mackay lands to another 'clan'; there was to be no such hesitation over handing over a part of the estate to his younger brother, John. In 1618 Sir Donald had granted a bond of £50,000 Scots to John, presumably in satisfaction of whatever provision their father had made. When payment was not forthcoming, John brought an inhibition against his brother and was given the lands of Dirlot in Caithness and Strathy in Sutherland.[32]

Despite these difficulties, Sir Donald was clearly intent on territorial expansion, and in 1624 purchased the estate of Reay in Caithness from Lord Forbes.[33] The acquisition may have been paid for by the large loan which Sir Donald obtained from Mackenzie of Coigach and for which a number of Sutherland landowners acted as cautioners, including John Munro of Obsdale, Robert Munro of Assynt, Gilbert Gray of Swordale and John Gordon of Embo. Sir Donald, along with several leading Mackay families, granted them bonds of relief, thus relieving their neighbours of their cautionry.[34] The following year Sir Donald acquired the Little Isles of Strathnaver (see above). Sir Donald enjoyed strong support from the Mackay gentry and every effort was made to preserve unity within the clan. In 1621, a dispute which arose between Sir Donald and William Mackay alias Neilson, wadsetter of Achness and a leading member of the Abrach Mackays over some salmon fishings, threatened to get out of hand. On examination, 'diverse and sundrie calumnious and evill reports' were found to have been 'maliciouse lies falslie inventit be weeked and evill dispoisit persones'. The parties came to an agreement whereby William undertook to 'love & s[e]rve ... Sir donald his cheife dureing all the dayis of his lyftyme as ane trustie & faithfull kinsman ought to doe his cheife', and Sir Donald in turn bound himself 'to discharge the duetie of ane chiefe'. Even this did not bring hostilities to a close, for in 1623 William signed a bond of lawburrows in the presence of Kintail not to harm Sir Donald. The following year, however, William renounced all claim to the salmon fishings and there the matter appears to have ended.[35]

In 1626, Sir Donald took the major step of raising, under a warrant from Charles I, a regiment to assist Count Mansfield in the Thirty Years War which was then raging in Europe. It was an opportunity to enhance his prestige and Sir Donald may have harboured ambitions towards the earldom of Orkney. Mackay's regiment served with the Danish king, Christian IV, and in 1628 Sir Donald was rewarded by being created Lord Reay. Thus encouraged, he sent his regiment to serve under the renowned Gustavus Adolphus of

Sweden. It is doubtful whether the regiment was a profitable venture. Its raising had been accomplished by several loans. In September 1626 an arrangement was entered into with Mackay's brother-in-law, Colin Earl of Seaforth, whereby Seaforth paid a total of 7,000 merks to satisfy the claims of an Edinburgh merchant and of Robert Munro, minister of Durness.[36] Wadsets were also granted to Duncan Forbes, provost of Inverness, (the lands were rented back to Mackay),[37] to Robert Farquhar, burgess of Aberdeen for 18,800 merks[38] and also to James and William Corbat for 1,100 merks.[39] All of these loans were still outstanding after Lord Reay's own involvement with the regiment was over, and it is probable that Charles I never paid all of Lord Reay's claims.[40]

Lord Reay returned north in 1632, not in the best of financial circumstances, and with the obligation to enter into a settlement with the Earl of Sutherland, who had not only attained his majority but had also managed to get Sutherland, including Strathnaver and Assynt, erected into a separate sheriffdom (it had previously been part of the sheriffdom of Inverness). Agreement was reached and the Earl, who continued to be guided by his uncle, Sir Robert, granted Lord Reay a feu charter of the lands of Durness in 1633. In recognition of his status as a vassal, Lord Reay bound himself to accompany the Earl of Sutherland to all Parliaments. It appears that the Earl's dubious claim to the superiority of Strathnaver itself was for the moment laid aside (it was to be eventually abandoned).[41]

The 1630s were to be a period of growing financial difficulty. In 1634, Lord Reay entered into several land transactions. Farquhar's wadset was repaid,[42] but the lands of Eddrachillis were wadsetted to Hugh Mackay (then designed of Eriboll), founder of the Mackays of Scourie.[43] Of greater significance, however, was the sale of the lands of Lochnaver and part of Mudale which were possessed by the Abrach Mackays to Sir John Gordon of Embo, who also received a wadset right to the salmon fishings.[44] This was the first alienation of clan lands to the Gordons, although Lochnaver was on the southernmost boundary of Strathnaver and Embo had at one time fallen out with the Earl of Sutherland. Over the following years, several small loans were raised from minor members of the clan. In 1635, Lord Reay and John Munro, the minister at Reay, with Murdo Mckay alias Neilsone of Growbmoir (an Abrach Mackay) and 'Dod Mckconill iein of Dauchow' as cautioners granted a bond for 1,000 merks to 'dod mckolekeane' from [Farr?].[45] The next year a wadset of Rossal was granted to Iver McConill Mcallaster in Achinduich and his son William McIver (later referred to as William Mckay Iverson) who were under pressure from the Murrays to relinquish their possessions in the parish of Creich.[46] In 1637, Lord Reay was forced into several drastic measures: part of Reay was sold to Innes of Sandside,[47] a wadset of 24,000 merks over Durness was granted to John Gray, the dean of Caithness[48] and a huge bond for 52,000 merks over much of Strathnaver was granted to the Earl of Sutherland.[49] Some of the proceeds would have gone to redeeming the wadset held by the Earl of Seaforth, another financially hard-pressed Highland landlord.[50] The following year, one David Dunbar was given a wadset right to the lands of Invernaver, then in the Master of Reay's own possession, for a loan of 3,000 merks.[51] Against this background, Lord Reay could not afford the action brought against him by Rachel Harrison, a lady with whom he had had an association prior to 1630 (not the first of a series of extramarital affairs).[52] The Privy Council found, largely on the basis of a document which may have been forged by Sir Robert Gordon, that she had been Lord Reay's wife and was therefore entitled to a very substantial sum for her maintenance. In 1638, Lord Reay was outlawed for non-payment.[53] The only comfort was that Robert Munro of Achness, a friend of the Mackays, had acquired several of the outstanding debts and obtained an apprising against the estate, thus affording Lord Reay a measure of protection from his other creditors.

In a sense, the Scottish revolution and civil war came none too soon for the Mackays. Lord Reay signed the National Covenant but was soon identified as not being true to the cause and indeed the clan was to adhere to the Royalist side throughout the civil war. Their position was probably less a matter of loyalty to the King or indeed of religious conviction, but rather a consequence of their desperate financial situation and the claims of the Earl of Sutherland who was a Covenanter.[54] The 1640s and 1650s were extremely difficult for many Highland families, partly because of the cost and devastation of war, but also because of the opportunities for creditors to seize possession of estates. There appear to have been few debts incurred by Lord Reay which may be directly attributed to the war apart from a sum owing in 1639 to John Lindsay, a gunmaker in Montrose.[55] However, by 1642 Lord Reay's finances had reached a critical point and he was forced to negotiate a sale of part of Strathnaver to the Earl of Sutherland. The Earl had received no interest on Lord Reay's bond of 52,000 merks, nor had been given possession of any land. In return for the cancellation of the original loan and outstanding interest of 16,640 merks, and for a further sum of 40,000 merks which the Earl undertook to pay to various creditors, Lord Reay sold him Invernaver and Borgiebeg and those parts of upper Strathnaver between Mudale and Langwell on the west and between Rossal and Skelpick on the east. The Earl also undertook to pay all Lord Reay's creditors in Sutherland, dispensed with the requirement that Lord Reay accompany him to Parliament, and instructed his factor not to collect any tax from Lord Reay nor to prosecute for arrears of feu duty for Durness.[56]

Survival depended upon keeping creditors at bay, and this required the full assistance of the clan gentry. In 1644, for instance, a group of leading men comprising the Master of Reay, John Mackay of Dirlot, William Mackay of Bighouse, Hugh Mackay of Scourie and Hector Monro of Eriboll granted a bond to Sir Robert Farquhar for one of Lord Reay's debts.[57] Farquhar was one of the merchants who provided substantial financial support to the Covenanters' cause and was responsible for tax raising in the north. He was also allied to the Sutherland interest; Sir Robert Gordon's eldest son married a daughter and co-heiress of Sir Robert Farquhar. The same year, the Master of Reay wadsetted the district of Oldshores to Robert

Munro of Achness in return for 12,000 merks; these lands were held by the Munros until 1678.[58]

In December 1646, Lord Reay and the leading Mackays were summoned to appear before the Commissioners of the General Assembly 'To ansr for ther complyance with the rebells and for ther uther malignant carriage, and to reseave such censure as ther offences sallbe found to deserue.'[59] Their support for the Royalist cause did not waver, and Mackay foot were even present at the Battle of Worcester under the command of William Mackay of Borley, though few returned.[60] After the death of the first Lord Reay in 1649, his son took part in Pluscarden's rising which ended with his capture at Balvenie.[61] Tongue House was garrisoned by the Commonwealth interest and creditors began to take action to seize possession of the estate.

In 1649, Robert Gray of Ballone obtained an apprising,[62] and the following year another apprising was obtained by Farquhar. The latter's claim rested on two bonds dating from 1639 and 1644 which had been acquired by Sir Robert Gordon of Embo and then transferred to the Earl of Sutherland.[63] In 1653 Alexander Gray of Creich obtained a further apprising.[64] The Gray families in Sutherland appear to have been making the most of the opportunities offered by the civil war period and were taking advantage of the financial problems of other families. Ballone, who was a younger brother of Creich, was a commissioner and became collector of cess for most of the northern Highlands and Isles.[65] The Earl of Sutherland paid for Gray's legal processes against Lord Reay: this may have been because the Earl was superior but it may indicate a deeper motive.[66] As might be expected, several minor families which had provided Lord Reay with financial assistance also suffered in the process. For instance, Hugh Mackay of Scourie's help to Lord Reay in the 1630s led to an apprising against him by Robert Gray of Skibo in 1654.[67] On the other hand, creditors who obtained apprisings did not necessarily gain possession of their victim's estates, or attempt to collect any rents, even after being granted a charter. Indeed, contrary to Grimble's interpretation, Farquhar did not obtain actual possession of any part of the estate.[68] Sometimes, an appriser did take matters a step further. In 1656-57, Alexander Gray of Creich obtained legal powers to eject the tenants of Torrisdaile, Skerray Torrisdale and Borgiemore. It is, however, very unlikely that any of the tenants were turned out of their holdings, but they may have been persuaded to pay Gray some rents.[69]

In the meantime, Lord Reay had participated in the royalist uprising in 1653 known as Glencairn's Rising. He surrendered in May 1655 but Tongue House was destroyed, either by Cromwellian troops or possibly by Lord Reay himself.[70] Lord Reay was in dire financial straits, and in 1658 he was forced to enter into another agreement with the Earl of Sutherland. In return for 41,660 merks which the Earl had paid to his Lordship or to his creditors (the most substantial being John Forbes of Culloden who received 22,000 merks), Lord Reay sold the Earl the salmon fishings of Naver and Torrisdale. Various financial claims between the parties were settled and they agreed not to trouble each other's tenants. On behalf of his 'haill freinds tennantes and followers', Lord Reay also undertook not to take any action for all 'horses kowes or uyr bestiall receivit or uplifted' by the Earl's tenants and vassals. The sale, which was ratified in 1664, brought a considerable reduction in the long-running disputes over the lands of upper Strathnaver.[71]

Although the Restoration protected the Mackays from unscrupulous claimants, it was not as advantageous as the family may well have hoped. Charles II, in time honoured fashion, decreed that Lord Reay should have reparation for his losses from Robert Gray of Arkboll (formerly of Ballone). It is doubtful whether Gray had, as Grimble claimed, made a fortune between 1645 and 1655[72] and it is clear that by the Restoration he was in no position to pay the claims of the Mackays. However, the more settled times in the north brought an improvement to the family's status. Lord Reay's wife, Barbara, the daughter of Mackay of Scourie, was 'a great historian, a smart poet, and, for virtue and house keeping, few or non her paralell.' In 1669 Lord Lovat paid a visit to Lord Reay who was then living at Durness. Lovat was entertained 'sometimes out at sea in berges afishing, sometimes haukeing and hunting, sometimes arching at buts and bowmarks, jumping, wrestling, dancing', and the visit culminated in a grand deer hunt in the Reay Forest. When Lovat left after over a month's stay Lord Reay gave him:

> a curious, curled, black, shelty horse, severall excellent firelocks, bowes, and a sword ... and two deer greyhounds. My Lady gifted him a plaid all of silk, party colloured, her own work, and a pair of truse of the same, neatly knit, and a dublet of needlework ... [Lord Reay conveyed Lord Lovat] out of his own bounds with twenty gentlemen in train, and set him on Sutherland ground.[73]

It was all the more remarkable as an illustration of the lavish hospitality which had obtained in a rapidly disappearing age.

Not a great deal was done to clear the burdens on the estate, although at least one debt was bought up by some of the clan gentry.[74] The family was saved, however, by Sir George Munro of Culrain, Commander in Chief of the Army in Scotland, whose daughter Anne married Donald, Master of Reay in 1677. Sir George bought up many of the debts affecting the estate, including an apprising which an Edinburgh merchant had obtained against the estate a few years previously, reduced some of the more questionable debts, and established a new title to the lands in his own person which he later settled on his grandson, the future Lord Reay.[75] Sir George also negotiated new agreements with some of the wadsetters on the estate. In 1678 he came to an agreement with Hugh Munro, wadsetter of Eriboll, who had assisted in the purchase of an apprising three years earlier. Munro not only agreed to restrict the amount on his wadset to 10,000 merks, but also accepted a 400 merks augmentation of the rents and made a further loan of 4,000 merks to the Master of Reay in return for a ratification of his wadset right.[76] This assistance allowed Lord Reay to move back into Tongue House which had been rebuilt.[77] However, he had only been there a year or two, when firstly the Master was killed in a hunting accident and then Lord Reay himself died. Fortunately, there was an heir, George who was brought up by his grandfather, Sir George Munro and then by Mackays in Holland. Their combined influences ensured that Lord Reay was to be a staunch presbyterian and supporter of the Government.

After returning from the continent the young Lord Reay stayed for a time at Balnakeil.[78] In 1701 Lord Reay settled with George Munro of Culrain for his father, Sir George Munro's, 'intromissions with the rents & duties of my lands & estate within the shyre of Sutherland & elsewhere'.[79] The following year he married Margaret, daughter of General Hugh Mackay of Scourie. Contrary to most accounts, Lord Reay did not acquire the lands of Scourie with this marriage. As will be recalled, these lands had been held on wadset and while Captain Hugh Mackay of Borley did, as eldest son of General Mackay, assign a claim on the lands to Lord Reay in 1703, the lands were immediately re-wadsetted to him and he took the designation of Scourie which he held until 1722.[80] Lord Reay's financial position continued to be a severe constraint. Indeed, his ambition to reacquire lands in the parish of Reay, no doubt with a view to restoring dignity to his title, was unfulfilled: the settling of long-overdue debts took priority.[81] A third marriage in 1713 may or may not have improved the position, and at the time of the Jacobite Rebellion in 1715, his letters to the Duke of Atholl 'breathed financial embarrassment'.[82] His loyalty to the Government was rewarded with a pension which the house of Reay was to enjoy until 1831.[83] The gift, however, was insufficient, and in 1718 Lord Reay sold the remaining coastal lands of Strathnaver, comprising Farr (except the lands of Ardbeg which were then occupied as a glebe), Swordly and Kirtomy, to the Earl of Sutherland.[84]

The sale appears to have brought a degree of financial stability, and Lord Reay was able to take a more active approach to the development of the estate. The surroundings of Tongue House were embellished with a terrace and bowling green to the front and kitchen garden (re-established?) to the rear, plantations were created and a new house was built at Balnakeil incorporating the remains of the old castle.[85] Lord Reay was an active member of the Society of Improvers in the Knowledge of Agriculture in Scotland. He wrote various communications on his experiments with sown grasses, inclosures and water meadows, and was latterly the Society's President.[86] He was also very supportive of the church in its efforts to bring presbyterian worship to the north of Sutherland (see below).

In 1732, on the marriage of his eldest son, Donald, Lord Reay executed a strict entail laying down the succession to the estate under certain conditions.[87] But the entail was never registered and when, in 1741, and 'Contrary to the inclinations of his friends', Donald took Christian the daughter of Sutherland of Pronsie as his second wife, it was surreptitiously cancelled. This, it was later alleged, was to allow Lord Reay to create fictitious votes to further his political opposition to the Earl of Sutherland within the county. However, it was probably also because Lord Reay was aware that his son was a very easy going person with little inclination for business or estate management. A new deed was executed, whereby the estate was placed under the management of trustees who were to settle the 'great Burdens' affecting the estate and pay the provisions for the children. Donald, who had under the previous arrangements been promised a liferent right to the whole estate, was only to enjoy possession of part of the lands of Durness, including the house of Balnakeil.[88]

The trust came into operation after Lord Reay's death in 1748. Donald found himself heavily dependent upon the generosity of the trustees, and with most of the estate let to his half brother, Hugh Mackay of Bighouse.[89] Donald's other half brothers, George and Alexander, were trustees and played an active part in the management of the estate. George had qualified as an advocate in 1737, obtained through political influence an army commission, and was MP for Sutherland from 1747 until 1761. He enjoyed an unofficial 'pension' of £300 during the 1750s, until given the office of Master of the Scottish Mint. He was initially designated 'of Strathmore' in virtue of a wadset right over those lands, but he later acquired the estate of Skibo in the parish of Dornoch.[90] Alexander enjoyed a successful army career, rising to Major General as well as becoming MP for Sutherland from 1761-1768 and for Tain burghs from 1768-1773.[91] A clearance with the trustees in 1755 revealed that the debts on the estate then amounted to about £5,700, including £3,600 in the form of wadsets and £700 incurred by Donald's father. The trustees recommended to Lord Reay and leading Mackay gentry that a renewal of Bighouse's tack 'would lead to the Interest and advantage of the Family and Estate'. Bighouse was subsequently given a 15-year tack of the estate from 1756 at an annual rent of £390.[92] Donald Lord Reay died in 1761 of, as Grimble plausibly suggests, syphilis; a condition which may well have affected the health of his offspring.

Donald's son and successor, George, an able but impatient and abrasive person, had already attempted to wrest control of the estate from the trustees. However, when Donald had died, the trustees had taken over the lands of Durness as well, and George 'became entirely dependent on these Trustees for any Support out of his own estate to himself his Lady or his Family'. He quickly came to the conclusion that the estate had been 'grossly abused' by the trustees, particularly his uncles, George and Alexander, 'two of the most artful interested and abandoned men that perhaps ever existed'. During the many years that the trust had been in existence, none of the family debts had been cleared off, the trustees had given 'uncommon nay unprecedented large discompts to Bighouse their darling Tacksman in open defiance of the trust ... and have also Lavished away Considerable sums'. Indeed, it was later estimated that the estate lost over £3,500 by virtue of Bighouse's tack, which had commenced in 1748 and subsisted until 1761. George's father had apparently threatened to reduce the trust but it had been felt that it was more in George's interest if the estate remained under tack to Bighouse rather than the trust terminated and the estate exposed to whatever additional burdens Donald might place on it. George failed to persuade the trustees to relinquish voluntarily but he discovered that a copy of the marriage contract of 1732, which had been kept secret from him, was in the hands of his uncle George of Skibo. He eventually succeeded in obtaining possession of the deeds and charter chest, and managed to overturn the trust in the Court of Session in November 1767. George had already began to take an active interest in the estate and had began to invest in new estate buildings at Tongue. He died, however, the following year.

He was succeeded by his mentally incapable younger brother Hugh, whose paternal uncles, Hugh of Bighouse, George of Skibo and Alexander were appointed as tutors and curators. Skibo was given the day-to-day management of the estate from 1768 until his death in June 1782 (after the death of Bighouse in 1770 he was heir to the estate). The sole surviving tutor and curator, General Alexander Mackay took over the management of the estate until his own death in June 1789. Although the General took decisions relating to the estate, most of the management was undertaken by his factor, Charles Gordon of Pulrossie (earlier of Skelpick). From 1789 until Lord Reay's death in 1797, the estate was managed by George Mackay of Bighouse in the capacity of factor *loco tutoris* to his Lordship.

After Skibo's death in 1782 in bankrupt circumstances, it was found almost impossible to disentangle the accounts relating to his management (following heroic efforts by a succession of accountants, a final state was eventually drawn up in 1829). On the whole, the tutors took a positive attitude to their responsibilities, arranging farm improvements at Balnakeil, developing fishing and kelp manufacture and also curbing the ability of the tacksmen to oppress their subtenants. Lord Reay lived in a modest manner with the Mackays of Skerray. The considerable burdens on the estate, however, were equivalent to an annual interest of almost £800 in 1768. Provisions for the two dowager Lady Reays and three daughters amounted to £472 per annum.[93] Between 1768 and 1782 the estate was not paying its way, and the position cannot have improved significantly after that. In 1788 Lord Reay's two surviving sisters brought an action for payment of their provisions.[94] An analysis of the financial position in 1792 revealed that there were debts of over £7,000 secured on the estate, including £2,000 of provisions to Lord Reay's daughters. The gross rent was almost £1,300 per annum, but after taking account of wadsets, public burdens (taxes, and ministers' and schoolmasters' salaries) and expenses of management, the surplus available for the payment of the debts was just £230.[95] It is unlikely that, without the very low personal expenditure of Lord Reay, the estate would have survived intact until the turn of the 19th century.

Eric, second but eldest surviving son of George of Skibo, inherited the estate and title on the death of his cousin in 1797. It was not, as he admitted to Mrs Louisa Mackay of Bighouse in January 1799, an easy prospect, 'It was I may say my misfortune to succeed to a very extensive Estate producing little, besides many Incumbrances, at the same time giving me a Rank which I would wish to maintain with becoming dignity'.[96] This desire to maintain a certain grandeur was to have enormous consequences for the people on the estate. All existing leases, some of which had been granted for excessively lengthy terms, were reduced – mainly by granting compositions, although court action was necessary in several cases.[97] This was the prelude to the reorganisation of the estate into sheepfarms and coastal townships for the resettlement of small tenants engaged in fishing or kelp manufacture. The process, which was spread over several years, brought an enormous increase in rental income. However, Lord Reay's lavish expenditure continued and by 1816 the debts on the estate amounted to £58,000; £17,100 represented annuities while the remainder was made up of bonds, bills and accounts. Almost £7,500 was owed to merchants as their share in the profits on kelp and fishing.[98] Lord Reay's financial circumstances worsened as the economic depression which followed the end of the Napoleonic Wars took effect. Not only did the proceeds from kelp manufacture collapse, but sheepfarming was also badly affected. Despite generous rent reductions, several sheepfarmers went bankrupt. In 1823, Lord Reay considered handing the estate over to trustees.[99] Two years later, £100,000 was borrowed from the Marquis and Marchioness of Stafford.[100] That same year, the House of Lords affirmed the judgement of the Court of Session freeing Lord Reay from any constraints to the sale of the estate.[101] A new factor was appointed to manage the estate on stricter lines. However, the task proved insurmountable, and Lord Reay sold the estate to the Staffords for £300,000 in 1829.

Mackays of Bighouse

The Mackay of Bighouse family was founded in the late 16th century by William Mackay, younger brother of Uisdean Mackay of Strathnaver [Figs. 4.6; 4.7]. William held lands in Durness – he was initially designed 'of Galdwell of Durness' and lived at Balnakeil – but led the Mackay offensive against the Murrays of Bighouse for their share of Strath Halladale. According to Rory Murray of 'Biggouris', in September 1587 William came to Bighouse in upper Strath Halladale and seized his goods:

> ejectit the said complenaris wyffe and bairnis furth of the saidis houssis; quhairthrou, thay being strangearis in that cuntrey, unacquented with ony of the cuntrey people, and wanting moyane to mak their awne provisioun, thay wer forceit to beg thair meitt, and at last miserablie deit throu hunger in the montane. ... [Five years later William was still in possession, and Murray complained to the Privy Council that he] ... hes continuallie sensyne withaldin and possest the said complenaris said hous and rowme, and hes baneist himselff the cuntrey, swa that he dar nocht repair theirunto for feir of his lyffe.[102]

Despite this seemingly horrific conduct, in 1597 the two parties entered into a contract whereby William, by then designed 'of Balnakeil', bought Strath Halladale. William was married to Isobel Mackenzie and the agreement appears to have been brokered by Rory Mackenzie of Ardafallie (Redcastle). William received a Great Seal charter of the lands the following year.[103]

The Mackays of Bighouse

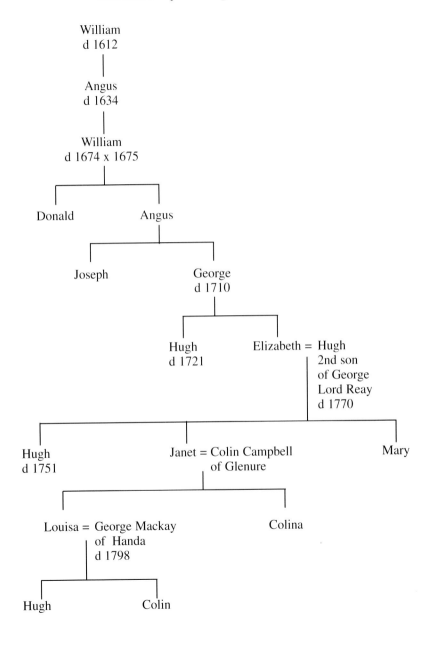

Fig. 4.7   The Mackays of Bighouse.

William was succeeded by his son Angus who incurred his chief's displeasure in 1618 when he and a number of his domestics shot 40 to 50 deer and fished for salmon in the water of Halladale.[104] As might be expected, Angus assisted with his chief's financial transactions in the 1620s.[105] In 1626, Angus granted a charter of upper Strath Halladale to his eldest son William, reserving his own liferent right as well as that of his mother who held at least half of the estate; this was confirmed by Charles II in 1633.[106] In 1631 Lord Reay granted a feu charter of lower Strath Halladale, of which he was superior, to Angus and to his son William who had married his Lordship's daughter Jean.[107] In 1632, following complaints to the Privy Council by the people of Caithness as to raids by one William Kennochbuyesoun and others, Bighouse became bound along with the Master of Reay and John Mackay of Dirlot, on behalf of the inhabitants of Strathnaver, to deliver up any stolen goods and to present a number of people who had supplied the rebels. William Sinclair of Berriedale, eldest son of the Earl of Caithness, and Sir Alexander Gordon of Navidale played a central role in ensuring that the dispute was settled at the local level without the intervention of the authorities in Edinburgh.[108] According to Gordon of Sallagh, Angus was 'a very active and able gentleman'. However, in 1634 'he was taken away be witchcraft. The witch was afterward apprehended and executed, who at her death confessed the crime.'[109]

His successor, William, was a major figure within the clan Mackay during the troubles of the 1640s. He was one of the leading men who undertook in 1644 to settle the debt owing to Robert Farquhar, and was amongst those who in 1646 were summoned to appear before the General Assembly to answer for their actions.[110] William was apparently involved in Pluscardine's rising, which for many Mackays ended with the 'incident' at Balveny in April 1649, although it is not known whether he was captured along with Lord Reay. It is against that background, however, and growing financial difficulties, that William settled the estate on his eldest son, Donald.[111] Several apprisings were led against the estate; by Robert Gray of Ballone in 1649,[112] by Robert Farquhar the following year[113] and by Forbes of Culloden by virtue of William's involvement in another debt of Lord Reay's.[114] William appears to have maintained two houses, one at Balnaheglis (which became known as Kirkton) and another at Forsinaird where he was to be found in 1646.[115] He survived until the spring of 1659 when the livestock on the estate were struck down by a 'grievous murrain or hastie death'; the tenants were not able to labour their lands or pay their rents.[116] Robert Gray, by then of Arboll, brought a process of removing against the tenants of Bighouse[117] and appears to have gained actual possession of part of the estate. An undated valuation roll of the period confirms William's difficulties: the wadset of Golval accounted for £151 of valued rent, Arboll's possession was worth £517 which left only £235, including Balnaheglis, in William's own hands.[118] In 1660, an apprising was obtained by Colin Mackenzie of Redcastle[119] and the following year a wadset of Torinver was granted to one James Grant there.[120] Times had changed, however, and men such as Gray of

Arboll were no longer able to take advantage of political upheavals to gain personal advantage. From 1664, despite continuing distractions of having to assist Lord Reay,[121] the Mackays of Bighouse began a slow a but steady recovery. The rescue operation was largely undertaken by William's son, Angus who had succeeded his brother as heir to the estate.[122] With the assistance of Angus's father-in-law, Patrick Sinclair of Ulbster, and Angus Mackay of Melness, the debts were paid off. By the time of William's death in 1674 x 75, the estate was largely free from apprisings and Angus was finally served heir to his brother in 1681.[123]

Having managed to avoid the worst possible consequences of their financial problems, the family suffered a series of natural catastrophes which brought the direct male line to an end. Joseph, who succeeded his father Angus, only possessed the estate for a few years before dying without issue.[124] He was succeeded by his brother George who died in January 1710 leaving 'considerable debts affecting the real estate, and also certain personal debts, which fell to be paid out of the executry'. George's only son Hugh died in April 1721 while still a minor, and the estate passed to his eldest daughter, Elizabeth, who was brought up in Tongue House. Lord Reay, who had been appointed Elizabeth's curator, proceeded to register an entail which George had made in 1709, providing that the eldest heir female should succeed to the estate without division:

> and the descandants of her body of the samen line being alwayes bound and
> oblidged to marry ane Husband of the name of Macky or who and the
> Descendants of his and her body succeeding ... shall be ... bound ... to
> assume the name stile and Designation and wear use and bear the armes of
> Macky of Bighouse.

In accordance with these provisions, Elizabeth was married to Lord Reay's second son, Hugh in 1728.[125]

The previous year, Elizabeth's younger sister, Janet, had married William Mackay of Melness, a descendant of the first Lord Reay and who had recently returned from Dutch military service. Melness felt that his wife had been unfairly treated: he later claimed that Lord Reay, 'taking advantage of the infancy of these two daughters, and of a false report industriously propagated, that the eldest daughter was alone entitled to the succession of the heritable estate, formed a scheme to secure that estate to his family' by marrying Elizabeth off to Hugh. Melness was, of course, mistaken over the succession to the estate, although Elizabeth's marriage would certainly have assisted his Lordship in providing for Hugh.[126] Melness, however, was very unhappy at the arrangements, went to the House of Tongue, and with a loaded pistol demanded that Lord Reay should hand over the title deeds to the Bighouse estate. But Lord Reay managed to escape and Melness was forced to retire.[127] In 1733, it was agreed by the two sisters that Elizabeth and her husband should have the estate, subject to the debts affecting it, while Janet should have the whole executry of their brother Hugh and their father George, relieved of various debts which Hugh Mackay proceeded to pay.[128]

Elizabeth and Hugh then took legal steps, using John Mackay of Clashneach as a trustee, to establish a new and secure title to the estate in the name of Hugh.[129] A good deal of the estate was liferented by George's widow, Katherine Ross, but in 1737 she surrendered possession of Kirkton to Hugh.[130] She lived at Trantlemore from sometime after the death of her second husband in 1742 until her own demise in 1757.[131] The whole episode provides a very good illustration of the considerable complexity of executry, minorities, succession and the liferent rights enjoyed by a widow.

Possession of Kirkton allowed Hugh and his wife to establish themselves there (see Beaton, this volume). The rental of the estate, however, was not large – in 1744 it amounted to only £129.[132] But Hugh played a major and very profitable role in the management of the Reay estate in the 1740s and 1750s (see above). He was actively involved in the cattle trade, attending the markets at Crieff, and was even experimenting with Tweeddale sheep. According to Rob Donn, he was a keen businessman. The poet's reference to Bighouse and the tacksman Iain Mac Eachainn is revealing:

> Surely their conscience is stifled
> When they are selling cattle to the Lowlanders.

There is a suggestion too, that this keenness was also applied to the tenantry. When commenting on a new suit worn by Bighouse, Rob Donn claimed that:

> There is not a button nor a button-hole in it
> That hasn't taken money off a poor man.[133]

During the '45 Rebellion, Hugh commanded one of the Independent Companies and, like his brothers, awarded himself prize money of £700 from the French gold captured from the Prince Charles (see below).[134] From about 1748 until 1758, the family lived in the House of Tongue.[135] In 1752, he asked his son-in-law to send various items north from Edinburgh, including some glasses, frames of 'Walnutetrie, or mohogny', grates for his room and the dining room, chairs, 'something gen[tee]l and to be covered', and a dozen prints including 'our Present King, ye Duke, Late & Present Dukes of Argyle, Lord Stair, Mr Pope, Prince of Orange, his Princess, her moyr the late Queen'.[136]

His children were to bring mixed blessings. In 1749, his eldest daughter, Janet, married Colin Campbell of Glenure in northern Argyllshire, who was half-brother to Campbell of Barcaldine and was to become famous as the Red Fox in Robert Louis Stevenson's *Kidnapped*, although he was generally known as *Cailean Ruadh* or Red Colin. Like many a daughter of a Highland laird at this period, Janet had probably enjoyed a season in Edinburgh.[137] She was about 18 or 19 years of age: Glenure was twenty years older with at least three illegitimate daughters.[138] Marriage for any landed family was a weighty concern and, as was customary, there were protracted negotiations between Bighouse and the Campbells. Hugh had already made enquiries through his lawyer into the financial standing of the prospective son-in-law: Glenure had an income of about £400 per annum which 'should afford a reasonable & Genteel settlement for Jenny and her children'. Glenure and his brother-in-law, Campbell of Achallader, paid a visit to Bighouse to discuss the terms of the marriage contract. The Campbells accepted some of the articles which Bighouse, on the advice of friends, had proposed, but considered that the level of provision for heiresses rather excessive. When agreement could not be reached, both parties agreed to submit their differences to lawyers. According to Achallader:

> Bighouse appeard extremely diffident of himself ... . He is a man of exceeding good parts, and capable of much greater affairs, very frank and Jocose, a good deall of the Highlander ... and values his clan more than any chief I ever knew.[139]

Bighouse though had formed a favourable impression of Glenure who:

> from a two Days Acquaintance was very aggreeable to me, and what might lessen his esteem wt oyrs raised it wt me, vizt that he does not want of the Highlandman in him; as I must do Jennie Mackay the Justice that she has acted her Part in this affair wt great Submission to my will, So I have remitted Glenure back to her, so as she may determine for or against him; as she sees most to her taste. I have no objection to the man himself takeing him in the Generall view, or to his Family & Circumstances, if equall to the Accounts I have ... . So if Mr Campbell is Jenney Mackay's Choice for a Companion in Life, I approve and consent frankly ... . And if she Loves the man, it would be imprudent to reject the proposal ... it would be cruell to take any advantage of Mr Campbell for the great regard he has for my Daughter, yet on the other hand, Affairs of this nature cannot be too minutely and Circumspectly gone about ... .

In Glenure, Bighouse gained a like-minded son-in-law who shared a keen interest in livestock farming. In 1751, however, Bighouse's eldest and only surviving son, Hugh, died while still relatively young, greatly mourned in the Reay country and the subject of one of Rob Donn's elegies.[140] At about this time, Mary, Bighouse's second daughter, became the second wife of William Baillie of Rosehall, who was probably in his forties and was to become a close family friend of Bighouse. Her portion was 5,000 merks.[141] In May 1752, Glenure, who was factoring for the Forfeited Estates Commissioners, was murdered, victim of the Appin Murder.[142] He left two daughters, but there was still the prospect of a male heir as Janet was pregnant. However, to her great disappointment, the child which was born the following February turned out to be another girl – who was named Colin or Colina in memory of her father. Janet reported to her brother-in-law Duncan, who had succeeded to Glenure, that she had 'been Luckie in getting a fine Nurse, wife to the famous Robb done the Poet, if you ever heard of such a man.'[143] In July, Janet made a 'Private Marriage' to her sister's step-son Charles, the eldest son of William Baillie of Rosehall. It was done,

Bighouse complained, 'wtout askeing me a single Question, till I found it out by ye mearest accident, on her way wt me to Tongue'. He was very fond of his daughter but:

> she has forfeit all that is dear to her for a young unexperienced boy that might have turned out well, had he followed out his Education. The moment I knew of her fate, I turned her of, & would not agree to our being under one roof.

He went to Achfary in the Reay Forest, to be 'in ye midst of ye hills a hunting ... to drive away sorrow'.[144] However, Janet's children stayed with him for several years, and he arranged for them to be inoculated for smallpox 'with great success' by Dr William Sinclair of Thurso.[145] Duncan Campbell of Glenure, however, was reluctant to pay for the upbringing and education of his nieces, and relations between the two families deteriorated.[146]

Bighouse and his family returned to live at Bighouse in the winter of 1758/59. Thereafter, Bighouse appears to have built a new and much larger mansion house at Tor (formerly Torinver) of Bighouse (see Beaton, this volume) – quite possibly using the timber which he had taken from the plantations at Tongue.[147] In 1767, the naturalist James Robertson found that Bighouse had 'a genteel dwelling house, adorned by a garden, which, for it's size, is the best & most elegant I have seen in the North'. Colonel Mackay had also 'enriched his moors with plantations of Forest-trees & is annually increasing their number.'[148]

Although appointed one of the tutors and curators for Lord Reay in 1768 (he was heir to the estate), Bighouse took no part in the administration as he was not in good health. However, in 1770, after the death of his wife, he married Isabella, daughter of Mackenzie of Lentron and 'a fine lively girl'. The marriage, almost certainly made with the aim of producing a male heir, would not have been welcomed either by his brother, Colonel Alexander Mackay, or by the heirs to his own estate. Unfortunately, Bighouse's health did not improve and he died at Bath later that year.[149] In 1767, he had made a settlement in favour of his brothers, George of Skibo and Colonel Alexander, which included various provisions to his descendants.[150] The settlement of his affairs in 1771 led to the sale of the 'mostly new' household furniture in the mansion-house of Bighouse along with the livestock – including 'The different species of cattle [which were] of a superior quality, being the stockings of the extensive grazings occupied by Col. Mackay'.[151]

The Bighouse estate passed to his daughters or their heirs. Colonel Campbell reported to Barcaldine that 'they will have good Plucking amongst them', although he feared that Hugh's widow would not 'come in for the share she ought Considering the Sacrifice she made, and the care she took of him': in the event she was to enjoy a substantial liferent annuity of £115.[152] Bighouse's grand-daughter Louisa (or Lucia), inherited a quarter share of Lower Halladale and the whole of Upper Halladale, and her husband, George Mackay of Island Handa, purchased the other shares and took the designation

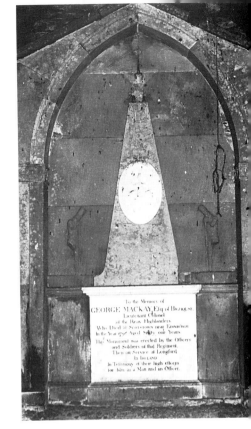

Fig. 4.8 Memorial to George Mackay of Bighouse, died 1798, in Reay churchyard.

Fig. 4.9 Memorial to the Mackays of Bighouse, Reay churchyard.

'of Bighouse'.[153] He had inherited a heritable security over Island Handa and also held other parts of the Reay estate on lease, including the lands of Scourie, Glendhu and later the Parph.[154] The late Bighouse's brother, Alexander, had 'tooth and nail opposed the marriage', but soon came to give a 'very good character' of Island Handa.[155] Between 1789 and 1797 George was responsible for the management the Reay estate (see above).[156] Like many of his contemporaries he served in the army: firstly as captain of the Bighouse company in the Duke of Gordon's Fencibles in 1778, and then as Lieutenant Colonel of the Reay Fencibles. Indeed, he played a major role in raising the regiment in 1794/95 but died while on active service in 1798[157] [Figs. 4.8]. He had placed his affairs in the hands of trustees who were to pay his debts, although his widow, Louisa, was sole accepting trustee. The entire stocking on the various farms he had held was rouped at Bighouse in June 1799.[158]

It had been the Colonel's wish that his eldest son, Hugh, should have the opportunity to buy his father's three-quarter share of Lower Halladale under burden of £4,000 to provide for other members of the family. Hugh, the eldest of a large family, was a merchant in Antigua and transferred this right to his mother who had liferent possession of the estate.[159] Louisa had already apparently moved to Edinburgh. Her portrait was painted by Raeburn and she made an impression on the social scene: 'Few ladies of her time displayed more grace and dignity in supporting her rank, or was more distinguished for her hospitality and benevolence in private life.'[160] The management of the estate was largely in the hands of her Edinburgh legal agent, James Horne of Langwell and her son-in-law, Gabriel Reid, who was a sheep-farmer in Sutherland. There was only a limited engagement with sheep-farming: one large farm was created in the upper parts of the estate (see below) which brought a substantial increase in rent, but it is clear that much higher rents were also levied on the small tenants. The gross rental of the estate rose from £232 in 1795 to a probable peak of £1,567 prior to 1819. Rents, particularly those of the small tenants, were quickly reduced with the onset of economic depression, and by 1822 the gross rental stood at £1,175.[161]

In the meantime, Hugh had died on Antigua in 1818. He was succeeded as heir by his brother Colin, a courageous army officer, who had initially served as a captain in the Reay Fencibles until disbanded in 1802, who formed the Bighouse Company of the Northern Battalion of the Sutherland Volunteers the following year, and in 1805 raised men from the estate to serve in the 78th Highlanders.[162] In 1829, his mother settled the estate on him, but he sold Bighouse to the Sutherland family only a year later for £51,650.[163] Not long afterwards, Colin bought an estate in Berwickshire and then a property in Arisaig – both of which he renamed Bighouse.[164] Louisa, who latterly appears to have lived in London, died in 1834. The family had effectively severed all links with Strathnaver [Fig. 4.9], although a descendant contemplated claiming the title of Lord Reay in 1875.[165]

Mackays of Strathy

The Mackays of Strathy were descended from John, a younger son of Hugh of Strathnaver [Figs. 4.6; 4.10]. John's education had included a spell in Saumur, and he received the lands of Dirlot (known as Dilret) in Caithness and Strathy in Sutherland from his elder brother, Sir Donald, possibly in 1619. He became known as Mackay of Dirlot.[166] From the 1620s to the early 1640s he assisted Lord Reay by becoming cautioner in several bonds,[167] and was also involved in dealing with the border disputes between Strathnaver and Caithness in 1632.[168] John settled his estates on his eldest son, Hugh, in 1633; his younger sons both became wadsetters on the Reay estate.[169] His eldest daughter married Patrick Sinclair of Ulbster, and in 1640 John promised them a liferent right to Dirlot.[170] His financial position was evidently becoming precarious, and in 1644 an attempt was made to sell the

The Mackays of Strathy

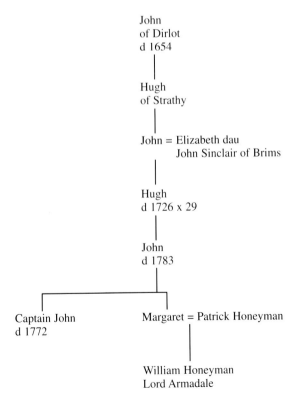

John
of Dirlot
d 1654

Hugh
of Strathy

John = Elizabeth dau
       John Sinclair of Brims

Hugh
d 1726 x 29

John
d 1783

Captain John   Margaret = Patrick Honeyman
d 1772

William Honeyman
Lord Armadale

Fig. 4.10   The Mackays of Strathy.

lands of Dirlot for 10,000 merks to John's 'cousin', Colonel Sir William Gunn, Gentleman of HM Privy Chamber and brother of Donald Gunn in Dirlot. John, however, refused to sign an agreement to transfer the superiority of the lands to the Earl of Sutherland which his uncle, Sir Robert Gordon, had proposed, and the sale fell through.[171]

After his father's death in 1645, Hugh was in reduced circumstances. Ulbster was apparently given a wadset of Dirlot; Hugh lived at Strathy, which he adopted as his designation rather than Dirlot, even though his mother possessed half the family lands in Sutherland in virtue of her liferent right.[172] Between 1669 and 1674 four apprisings were led against the estate, forcing a rescue operation to be put in hand. In 1679, Hugh and his eldest son, John handed over Strathy and the reversion to Dirlot to John's father-in-law, John Sinclair of Brims, who proceeded to buy up three apprisings. In 1681, John Sinclair of Ulbster, one of the apprisers, was sold the lands of Braegael in Halkirk. In 1690, after Hugh's death, Brims disponed the estate of Strathy to his daughter Elizabeth and her eldest son, Hugh. It was a rescue operation which was similar to that performed by Sir George Munro for the Reay estate, although relatively more expensive since it involved the loss of all the family's lands in Caithness.[173]

The experience of the family in the 18th century typified that of a small Highland laird. Two of Hugh's sons emigrated to Georgia in the 1730s: James, who once fought alongside Washington, acquired an estate which he named Strathy Hall; and Hugh, who ended up in Jamaica.[174] Hugh of Strathy's successor, John, borrowed 4,000 merks on the security of the estate in 1751.[175] This may have been to pay for some improvements. In 1760 Bishop Pococke found, on the east bank of the Strathy river, 'a good house and offices, and I was received with great politeness by Lady Strathy', and seven years later it was reported that Strathy 'has begun to plant his moors with forest-trees, which seem to thrive extremely well.'[176]

Following the death in 1772 of his only surviving son and heir, Captain John Mackay of the Sutherland Fencibles, John of Strathy settled the estate on his grandson, William Honeyman, the son of his daughter Margaret and Patrick Honeyman of Graemsay, a prominent landowner in Orkney. Honeyman entered upon a legal career, became an advocate in 1777 and, through his political support for Henry Dundas and marriage to the eldest daughter of Robert MacQueen, Lord Braxfield, was made about twenty years later a Court of Session judge. He took the legal title of Lord Armadale and was made a baronet in 1804 as Honeyman of Armadale.[177] He had succeeded to Strathy in 1783, but appears to have channelled his energies into lands which he bought in the central Lowlands.[178] A sheepfarm was created in the early 1790s, and by 1807 the 'old mansion house, and offices, [were] in a ruinous state'.[179] His second son, Robert, however, was major in the Reay Fencibles and afterwards served in the 93rd Sutherland Highlanders.[180] By early 1812, if not before, the Sutherland estate management was looking to buy the estate and use it as a resettlement area for people cleared from Kildonan and Strathnaver. Sir William's own circumstances necessitated a sale, but he wanted a proper valuation of the estate. A report, drawn up under the supervision of Robert Brown, a well-known estate manager and consultant, drew attention to the potential for the creation of large farms and the establishment of fishermens' holdings at Portskerra. His views coincided with the policies being pursued on the Sutherland estate but the estate management was reluctant to pay too high a price. However, in January 1813, Sir William who was faced with debts of about £75,000, handed over his estates to trustees who promptly sold Strathy to the Sutherland family for £25,000.[181] Sir William retired from the bench and was given a pension of £150. He died at his seat near Lanark in 1825.[182]

The Lands of Lochnaver under the Gordons of Embo and the Sutherlands of Duffus

In 1634, Lord Reay had sold the lands of Lochnaver to Sir John Gordon of Embo. Sir John's involvement in Lord Reay's affairs led to an apprising being obtained against his estate in 1647 by Duncan Forbes of Culloden. John Sutherland of Kellas (later in Skelbo) obtained a further apprising,[183] and in 1654 Robert Gray of Arboll obtained an apprising against his successor, Sir Robert Gordon on the basis of a contract made in 1648.[184] Embo entered into a submission with Arboll. Embo owed 44,800 merks and the arbiters decerned that Arboll should have possession of Lochnaver and of various lands in Ross-shire. However, Embo was given the opportunity to 'find out a merchand' for Lochnaver for 16,000 merks. Embo apparently managed to do this and as a consequence undertook Gray's side of the agreement. This included granting a wadset of Achness to William Munro of Achness and his brother, George Munro of Teaninver, for 5,000 merks. Two thousand merks was later repaid, and the remaining debt was assigned to William Sutherland of Rearquhar in 1664.[185]

In the meantime, Kellas's brother and heir, Alexander Sutherland of Torboll, had disponed the earliest apprisings to James Sutherland, son of Lord Duffus, the owner of Skelbo in east Sutherland as well as an estate in Morayshire.[186] In 1668, Embo sold the lands of Lochnaver to Lord Duffus.[187] Lord Duffus subsequently faced growing financial trouble – exacerbated by his murder of William Ross of Little Kindeace – and was forced to flee to London. He raised loans by granting a number of wadsets over Skelbo, as well as a heritable bond to Munro of Culrain over Lochnaver which later came into hands of Captain Hugh Mackay younger of Borley.[188] In 1692, the lands of Lochnaver were let to Alexander Sutherland of Pronsie and Hugh Sutherland of Kinauld, wadsetters on the Skelbo estate. An attempt by them to institute removals in June 1693 met with armed resistance from the possessors, who were joined by some of Lord Strathnaver's tenants from nearby farms. In 1694, Duffus entered into a contract to sell the lands to Lord Strathnaver for 20,000 merks, subject to the burdens secured over the lands. If Duffus could not persuade Pronsie and Kinauld to renounce their tack, he was to pay 300 merks per year until their right expired. The difficulties with the possessors continued, however, and it was not until 1700 that Lord Strathnaver became owner of Lochnaver.[189]

Sutherland Take-Over

A full assessment of the effects of the Sutherland take-over of Farr has not been attempted here; the task is, of course, complicated by the fact that the acquisition of Farr took place in three stages – in 1642, 1700 and 1718. Initially some Mackays were dispossessed, but this policy does not appear to have endured. For instance, William Mackay Iverson's wadset of Rossal was formally terminated and the lands given to one John Gordon. However, in 1653, Iverson was granted a five-year tack on condition that he 'benefeitt & acknowledge the ... Earle his hous Tuyce ilk yeir' as other possessors of Strathnaver did, and also that he and his fencible men followed and accompanied the Earl in all 'hoistingis hunteings & waponschawes' whenever required.[190]

The marriage between Lord Strathnaver's brother, Robert Gordon and Lord Reay's daughter Jean was made to further good relations between the families. Robert was given a long-term wadset for 18,000 merks over the lands of Grummore, Grumbeg, Syre and Langwell, and took the designation 'of Langdale'. However, from 1659 until 1665 he had run up a number of debts living in some comfort in Edinburgh. He died soon after his marriage from drinking to excess after a Dutch ship had been wrecked on the north coast. One of his creditors gained right to the rents of his lands until Lord Strathnaver settled the claims.[191]

When Lord Strathnaver acquired Lochnaver in 1700, he appears to have been successful in bringing legal proceedings against the possessors for the rents they had withheld from the previous owner, Lord Duffus; but it is significant that in 1708 a nine-year tack of the lands was given to Donald Mackay of Sandwood, possessor of Eriboll.[192] A list of tenants in lower Strathnaver in 1700 contains a mixture of Gordons, Mackays and others; a balance appears to have been struck between introducing Gordon families and accommodating the existing possessors.[193]

After the acquisition of the coastal lands of Farr in 1718, there were no more opportunities for the Sutherland family to buy lands in the province of Strathnaver until the early 19th century. The inheritance of the Bridgewater Canal fortune changed the family's financial position completely. The purchase of Strathy, in 1813, fitted in with the reorganisation of the Sutherland estate and provided vital resettlement areas to accommodate people cleared from inland farms. It was a good investment, and it is not surprising that thoughts were had of buying Bighouse as well.[194] Some tidying up was achieved by the purchases from Lord Reay of Ardbeg in 1813 and Borgiemore in 1820. The acquisition of the Reay and Bighouse estates in 1829 and 1830 was of a different order, however. James Loch, the commissioner for the Sutherland estates, largely justified them on the grounds of family aggrandisement or looked for connections with the ancient earldom of Sutherland.

SOCIETY AND ECONOMY

Landholding

Although the Reay estate was quite extensive, its value was only a third to a half that of the Sutherland estate – which included richer agricultural lands in the east of the county. Lord Reay was a substantial landowner, however, and, even after the sale of Farr to the Earls of Sutherland, the province of Strathnaver continued to be dominated by the greater landlords. By comparison, the Mackays of Bighouse and Strathy, the only cadet branches of the clan Mackay to own land in Sutherland, were but lairds. Indeed, Mackay wadsetters formed a significant part of the Mackay interest.

Most wadsets were granted to assist needy landlords, but some were granted to promote the various political interests by the creation of 'fictitious' votes. The endurance of these rights over many years often meant that wadsetters such as the Mackays of Scourie could be regarded as landlords. There were very few wadsetters, however, who made the transition to full ownership; many were effectively tacksmen and resided on their wadset lands. Some resided elsewhere; James Maclean of Capernoch, who held a wadset of Skail and other lands from 1744 until 1764, lived in east Sutherland.[195] On the other hand, a good number of wadsetters, particularly on the Sutherland estate in the 18th century, were absentee and their lands were managed by the estate factors. Examples are Captain, later Sir Harry Erskine, who held a wadset of Grummore from 1745 to 1757 and Lord Duffus, who held a wadset of Farr from 1757 to 1763. A wadset of Grummore and Grumbeg was held by Dugald Gilchrist, factor on the Sutherland estate, tacksman of Loth and later owner of Ospisdale, from 1757 until 1767, when it was transferred to Sir Adam Fergusson of Kilkerran who held it until 1794.[196]

By far the main source of income for Sutherland landowners were estate rents. Most landlords, however, also farmed on their own account. On the Reay estate there were mains or home farms at Tongue, Balnakeil and, prior to 1642, at Invernaver, which had probably been formerly attached to Castle Borve. The mains on the Bighouse estate was at Kirkton although there appears to have also been a home farm at Forsinaird in the 17th century.[197] Furthermore, the landlords often also possessed extensive grazings for their large herds of cattle, which could be very profitable.

The rights to hunting and hawking were restricted to landlords, and the province of Strathnaver contained several well-known forests or reserves including Ben Clibrig, Ben Loyal and Ben Hope, the Diri Mor (also known as the Reay Forest) and the Parff. The tradition of grand hunts in August in the Reay Forest lasted well into the 18th century.[198] These were activities reserved for the clan gentry; others were only allowed to hunt with a licence, although the tacksman of Scourie was generally allowed to take 12 deer from 'Hills of Arkle & Stack' and their bounds.[199]

The majority of farms in the province of Strathnaver were held by tacksmen, who occupied an intermediate position between the leading members of the clan gentry and their subtenants. It follows that most of the population were subtenants living on tacksman farms, although there were some tenants holding directly of the landlord. Tacksmen and tenants paid rents in money and in kind, especially sheep, butter and cheese. Most were liable to various services including providing peats, working on the mains farm (particularly at shearing and harvesting), wintering the landlord's cattle and assisting with the maintenance of the mills and salmon fishings.[200] With growing absenteeism, there was a tendency for landlords to convert rents in kind and services into money payments. However, 'arbitrary and oppressive services' were mentioned as a factor behind the emigration of the early 1770s, and there were still services performed on the mains of Tongue as late as the 1790s.[201]

Trade and Economy

In the 17th and 18th centuries, Sutherland exhibited a contrast between the more upland areas (where rents were paid in money mainly from the proceeds of cattle), and the lowland areas in the east (where rents were paid in grain).

Arable Crops and Livestock

In the early 17th century, Strathnaver was described as 'a Countrey full of Bestial and Cattel, fitter for Pasturage and Store than for corns, by reason there is little manured land there'.[202] This does not mean that the economy was wholly pastoral – the arable land was important, as years of poor harvest proved, although Strathnaver generally imported grain, particularly from Caithness. Problems could arise after a poor harvest and when sources of money income failed. The very bad harvest of 1740 meant that supplies of grain had run out by the summer of 1741. People starved and tried to exist on fish and milk, with the result that dysentery became rife and many, possibly as much as a tenth of the population, died. The presbytery of Tongue appointed the ministers 'to take some effectual course to get their poor provided within the bounds of their respective parishes'. Poor persons transgressing the regulations concerning vagrants would lose their right to a share in any collection. The presbytery wrote to neighbouring presbyteries 'intreating them to take some effectual method to keep their poor from us'. Fortunately the following harvest was plentiful.[203]

However, not only were there difficulties in the early 1770s, but in 1783 there was a 'universal failure of crop ... [and] ... many Families were in danger of dying'. The kirk session of Tongue 'appointed an Elder in every District of the parish, to collect some meal and Barley, or Money; which when done, there was a meeting for distributing the same. They collected several Bolls.' General Mackay sent 20 bolls of mixed meal for the poor on the Reay estate, half of which was distributed in the parish of Tongue and the parish also received 20 bolls of Government meal.[204]

Most tenants kept a variety of stock: cattle, horses, sheep and goats. In the early 17th century, great numbers of cattle were sold at fairs on the north and east coasts, along with young horses. But there was also an important trade in animal products or deadstock, and many cattle were sold in the form of barrelled beef shipped to lowland ports along with their hides and the skins of deer. A contract made in 1634 between Lord Reay and Duncan Forbes, a merchant in Inverness, included a quantity of 'ky slaughter marts gud & sufficient full laidin ky, haveing ane stone taloue at least in ilk ane of yr bellies' and 'slaughter mart and deir hyds hartt & hynd'.[205] The trade was superseded by the droving of cattle to southern markets, either in lowland Scotland or in England.[206] It is not known when the droving of cattle from Sutherland took off, but it was certainly established by the mid-17th century and expanded after the Union of 1707. All levels of society, from landlord to small tenant, relied on the cattle trade as a source of money income although, in the long term, the nature of the trade benefited the larger farmers the most.

The business of cattle droving required capital, and was dominated by tacksmen farmers such as Charles Gordon of Skelpick and Donald Mackay of Eriboll. It was financially hazardous and many failed. Angus Mackay, a drover from Syre in Strathnaver, went bankrupt in 1807 owing money to a number of local tacksmen and tenants. He was a cottar without any land, and his principal means of livelihood had been as a cattle dealer and drover. He appears to have been back in business by 1818.[207] Not only did the drovers buy from tenants all over the north but they also entered into contracts to take the Reay drove of cattle handed directly over to the landlord as payment for rent. The usual place for delivery was at Mudale in Strathnaver. In 1792 several new cattle fairs were established on the Bighouse, Reay and Sutherland estates.[208]

Fisheries and Kelp

The province of Strathnaver contained a number of fine salmon rivers, and the fishing rights were zealously guarded by their owners as the earnings from fishings could make a significant contribution to estate income. The salmon were caught using a variety of methods: principally cruives, a form of trap using wooden chests set into stone dykes across the rivers; netting with cobles in the mouths of rivers or pools; and yairs, wattle fences in the estuaries which trapped the fish with the falling tide. Bag-nets were introduced in the first half of the 19th century. Once caught, the salmon were placed in large vats, with salt, prior to being packed in barrels with more salt. New methods of preserving, using ice or boiling and processing the fish with vinegar, were introduced in the 19th century. The fishings were sometimes managed directly by the landlord with the fish being sold to a merchant, or they were let to a merchant to operate. Salmon fishing required investment in equipment and processing materials, and also a seasonal labour force; very often land near to the estuaries was reserved for salmon fishermen.[209]

The herring, cod and ling fisheries were important for many coastal communities, not only for their subsistence but also as sources of money income. Not surprisingly, the right of having a fishing boat at a recognised creek was included within the landlord's title to many coastal lands. A 1668 wadset of the lands of Kirtomie included the 'freedome of ane fish boat ane or more at the ordinar port of kirtomie'.[210] Commercial exploitation of the fisheries, however, required capital for equipment and access to markets, and tended to be dominated by merchants. In 1650, for instance, Oliver Mowat and Robert Pettin, merchants in Thurso, contracted to supply Alexander Johnston, an Edinburgh merchant, with herring, 'keilling' (cod) and ling from the Western Isles, Orkney, Caithness and Strathnaver. The Thurso merchants were to provide 'sufficient boattis with skeiled men nettis lynes huikis' and other necessary materials.[211]

For many centuries, ships from the Lowlands of Scotland and from Europe had followed the erratic visits of the herring shoals to the Western Highlands. The expansion of the Scottish fleet of herring busses (large fishing vessels) in the 18th century, brought sometimes hundreds of ships from the Clyde and eastern ports to the coastal lochs of north-west Sutherland. In general, local effort was organised by the landlords who bought fish from their tenants, cured it onshore and then supplied it barrelled to merchants. In 1724, Lord Reay contracted to sell herring, salmon and other produce to Messrs Falls, merchants in Dunbar.[212] In the 1730s, Lord Reay sold herrings caught by his tenants, ready-cured, to merchants from Glasgow, Renfrew and Dunbar, who sent vessels to take them away at a fixed price agreed by contract. During the 1740s the herring deserted the north-west coast.[213] However, they later returned, and in 1775 the tutors of Lord Reay gave a 21-year lease of the salmon fishings to Thomas and James Arbuthnot, merchants from Peterhead, and their local manager, James Anderson, who had received a lease of various coastal farms and a storehouse on Island Rannich, near Kylesku, to pursue the herring and cod fisheries. Island Rannich was found to be inconvenient and, under a new lease granted in 1787, the merchant partnership built a fishing station at Rispond (Loch Eriboll) including a harbour, houses for the manager and ship-master, cooper's shed, salt cellar, sail-loft, net room and two store houses [Fig. 4.11]. Another storehouse was maintained at Laxford.[214] For the inhabitants, there were opportunities for supplying the merchants and visiting herring busses with fish, as well as employment in gutting and packing.

Another potential source of income was to be provided by kelp manufacture. In about 1735 kelp was made on the Reay estate by Alexander Mackay, who came from Orkney, one of the earliest kelping areas. Hugh Mackay, who was later the tenant of the first sheep-farm on the Reay estate in the 1770s, after returning from America, manufactured kelp in 1739 and possibly 1740. There then appears to have been a period of inactivity until Hugh Mackay of Bighouse recommenced kelp manufacture in the early 1750s. Initially, Alexander Morrison from Skye was the organiser, but in 1754 Bighouse placed kelp manufacture in the hands of Donald Forbes, tacksman of Ribigill.[215] In 1764, Forbes took over the manufacture of kelp himself under a 10-year lease of the:

> whole ware and Tang ... in the Parishes of Edderachillis and Durness ... excepting that ware and Tang as will be indispensibly necessary for manuring the Arrable Lands of the respective Inhabitants of the said Shoars.

Lord Reay undertook not only to encourage the possessors of the coastal farms to manufacture kelp, but also promised to gain the consent of the tacksmen to the cutting of ware and burning of kelp. Forbes was to provide meal and iron to the kelp-makers, and to pay an agreed levy to Lord Reay for each ton of kelp.[216] Forbes continued to manufacture kelp until a dispute arose with Lord Reay's curators in 1773 and his lease was not renewed.[217] The kelp shores were afterwards let to the merchant partnership who were later based at Rispond.[218] The Reay estate, particularly in the parishes of Eddrachillis and Durness, became one of the main centres for kelp manufacture on the mainland. Direct involvement by the landlord was limited as the lead was

Fig. 4.11   Fishing station at Rispond, Loch Eriboll.

taken by merchants or local tacksmen, but kelp manufacture was central to the resettlement policy pursued during the Clearances and continued into the 1830s.

Tacksmen, Tenants and Subtenants

Many of the tacksmen on the Reay estate were related, if distantly, to their chief. John Mackay, Iain Mac Eachainn 'Ic Iain, well-known through the songs of Rob Donn, was a younger son of Mackay of Strathy (and thus a third cousin of Lord Reay).[219] Robert Mackay, known as the tutor of Farr, was a grandson of Donald 1st Lord Reay, held extensive tacks, and acted as one of the estate factors. However, a number of other families, such as Sutherlands, Forbes, Scobies and Clarkes, rose to prominence in the 18th century. Although there were still Mackay tacksmen on the Sutherland lands of Farr at the end of the 18th century, there were also several Gordon families who had been introduced by the Earls of Sutherland.

As befitted their traditional role, many tacksmen served as officers in the armed forces raised in the north, particularly the Independent Companies of the '45, the Reay and Sutherland Fencibles, and the 93rd Sutherland Highlanders. They also organised the various militia and volunteer companies during the Napoleonic Wars. Many, however, were involved in the cattle trade and took an increasingly commercial attitude to their farming operations. Some looked for better opportunities abroad, and several Mackay tacksmen/gentry led an emigration from Strathnaver to Georgia in the 1730s.[220] But those who stayed began to emulate the landlords in the enjoyment of higher, and more ostentatious, standards of living. From the 1760s a number of tacksmen built new and better houses, and several made the transition to sheepfarmers.

Donald Forbes of Ribigill was a central figure on the Reay estate in the mid-18th century. Born in about 1713, he set up, probably under the patronage of Lord Reay, as a lawyer in Tongue when hardly 20 years of age. For several years he lived at Kinloch and in addition held the lands of Dheruemeadie (between Loch an Dherue and Loch Meadie).[221] In 1744, he stated that he had 'been these sixteen years past concerned in adjusting the factors accompts with Lord Reay and dureing that space kept his Lordships rentall Book'.[222] At the time of the 1745 Rebellion, he served as a Lieutenant in one of the Government's militia companies and played an important part in the capture of French troops who had been forced to land near Melness with, it was claimed, £12,000 in gold for Prince Charles. According to traditional accounts, the French scattered the money, throwing some into Loch Hakel near Ribigill, and Forbes is said to have laid hands on £1,000 for himself. However, he was officially given £100 in prize money and later made strong complaints about how the money was shared out.[223] In 1747, Forbes obtained a 19-year lease of the lands of Ribigill, then in the hands of several tenants. He was encouraged to improve the buildings on the understanding that Lord

70

Reay would pay for any improvements not exceeding 200 merks. The lease, and another relating to his possession of Dhirumeadie, may well have been granted at the time of his marriage to Jane, the daughter of Robert Mackay, the tutor of Farr.[224] In 1751 he had prospered sufficiently to be able to lend 4,000 merks on a heritable bond to Mackay of Strathy.[225]

In 1752, Forbes obtained a lease of the salmon fishings of Inchard and the district of Oldshores (which reached from Sandwood to the River Laxford). Forbes was given leave to graze 'yell' or non-milking cattle on part of the Parph, and was also allowed a deduction of rent for damage done by blowing sand. The rent included a large entry payment of £50. In 1764, he was given a lease of all the salmon fishings on the rivers and coasts of Durness and Eddrachillis. As has been noted, he was involved in kelp manufacture for almost twenty years and also traded as a merchant, importing raw materials and luxuries. He supplied Lord Reay with coal, meal and iron and a variety of more exotic goods such as rum, port, brandy, sugar, cinnamon, currants and breakfast and evening tea. Like many of his contemporaries Forbes was engaged in both legal trading and smuggling.[226] In 1766 Forbes renewed his lease of Ribigill, albeit at a slightly higher rent. Five years later he made a new agreement with Lord Reay's tutors. The house at Ribigill had become ruinous and Forbes was allowed £35 for repairs, although his rents were further increased. It would appear that Forbes built himself a new house, probably a three-bay one-and-a-half storey house of stone and lime construction.[227] Despite all these activities, he had continued with his legal work and in 1765 he had been made sheriff-substitute within the bounds of Strathnaver.[228] The devious Forbes – he was apparently known as Donald of the quirks – and his sharp-tongued wife appear in the works of the Gaelic poet Rob Donn; he provides a good illustration of the numerous activities and varied life of a successful tacksman.[229]

Donald Mackay, tacksman of Eriboll, combined the traditional role of the tacksman as a respected figure in the local community with a successful career as a drover. He served in the Duke of Gordon's North Fencibles, and in the 1770s built a new house and made various improvements at Eriboll. The renowned Dr John Kennedy, whose father served as missionary at Eriboll, described Mackay as 'A gentleman, a soldier, a Highlander, and a Christian at once', who was 'loved and respected' by the people. His daughter, Barbara, married Captain Mackay John Scobie in the East India Company Service, who became tacksman of Melness and later of Keoldale sheep-farm. The Scobie family were all descended from a minister who came to Assynt in the late 1720s, and Captain Scobie's father had taken over the farm of Melness in 1770 after the death of the bankrupt wadsetter, William Mackay 'of Melness'. Barbara Scobie, 'generally regarded as the model of a Christian Highland gentlewoman', was well-known for her knowledge of traditional Gaelic songs. James Loch was greatly impressed by 'the most talented Highlander I ever saw ... she and her daughters singing some of Rob Dons songs was very wild and beautiful'.[230]

The onerous services which many tacksmen exacted from their

subtenants were socially divisive. During the early 1750s, the Sutherland estate management was concerned at the 'poor peoples usage in time past under a tacksman', and the subtenants of Lochnaver petitioned to be given their own possessions.[231] A rising tide of complaint culminated in the emigrations of the early 1770s; as commercial opportunities grew the people found such services irksome. Unlike other areas of the Highlands where the tacksmen led their followers to new lands,[232] in Sutherland these emigrations were organised by the tacksmen for profit. Both the Reay and Sutherland estate managements took steps to curb the power of the tacksmen; restrictions were placed on the number of subtenants who could be removed and on the rent increases which tacksmen could impose. Many of the tacks which were granted in 1787 on the Reay estate only allowed the tacksmen to charge their subtenants 5% on top of their own rents for 'trouble and risk'. The tacksman of Duartmore, was given particular warning: 'This clause never to be forgot by David Nicol'.[233] At the same time, the tacksmen greatly assisted the landlords by taking on the burden of managing a growing and relatively poor tenantry.

While there is some evidence that population was growing from the earlier part of the 18th century, it was certainly expanding in the second half of the century. In Durness, the number of registered births rose from 25 per annum in the 1760s to 45 per annum in the 1790s when recruitment for the Napoleonic Wars and farm reorganisation reduced it considerably.[234] A number of factors were involved in the growth of population: the colonisation of new land through the transformation of shielings into permanent settlements; the development of the cattle trade; and the opportunities for earning income through fishing, kelp manufacture, seasonal work in the south and military service. These factors, along with the introduction of the potato, meant that less land was required to set up a family. The creation of a crofting population reliant on by-employment was not solely the result of people being resettled in crowded townships during the clearances; population expansion and the growth of money income in the 18th century played a part as well.

Sheep and the Clearances

Apart from some early experiments with 'southern' sheep in the 1740s and 1750s, the first sheepfarm in Sutherland appears to have been established on the Parph peninsula in the mid-1760s by Lord Reay.[235] It was not until the early 1790s that Armadale on the Strathy estate was let to the Kerrs from Northumberland. A good deal of the initiative was taken by local tacksmen who, in introducing sheep and displacing subtenants, acted independently of the various estate managements. One example would be William Munro of Achany, a small landowner with extensive farming interests, who took a lease of Auldinriny in 1787. On the other hand, wholesale clearances did not take place until the early 19th century.

On the Reay estate a number of sheepfarms were established in 1801, but were further extended between 1805 and 1809 and again after new leases were granted in 1815. This, along with the fact that many former possessors were allowed to remain as subtenants for varying periods, led to a rather complex pattern of clearances. On the Bighouse estate, a sheepfarm was created at Forsinain and Forsinaird on the early 1800s; 18 families were removed and rents rose from £185 to £400 per annum. But a subsequent attempt to establish sheepfarms over the remainder of the estate was not pursued.[236] Broadly speaking, the clearance of Strathnaver, which was subject to the wholesale programme of reorganisation pursued on the Sutherland estate, took place in three phases. The first phase commenced in 1807 with the creation of the Great Sheep Tenement, which reached from the south shore of Loch Naver to near Lairg and also included the detached lands of Letterbeg. The second phase centred around the farm of Rhiloisk, let to Patrick Sellar, and which was cleared between 1814 and 1816. The third phase lasted from 1819 to 1822 and saw the establishment of the farms of Langdale, also let to Sellar [Fig. 4.12], and Skelpick. Several 'Southern Graziers' moved into the region, but a few of the local tacksmen, such as the Clarkes of Keoldale and Eriboll, became sheepfarmers. However, during the severe depression of the 1820s, a number went bankrupt, including Munro of Achany and Forbes of Melness (previously of Ribigill); and in their wake came incomers such as Mitchell of Ribigill.

Fig. 4.12   The farmhouse at Syre, Strathnaver, said to have been used by Patrick Sellar. 1984.

There were further clearances and sheepfarm reorganisations after the purchase of the Reay and Bighouse estates by the Sutherland family. Rearrangement of the Bighouse estate in 1831 included the clearance of 126 people to the coast.[237] The most well-known clearances of this period were instigated by James Anderson, the fish merchant at Rispond, who had decided to turn his attention to sheepfarming. Between 1839 and 1841 he cleared 32 families from various farms, but met with strong resistance when he attempted to clear another 31 families in 1841. The military were called in but, following arbitration by the local minister, the people were given a respite until the next year. The whole episode was extensively reported in the newspapers and was highly embarrassing to the Duke of Sutherland. This was unfortunate as the estate management considered that the people were partly justified in their response to a rapacious middleman.[238] In 1848, various lands, including the Isle of Handa, were cleared and added to Scourie sheepfarm for Evander MacIver, factor for the Scourie district, and the township of Shegra was also cleared and made into a small sheepfarm.

In the early 19th century, the complete clearance of the population was not sought as, under the prevailing economic conditions, it was financially advantageous to landlords to resettle the bulk of the population on the coast, either in existing townships or in new settlements. Holdings were deliberately made small in order that the people would be forced by necessity to look for earnings from kelp manufacture or the fishing. The main areas of resettlement were around Scourie, on the north shore of Loch Laxford, around Durness, and on the coasts of Tongue and Farr. Resettlement, combined with continuing population increase, saw townships grow enormously.

In the parish of Farr, the resettlement of families cleared from the interior was accomplished through the laying out of a large number of crofts; individual holdings in contrast to the centuries old runrig system of intermixed strips.[239] The experience there exemplifies the close relationship between the clearances and the creation of crofts.[240] However, in Tongue, Durness and Eddrachillis the crofts were largely created in the early 1830s (though not without some resistance from the people), well after the main clearances were over.[241] The prosperity promised by kelp manufacture and fishing failed to materialise and the landlord was faced with a 'redundant population'. Emigration was subsidised, but fishing remained a priority, although the main response of the Sutherland estate management was to encourage the crofters to make the most of their arable land.

THE CHURCH

From the Reformation to 1690

In the medieval period, the province of Strathnaver was divided into three parishes – Durness, Farr and Reay (straddling the border between

Sutherland and Caithness).[242] The whole province was thus effectively served by only two churches, Farr and Durness, although there was a considerable number of chapels, including Kirkiboll near Tongue, Skail (where the priest for the parish of Farr resided), Strathy, and Balnaheglish or Kirkton near Bighouse.[243] All of the revenues of the parishes were devoted to supporting the bishops and other dignitaries at the cathedral in Dornoch.[244] The precise boundary between Farr and Durness is not known.

Not only did the churchlands of Durness feature in the feuds between the Earls of Caithness and Sutherland, but in 1549 the Earl of Caithness was accused by the bishop of invading the 'kirk and sanctuarii of Far', seizing the 'chalice chrissumstok Eucharest and ornamentis of the altaris', and violating the sanctuary by taking away 18 persons 'agit and decrepit men and bairnis onder colour of saifty'. The sacraments could not be ministered, and the bishop demanded the Earl to cause 'Marie Geolachis sone callit Johne Sutherland in Barredale restoir the messe buik of the kirk of Far, and other Cathenes men the ornamentis of the altar thairof'.[245] Robert Stewart was one of the three bishops in Scotland who supported the Reformation, and although he had handed over the church lands of Durness to his brother-in-law, the Earl of Sutherland, he continued to take an active interest in his diocese. Within a decade of 1560 most of the parishes were supplied, if not with ministers, then with exhorters or readers who were allowed to read prayers and sermons. Further progress, however, was gradual, and it was not until the early 17th century that the majority of parishes were supplied with ministers.[246] The three northern parishes of Durness, Farr and Reay appear to have been included within the presbytery of Caithness.[247]

Even in the 17th century, there were to be continuing problems over the shortage of qualified ministers. Eventually a new church was built at Durness in 1619 [see Fig. 3.2], and the chapel at Kirkiboll was later repaired. These may be taken as signs of local confidence in the new church, though the example of Sir Robert Gordon, who was repairing churches throughout eastern Sutherland, may well have been influential.[248] It is, of course, very difficult to gauge the impact of the Reformation on people's beliefs, although the work of Alexander Munro, who became minister of Durness in 1634 and who translated a good deal of the Bible into Gaelic verse – known as Sandy Munro's verses – suggests that the new religion could make a strong appeal to the local people.[249]

The pre-Reformation parishes continued to provide the framework of ecclesiastical administration, although there was an attempt in 1638 by the largely absentee John Abernethy, bishop of Caithness, to reorganise Durness and Farr into three parishes. The chapel at Kirkiboll had already been transformed into a church, but no additional minister was provided and the minister of Durness continued to serve both Durness and Kirkiboll (for some time known as the parish or parishes of Durness and Kintail).[250] The political troubles of the mid-17th century set back the progress of the reformed church, and by the 1650s there were no ministers in the parishes of Durness, Farr and Reay. The parish of Reay was the first to be provided: initially by a preacher who served both Halkirk and Reay, and then by the admission of David Munro in 1657. Gaelic-speaking ministers were in short supply. However, the presbytery of Caithness responded to pleas from Lord Reay, and sent ministers to Strathnaver to preach and to exercise discipline.[251]

The Restoration of the king also saw the reintroduction of bishops acting in concert with synods and presbyteries. In Caithness, as opposed to Easter Ross, opposition to the episcopal settlement was subdued.[252] In line with colleagues elsewhere, the bishop of Caithness was keen to accelerate the presentation of ministers to parishes, although there is little evidence that this brought in ministers of poor quality.[253] Durness was provided with a minister in 1663, and Farr the following year. The minister of Reay was actively involved in presbytery business, the minister of Farr much less so, and the minister of Durness hardly attended any meetings of presbytery.

In imposing church discipline, the presbytery of Caithness dealt with cases of sabbath breaking, piping at lykwakes and superstitious customs. It concentrated, however, on sexual misbehaviour and a great deal of its time and energy was expended on investigating unmarried pregnancies.[254] In view of the distance involved in bringing delinquents to the presbytery at its normal meeting place in Thurso, in 1665 the synod of Caithness and Sutherland ordered some ministers to go to Strathnaver and, in concert with the ministers there, to exercise discipline against fornicators, adulterers and other delinquents. The ministers subsequently reported that they had convened at Farr and 'went about discipline w[i]t[h] all possible diligence and zeall'.[255] The establishment of an active kirk session appears to have brought such expeditions to an end, although weightier cases continued to be remitted to the presbytery. One such case concerned William, brother to Mackay of Bighouse, and Margaret, daughter of Mackay of Strathy. When brought before the session of Farr in 1676, William had confessed to the sin of fornication but denied being the father of Margaret's child, 'because as he alledged the child was born ane moneth & five weeks within the nine moneth after his being guilty with her.' The presbytery was persuaded to invite the minister to search for another man who had been 'scandalously conversing' with Margaret.[256]

Presbyterianism Re-Established

When presbyterianism was re-established in 1690, there was a severe shortage of suitably qualified ministers in the presbytery of Caithness; it was not until 1697 that there were four ministers and a presbytery could be formally established. A minister for Farr was ordained that year. Although the province of Strathnaver appears to have been mainly presbyterian territory, there were problems with the minister of Durness, Hugh Munro, and in 1699 the presbytery considered instituting proceedings against him. However, Lord Reay found that the parishioners were so violently set against the presbytery's suspension of the minister of Latheron, that he advised 'if the presbitry hade a suitable and well qualified person ... they might proceed against Mr Hugh Monro ... otherwise the paroch would be redacted to great straits in baptiseing their children and in their marriages'.[257] His Lordship's view prevailed, and Durness remained under an episcopalian incumbent for a few more years. In 1701 the presbytery, minded of the 'clamant condition' of the parish, decided to investigate the parishioners' 'Inclination to have a presbyterian minister'.[258] However, the parish was vacant until 1707, when John Mackay (who was related to Lord Reay) was ordained at Kirkiboll. Mackay, however, left after it became evident that promises to divide up the huge parish were not going to be fulfilled.

Kirk sessions and the presbytery continued their struggle to deal with fornicating and adulterous parishioners, and abolish such practices as promiscuous dancing at weddings. In 1715, Hugh Mackay of Strathy was hauled before the presbytery accused of adultery with one Margaret Bain. Lord Reay took a personal interest and removed Margaret from Strathy's estate to his own. She was disallowed from going to Strathy without her husband's permission and, if she had to go, he was to 'send one with her to watch her carriage'.[259] Lord Reay's support contrasted with the behaviour of the Caithness lairds who ignored the presbytery's censure of their sexual adventures.[260] Less evident is the effect of the new church on the traditional tales, the Fingalian legends which were still a part of the local folklore in the 1730s.[261]

The difficulties of administering to a large parish were particularly acute in the case of Durness. In the 1720s, there were already 2,500 catechisable inhabitants in the parish. Although there were five places of public worship, yet both the minister and the people were:

> under great hardships and inconveniences in travelling ... . It being impracticable to travell on Horseback ... often endangers their lives ... and the Minister is frequently seven or eight weeks at once absent from his house on goeing about his ministeriall work, and not only many children dye in his absence without Baptisme, but people come to age, dye without haveing the benefite of a Minister to visite them when most earnest for the same.

In 1721, after Lord Reay had petitioned the General Assembly, an act was passed ordering a collection to be made throughout Scotland, the proceeds of which were to be used in supporting new ministers. Three years later, the General Assembly authorised both the splitting of Durness into three parishes (Tongue, Durness and Eddrachillis) and the creation of a new presbytery of Tongue which was to contain the parishes of Farr, Tongue, Durness, Eddrachillis and, for a few years, Assynt. The kirks at Tongue and Durness were largely rebuilt, and a completely new church was built at Badcall.[262]

The parish of Reay, however, was not so well provided for and Alexander Pope, who became minister in 1734, had to strive hard to obtain a decent stipend and persuade the heritors to build a church and manse. The church consisted only of bare walls which were ready to fall, and there had apparently not been a manse since the Reformation. Pope complained that he had been forced to live in a little barn belonging to a brewer, and had been chased out every morning before he had time to put on his clothes. The heritors tried to play down his responsibilities but, as Pope pointed out, Reay was a sizeable parish with over 500 catechisable persons within the sound of the church bell. Moreover, Strath Halladale itself, was 'a Glen of 12 miles in lenth, besides the shellings at 3 miles distance therefrom, having therein 500 Catechisable persons whereof only 13 can read, and the minister is obliged to preach once every 5th or 6th Sabath there'.[263]

Of the ministers, none was to be more conscientious than Murdo Macdonald, the minister of Durness, an evangelical whose sternness was moderated by his deep and sincere compassion.[264] Not all ministers were to command the people's respect. The worst was John Skeldoch, appointed to Farr by the Earl of Sutherland in direct opposition to the wishes of the congregation. In 1732, some of the parishioners of Farr had presented a petition to the presbytery against the call and claiming that:

> upon a Sabbath after he had preach'd at Keankyle he had a long Conversation upon the Method of improveing Land and Grass in the Highlands and concerning the manly feats of some Highlanders in his own Countrey; and that this Conversation continu'd from two oclock in the afternoon till Sunset in a June day.

Influence was brought to bear through the synod, and Skeldoch was admitted in 1734. However, he was very inattentive to his duties, preferring to concentrate on his farming interests, and was the subject of various proceedings for oppressing his subtenants. He was eventually suspended in 1748.[265] His parishioners did not attend his services, instead they held their own fellowship meetings.

The Reay estate, on the other hand, tended not to exercise the right of presentation but its views were sought by the presbytery. In 1769 there was some opposition to the choice of William Mackenzie, missionary in the heights of Farr, for the parish of Tongue. A number of parishioners dissented and presented a petition asking to hear two other preachers. The presbytery refused – there 'would be no end to such work' – and indeed the subsequent call to Mackenzie revealed that the protesters were in a minority.[266] The opposition to certain ministers should be considered alongside the lengthy controversy over 'the mens' day', or fellowship meetings held on the Friday of the Communion season which, between 1737 and 1758, the synod tried unsuccessfully to suppress.[267]

All parishes appear to have had active kirk sessions. The records have not always survived and were sometimes irregularly kept. One of the earliest surviving entries in the session book of Tongue relates to Hugh Ross, the former parochial schoolmaster and session clerk, whose unpaid salary on his death for services to the session was 'something considerable'. The session took a hard line, and on the grounds that there could be no legal claim, gave his son a guinea.[268] The sessions tended to be filled by parish schoolmasters and tacksmen, although small tenants served as well. The session of Durness included assessors who attended meetings without taking part in the proceedings. In 1767, four 'promising young men of grave and decent Deportment' were selected to 'assist the Elders who are some of them tender and elderly men'. Seven years later these assessors were appointed as elders.[269] There can be no doubt that this was a grounding for future leaders within the crofting community.

The kirk sessions continued to concentrate on matters of discipline, particularly sexual ones. The usual punishments were applied: appearing before the congregation in sackcloth, fines and excommunication. A man who falsely accused another of indecent familiarities was 'ordered to stand in Sackcloth next sabbath before the Congregation, to lay his hand on his Mouth and own that he told a lye'.[270] The Durness session exercised discretion in levying fines. A married man found guilty in 1765 of fathering a bastard was excused: he was 'in low Circumstances and that it would be doing a manifest Injury to his weak throng helpless Family to exact his Fine'.[271] The session also allowed a young lad, Donald Mackay alias MacEnicalister Roy in Balnakiel, to marry Mary Down, daughter of a certain 'Robert Down Poet in Balnaceill' and who was visibly pregnant, despite the objections of the boy's father.[272] The more difficult cases, especially when the charge was denied, were remitted to the presbytery. These included a number of cases involving tacksmen who resisted the church's authority (maidservants of tacksmen often suffered from the attentions of their masters or their sons).[273] Occasionally, something of the tone of the presbytery's proceedings is revealed. One case from 1770 concerned a young unmarried girl who killed her baby and then absconded. The father, who was a married man, was summoned before the presbytery which:

> spent long time in laying before him both the Nature, & awful Consequence of his gross deviation from the divine Law, if unpardoned, and unrepented of: therefore, urging him importunately by faith & prayer, to apply to the Merits of a Saviour for remission of Sin, & that repentance, which is unto Life – exhorting him, for the future, to be more watchful, & circumspect – abstaining from Fleshly Lusts which war against the Soul.

He was then remitted back to the session to satisfy discipline in the usual manner.[274]

The kirk session of Durness raised a modest income, mainly from fines, but also from church collections, the interest on a bond granted by Lord Reay and from lending out the mortcloth. This was spent on the wages of the clerk and kirk officer, minor repairs to the kirk and schoolhouse, and meal for the poor. The session also provided limited assistance to the indigent: in 1771 it paid a surgeon for 'Curing 2 poor men', and the following year gave money to Barbara Munro [probably a widow] 'to help her son going to a Trade'.[275] The session of Tongue distributed the limited funds from the poor box to needy parishioners, including two 'reduced and superannuate' elders.[276]

Education and Missionary Activity

The Reformation ideal was for every parish to have a school. Although this was enshrined in various Acts of the Scottish Parliament during the 17th century, which placed an obligation on heritors to pay for a schoolmaster, educational provision in the Highlands remained poor. It has been suggested, however, that there were more schools than has been realised,[277] and a search of the records has revealed the names of several schoolmasters on the north coast: 'Mr Andrew Morisone school Maister at Rhae' in 1635;[278] James Taillor schoolmaster there in 1666;[279] Donald McMarcus in Farr in 1681;[280] and John Fullartone in Strathy in 1705, who was probably employed by the Mackays of Strathy.[281] Regular provision of parochial schools was not achieved until the 18th century when Lord Reay took an interest, although even then provision could be patchy; there was, for instance, no school in Tongue in 1755.[282]

The insufficient coverage afforded by parochial schools attracted the attention of the SSPCK (Society in Scotland for Propagating Christian Knowledge), and the Society's sixth school was established at Durness in 1712. Two years later, the school had 67 pupils 'reading the Bible, writeing, learning arithmetick & musick &c'. The Society's schools tended to be moved about: in 1720 the Durness school was transferred to Ribigill, in 1721 to Langwell in Strathnaver and in 1725 to Strath Halladale. In the meantime, a new school had been established in the parish of Eddrachillis. By the 1730s, the Society was maintaining two schools: one in the parish of Tongue and another in the parish of Durness.[283] Considerable emphasis was placed on religious education and the 'rooting out' of the Gaelic language; and until 1767, the Society had a policy of only teaching in English.[284]

There had been considerable concern over the religious state of the Highlands, and in 1725 a Committee for the Reformation of the Highlands, otherwise known as the Royal Bounty Committee, was established to assist with the supply of Gaelic-speaking ministers and catechists. Joint-funding by the SSPCK and the Committee of schoolmaster/catechists who would also visit and pray with the sick, became common.[285] In 1736, for instance, these organisations funded the following posts: John Macdonald, schoolmaster and catechist at Knockbreck, Durness; Robert Mackay, schoolmaster and catechist at Grumbeg; Aeneas Mackay, catechist in Eddrachillis; Donald Sutherland also known as Donald Happie, catechist in Tongue; and Mr William Henderson, itinerant preacher or missionary in the parish of Farr.[286]

Most schoolmasters intended to train for the ministry, but the shortage of qualified Gaelic speakers could lead to unsuitable appointments. Although John Ewing, appointed schoolmaster and catechist at Knockbreck, Durness, ca 1740, was able to read the scriptures in church and translate them from English into Gaelic, what he had of the Gaelic was 'very unintelligible'. He was unable to sing the church tunes or to teach them. Moreover, he refused to teach children who only turned up for part of the day, which was hard on tenants who did not have servants and relied on their children to perform many household and agricultural tasks. The few children who did go to his school were made to translate from English to Gaelic. He was advised to leave, and when he did not, the people stole his peats leaving him not 'one dry peat to put on the fire, my wife & I are obliged to go a mile, & pull heather, & carry it home on our backs.' As Ewing himself admitted, he was 'useless to the people indeed, because they do not keep yr children at ye school'. His shortcomings, which included an 'unmanageable Temper', were brought to the attention of the SSPCK and Lord Reay, who suggested Donald Mackay, son of the late catechist William Mackay, as a suitable replacement. Donald was a 'sober pious lad and has taught this parish school here with success for several years it's true he cannot sing but that deficiency can be made up.' Ewing's employment was terminated in 1741.[287]

Private schoolmasters continued to be employed by tacksmen in the more remote districts. For instance, Patrick Ross, who taught at Achness in 1773, was probably employed by Robert Gordon of Achness.[288] Although there is some evidence of increasing literacy, the provision of schools did not match the growth of population. In 1811, it was reported that there was no society school in upper Strathnaver and the children were very deficient in learning; less than 40 persons out of a population of about 900 could read the Bible in Gaelic.[289] However, a number of charitable societies were established to further Gaelic education, and although the Gaelic School Society schools placed considerable emphasis on religious education, they appear to have had a significant effect on the general level of literacy. The schools moved around, enabling old as well as young to learn to read. In 1825, the parish of Eddrachillis contained three society schools in addition to the parochial school: an SSPCK school at Oldshores established ca 1800; an Edinburgh Gaelic Society school at Kinlochbervie dating from 1821; and a Glasgow Gaelic Society school at Achrisgill established in 1823 (both of the Gaelic Society establishments were circulating schools).[290] By 1826, there were only 1,413 people over the age of 20 in the province of Strathnaver who could not read either English or Gaelic, out of a total population of 5,487. As yet, about one in ten families were without someone who could read. As people acquired the ability to read Gaelic, their desire grew to learn and understand English.[291]

In 1755, there were 3 preaching places in the parish of Farr: the church at Clachan; Achness, where the minister preached every fourth sabbath; and Strathy where the minister preached but once a quarter.[292] By the 1760s, there was a missionary minister permanently based in the heights of Strathnaver who spent one third of his time administering to Strath Halladale.[293] A generous donation allowed the SSPCK to set up missions, and in 1794 one was established at Eriboll to serve the districts of West Moine, Melness and Oldshores. The missionary preached at 'Cambusnadun' near Eriboll and Melness in winter and spring, and preached 12 sabbaths in summer and autumn at Kinlochbervie.[294] A new mission church [Fig. 4.13] was built at Eriboll in 1804.[295] In 1797, the presbytery greatly disapproved of the government move to prevent the erection of chapels of ease as it would prevent the 'spread and furtherance of the Gospel – since population is rapidly increasing'.[296] Population growth and the movement of people associated with the clearances created considerable pressure for additional places of worship. Eventually, in the late 1820s, the government funded a number of 'Parliamentary' churches in the Highlands – including Strathy and Kinlochbervie[297] [Fig. 4.14]. The Eriboll missionary was then restricted to West Moine, Eriboll and Melness. Provision continued to be poor in some districts. Until a new building was built in the mid 1830s, services in Talmine took place in the schoolhouse, with people 'standing upon the windows and about the doors'.[298] Another missionary minister, who also worked in Watten and Halkirk in Caithness, took care of Strath Halladale – where ca 1830 near Comgill, a thatched church was built by the people, with assistance from the Sutherland family.[299]

The Role of the Ministers During the Clearances

The ministers of Sutherland have been extensively criticised for siding with the landlords during the clearances, and none more so than the Rev David Mackenzie of Farr.[300] Recent years have seen a re-assessment of that role. It has been pointed out that Mackenzie refused to deny the circumstances leading to Sellar's trial, on the grounds that there was some foundation to the allegations made against the factor. Moreover, it has been argued that the letter which the minister wrote to James Loch in 1818, criticising the resettlement arrangements, 'was probably the most comprehensive rejection

Fig. 4.13   Mission church at Loch Eriboll.

Fig. 4.14   The T-plan 'Parliamentary' church at Kinlochbervie (now the Free
Presbyterian Church), built in 1829.

of the assumptions of the Sutherland policy uttered during these years'.[301] One study has emphasised the diversity of actions and attitudes among the clergy, but suggested that the Sutherland estate papers corroborated Donald MacLeod of Gloomy Memories' account of the very poor opinion enjoyed by the ministers during the clearances. Mackenzie was not an active opponent of the clearances, but was critical of the way in which the policy was carried out. Attention has also been drawn to the ambivalent position adopted by William Findlater, minister of Durness, during the riots which took place in 1841.[302]

Mackenzie's behaviour has been contrasted with that of Donald Sage, missionary minister at Achness in Upper Strathnaver, who left a very influential account of the 1819 clearances and has enjoyed a better reputation.[303] Sage's father, Alexander, minister of Kildonan, was singled out for praise by Donald MacLeod for his opposition to the clearances.[304] On the other hand, although Donald Sage had undoubted concern for his congregation, his position as a missionary minister was precarious and he did not protest. Indeed, in 1818, the Sutherland estate factor wrote to him that he was pleased that the people were preparing to leave their possessions: 'I never doubted their regular behaviour and I am sensible much of that regularity & good order is in part owing to the constant advice of their minister'.[305] Sage appears to have followed the line adopted by his predecessor, the Rev Duncan MacAulay, whose induction to Assynt in 1813 was highly unpopular as the people thought that he had acted as a spy for Sellar when missionary at Achness.[306]

In a thorough examination of Mackenzie's case, Paton has argued that, even though the influence of the church was not as pervasive as it later became, Mackenzie faced no threat to his authority: there were no separatist movements in his parish and he led his congregation into the Free Church at the Disruption. Mackenzie's position was based on the standard church doctrine of the time, which accepted Divine Will no matter what degree of suffering this entailed.[307] The lack of action by individual ministers during the clearances is to be expected, given the church's uncritical stance on social issues in general.[308] As has been pointed out, the move by whole congregations into the Free Church was not attributable to the role of the ministers during the Clearances.[309] It is important to understand the complexity of these issues. The ministers of Tongue could be sincere evangelicals capable of passing critical comment on the poverty of the people following the clearances, while at the same time taking an evident interest in the improvement of their glebe and displacing some of their neighbours.[310]

The Rise of Evangelical Protestantism

Like many other parts of the Highlands during the first half of the 19th century, evangelical protestantism came to play a central role in many people's lives in north-west Sutherland. In part, this was the culmination of the efforts of evangelical ministers, missionaries and the influence of the 'Men', *na daoine*, lay preachers renowned for their religious intensity. The availability of a Gaelic Bible in the early 19th century, and the assistance provided by organisations such as the Reay and Strathnaver Auxiliary Bible Society in distributing bibles, combined with the work of the Gaelic School movement which enabled people to read the Bible for themselves.[311] The strength of evangelicalism in the 19th century suggests that the social and psychological consequences of the collapse of the old order in the Highlands were important factors. The evangelical faith gave people a sense of purpose and a way of coping with the immense changes sweeping the Highlands.[312]

Something of the strength of this faith – and the landlord reaction – is gained from James Loch's astonishment when, in 1835, he came across a crowd of 3,000 people on a rain-drenched hillside in north-west Sutherland, 'to hear preaching; the rain pouring incessantly. The English service in the Church was attended by about 12 individuals.'[313] People walked great distances to hear well-known preachers, and individuals such as Margaret Macdiarmid (Mrs Mackay of Shegra) were renowned and long remembered for the intensity of their beliefs and devout way of life.[314] However, poverty, seasonal work elsewhere and inaccessibility continued to affect church attendance; in the 1830s it was reported that 'all the parishioners occasionally attend, though many of them are, from circumstances, very irregular.' Much worship took place outwith normal church services. In Tongue, the minister infrequently went to remote districts and either preached 'in the open air or in some large byre or barn'; and in Eddrachillis, there were meetings on the sabbath for prayer and readings 'conducted by pious persons' in distant parts of the parish. Similar meetings were taking place in the Skerray district but 'it is not under the superintendance of any person officially connected with the congregation, and he [the minister] considers it irregular' (such activity could well foster separatism – the breakaway of people from the established church). In Durness and Tongue, most townships held meetings on Sabbath evenings for readings from the Bible and religious works.[315]

There were still individuals who disregarded church discipline. Activities which were so important to peoples' livelihoods such as fishing tempted some to sabbath breaking – although it was said that most fishermen who broke the sabbath were not local. Cases coming before the presbytery appear to have been restricted to the likes of Alexander Bain, the ground officer and Thomas Mackay, merchant in Torrisdale who got drunk in Kirkiboll inn on the sabbath; and two servants of the sheepfarmer at Ribigill, who were found guilty of fornication sometime after the July Heisbreacky market. The impression is gained that the level of indiscipline had not only diminished since the mid-18th century, but that censorious behaviour was more prevalent outwith the crofting community.[316] Ironically, the presbytery faced most trouble from two of its own members. The case of the Rev John Mackenzie of Eddrachillis first came to official light at a meeting of the synod in 1822, when 'there appeared an apprehension of Great irregularity, and frequent want of Church ordinances'. The presbytery, which appears to have been aware of the situation (possibly for some time), managed to persuade Mackenzie to agree to the appointment of an assistant. Mackenzie did not co-operate, and in 1824 a complaint was made by certain elders and heads of families accusing their minister of drunkenness and neglect of duties for several years, to such an extent that the 'whole discipline of the parish [was] come into confusion'. They also accused him of frustrating the efforts of his assistant. Mackenzie eventually agreed to the continuance of the assistant and the parishioners dropped their complaint. The problems resurfaced when the assistant moved to another parish, and in 1831 the congregation petitioned presbytery that, 'in a population of about 600 Souls, at no great distance from the Parish Church [at Badcall], scarcely above a score are found entering its walls on Sabbath days'. Faced with a visitation by the presbytery, and with the Sutherland family's agreement, Mackenzie accepted the appointment of an assistant and successor.[317] These arrangements were hardly in place when the presbytery had to deal with the *Fama Clamosa* surrounding the minister of the Parliamentary Church at Kinlochbervie. Donald Mackenzie, who had suddenly dismissed his servant maid in October 1830, then returned with her as his wife eight months later, having married at the Gaelic Chapel in Greenock. Many members of the congregation had deserted the church, and the presbytery commenced an investigation to decide whether Mackenzie was guilty of antinuptial fornication. No-one had personal knowledge of any indecent behaviour prior to the marriage, apart from Mackenzie's 'unbecoming and indecorous habit, of letting her sit with him at meals'. However, Mackenzie was unable to supply any references as to his wife's whereabouts in the months prior to her marriage and eventually emigrated to Canada.[318]

A major aspect to evangelicalism was the strength of feeling against patronage which was shared by ministers and people alike. In 1825, the presbytery of Tongue made an overture to the General Assembly on the evils of patronage.[319] Two years later, however, the presbytery had to deal with John McIntosh, catechist and elder of Farr, who had withdrawn from the church because 'it was a matter of Conscience with him, to separate from a Church in which there were so many things contrary to the Word of God, especially forcing Ministers on Congregations'. A sympathetic presbytery eventually persuaded him to repent.[320] Such sentiments, however, led to two patronage disputes: firstly in 1828, when there was opposition to Stafford's choice of minister for the Parliamentary Church of Strathy;[321] and then in 1834, when Kinlochbervie fell vacant. A Royal Presentation to Kinlochbervie was received in favour of one Robert Clarke, then a minister in Glasgow, but the inhabitants petitioned in favour of Archibald Cook. The congregation was aware that Cook had been represented to the Sutherland family as 'deficient in ministerial qualifications', but hoped that the presbytery alone would judge whether 'he is not by his principles and habits of life peculiarly fitted for the people of Kenlochberuie, among whom there are none of a higher rank, than schoolmasters and Fishers.' Despite its evangelical character, the presbytery recognised the legal right of the Crown as patron and refused the petition. When the call to Clarke was administered, 'a leading individual in the Parish did repeatedly attack the public & private character of those who came forth to sign the call, while in the act of signing'. Only the factor and ten heads of families signed, but nevertheless Clarke's admission went ahead. The presbytery afterwards expressed its hope to the General Assembly for 'measures to restore to the Christian people that voice in the settlement of their ministers which originally belonged to them by the constitution of the church.'[322] Against this background, it is not surprising that, at the Disruption of 1843, most of the ministers and the bulk of the population in north-west Sutherland left the established church for the Free Church. It was said that the church bell of Durness was muffled with an old sock and that a dead dog was left hanging over the pulpit in Farr church.[323]

CONCLUSION

The rise of the Mackays to become a significant force in the northern Highlands invites comparisons with other expanding clans such as the Mackenzies of Ross-shire. However, the competition faced by the Mackays from the Sutherland/Gordon interest and the earls of Caithness, effectively blocked the advances of the Mackays, leaving them without a permanent presence in the richer arable lands of eastern Sutherland or the Caithness plain.

The period of the civil war and interregnum was particularly disruptive to the fortunes of the Mackay clan, but this must be seen against the changes taking place before the 1640s.[324] Although sales of land were made from the 1630s, the assistance of the clan gentry, especially in providing loans in return for wadsets, made a significant contribution to the survival of the house of Mackay.[325]

The rise of indebtedness was a central feature in the history of the Mackay gentry and largely explains the various land transactions. It is tempting to attribute the financial difficulties to the predatory actions of Sir Robert Gordon and the house of Sutherland. But more general causes should also be sought. We do not know so much of the daily lives of the Mackay families as we do of their Caithness counterparts, whose lavish entertainments and often riotous living is well documented.[326] However, there is sufficient evidence to suggest that the cultural integration of the Mackay gentry into Lowland ways was obvious by the early 18th century. The concerns of the Mackays of Bighouse over marriage provisions, the management of the family debts and their interest in estate improvements are typical of landlords throughout Scotland. Attention should also be drawn to the search for opportunities outwith the Highlands; a quest which was shared by the younger sons of the gentry and the smaller lairds alike.

Landlords, including the most traditional of clan chiefs, had always adopted a commercial attitude towards their estates and had been alert to trading opportunities.[327] Indeed, attention is now being drawn to the penetration of economic forces into the Western Highlands in the 16th century, and the evidence would suggest that this is true of northern Sutherland as well.[328] This does not mean that we should lose sight of the continuing importance of kinship and military strength. However, the ground was well prepared for a quickening of the commercial impulses in the 18th century with the development of the fishing and kelp industries and the expansion of the cattle trade.[329] In this process, the role of the Sutherland tacksmen, not as reactionaries, but as commercial middlemen, was to be crucial. The climax to this transformation came with the introduction of sheepfarming, the clearances, and the creation of the crowded crofting townships of the coastal margins.

Accounts of the religious history of the Highlands in the 18th century have tended to paint a picture of a church dominated by lukewarm ministers. In fact, most ministers of northern Sutherland were conscientious, and all parishes had functioning kirk sessions. The opposition to Skeldoch's induction and the controversy over the fellowship meetings suggests that the church had put down strong roots. Of course, there was still much superstition and an enduring tradition of practices which harked back to the pre-Reformation period and which may have drawn upon an even older pagan past. Moreover, the incident known as the 'lapse of Halmadary', when a prayer meeting went out of control and came close to sacrificing a man's son, presents an intriguing insight into religious beliefs.[330] However, the foundations had been laid for evangelical presbyterianism to take a firm hold in the late 18th and early 19th centuries, and to play a part in nurturing leadership within the crofting community.

The process of change, however, was to be long drawn-out and complex; commercial pressures coincided for a considerable period with both kinship-based and feudal relationships. Grimble's assessment of Rob Donn's world as having preserved its immemorial way of life, unaffected by external influences, cannot be sustained.[331] On the other hand, the century after 1750 was to bring about a radically different set of social and economic relationships.

Acknowledgement

I would like to thank Hugh Cheape, Dr Barbara Crawford and Elizabeth Beaton for their helpful comments; John Ballantyne for supplying many useful references; R.W. Munro for sight of an unpublished paper on the Munros in Strathnaver. I am particularly grateful to the staffs of the National Library of Scotland and Scottish Record Office for their assistance over many years. Figure 4.3 was kindly provided by Dr. J. Close-Brooks and Figure 4.12 by J.A. Johnston, Bettyhill. Figure 4.14 is Crown copyright, courtesy of the Royal Commission on the Ancient and Historic Monuments of Scotland.

References and Abbreviations

Manuscript:

Highland Council Archive, Inverness (HCA):

Sutherland 1/1/7   Sutherland Book of Disjunctions

National Library of Scotland (NLS):

Acc.10824	Cumming-Gordon Accession
Adv. MS 37.2.4	John Philip Wood Legal Biographies
Dep.175	Cumming-Gordon Deposit
Dep.313	Sutherland Papers
MS 1149, 1483	Delvine Papers
MS 3430	Lee Papers

Scottish Record Office (SRO):

CH1/2	Church of Scotland General Assembly Papers
CH2/47	Presbytery of Caithness
CH2/508	Presbytery of Tongue
CH2/509	Kirk Session of Tongue
CH2/876	Kirk Session of Durness
CS	Court of Session Records (Warrants and Processes)
DI63	Particular Registers of Inhibitions, Inverness
E326	Exchequer Records: Assessed Tax Schedules
GD84	Reay Papers
GD87	Mackay of Bighouse Muniments
GD95	SSPCK Records
GD136	Sinclair of Freswick Papers
GD170	Campbell of Barcaldine Muniments
GD214	Professor Robert Kerr Hannay's Papers
GD268	Loch Muniments
RD	Registers of Deeds (Registers and Warrants)
RH6	Register House Charters
RH15	Register House Papers
RS37, 38	Particular Registers of Sasines, Inverness
RT	Register of Tailzies
SC9	Dornoch Sheriff Court Records
SC14	Wick Sheriff Court Records
SC34	Tain Sheriff Court Records
TE	Teind Court Records

Printed:

OPS	Origines Parochiales Scotiae (Bannatyne Club, 1851-55).
SAS	Sutherland Abbreviated Sasines.
RMS	Thomson, J.M. et al (eds) Registrum Magni Sigilii Regum Scotorum. 1882-1914.
RPC	Burton, J.H. et al (eds) The Register of the Privy Council of Scotland. 1877-.
RRS	Barrow, G.W.S. et al (eds) Regesta Regum Scottorum. 1960-.

Notes

1. Grimble, I. *Chief of Mackay*. 1965 (reprinted 1993); *The World of Rob Donn*. 1979; *The Trial of Patrick Sellar*. 1962 (reprinted with additions 1993). The latter work has been highly influential although the other volumes are perhaps more distinguished works of scholarship.

2. Mackay, A. *The Book of Mackay*. 1906. An essential contribution to the history of the province of Strathnaver which appeared too late to be taken account of is Mackay, W.R.

'Early Evangelical Religion in the Far North: a *Kulturkampf*', in *Records of the Scottish Church History Society*. 1996. vol 26.

3. See eg Cheape, H. 'Caisteal Bharraich, Dun Varrich and the Wider Tradition', in *Northern Studies* 30. 1993: 56.

4. Pope, A. 'Of Caithness, Strathnaver, and Sutherland', in Pennant, T. *A Tour in Scotland 1769*. 1774: 320, 323.

5. Crawford, B.E. 'Scots and Scandinavians in Medieval Caithness: A Study of the Period 1266-1375', in Baldwin, J.R. (ed) *Caithness: A Cultural Crossroads*. 1982: 65.

6. NLS Dep.313/35/101/12 for an example of the payment of feu duty to the Bishop of Moray in the 17th century.

7. Crawford, B.E. 'The Earldom of Caithness and the Kingdom of Scotland 1150-1266', in Stringer, K.J. (ed) *Essays on the Nobility of Medieval Scotland*. 1985: 34-36. The gift of 4 davochs in Strathnaver by William Federeth to Reginald Cheyne suggests that the lands in Strathnaver were split between Joanna's daughters, and were thus subject to the same rules of inheritance as the remainder of the Caithness earldom.

8. Crawford, B.E. 1982: 65.

9. Gordon, R. *A Genealogical History of the Earldom of Sutherland*. 1813: 32.

10. Traditional accounts of the 'red priest' point to the presence of St Maelrubha and it is noteworthy that the monastery he founded at Applecross appears to have enjoyed lands of similar extent to Durness.

11. Cheape, on the other hand, argues that Castle Varrich should be associated with Angus Dubh Mackay: Cheape, H. 1995.

12. *RRS* II. no.520.

13. Fraser, W. *The Sutherland Book*. 1892. I: 71-2, 86, 140; *OPS* II ii 697.

14. Morrison, A. *The MacLeods – The Genealogy of a Clan*. V. c1977; SRO GD84/1/23/1-3. Donald MacMurdo, the wild man of Hope, buried at Durness, is claimed to be one of the MacLeods of Eddrachillis by MacLeod historians, and as a Mackay by the Mackays: Morrison, A. ca 1977; Mackay, A. 1906: 280-82.

15. Crawford, B.E. 1982: 69-71; Mackay, A. 1906: 57-59; Munro, J. & Munro, R.W. (eds) *Acts of the Lords of the Isles* (Scottish History Society). 1986: 30-31, 45-47, 141-43; *RMS*. II. nos. 148, 149.

16. Munro, J. & Munro, R.W. (eds) 1986: 141-43; NLS Dep.313/462 Inventory; *OPS* II ii 744-45. The Mackays of Strathnaver obtained the superiority of lower Strath Halladale in 1570 and retained it after the lands were acquired by the Mackays of Bighouse.

17. Bannerman, J. *The Beatons: A Medical Kindred in the Classical Gaelic Tradition*. 1986: 62-64.

19. SRO RH6/772.

21. Mary Beith. 'Making the Cure', in *West Highland Free Press*. 5 May - 30 June 1995.

22. SRO RH6/1213, 1218; *RMS* III 2048.

23. SRO RH6/1240, 1241.

24. Donaldson, G. *Reformed by Bishops*. 1987: 56.

25. This would apparently explain why there were investigations in the 1640s into lands in Strathnaver belonging to the bishopric of Orkney: Peterkin, A. *Rentals of the Ancient Earldom and Bishoprick of Orkney*. 1820. iii 11; Anderson, P.D. *Black Patie: The Life and Times of Patrick Stewart Earl of Orkney, Lord of Shetland*. 1992: 28. The Queen also made Reid tenant of the churchlands of Durness: *OPS* II ii 703.

26. Fraser, W. 1892. I: 140-41, 145; Wormald, J. *Lords and Men in Scotland: Bonds of Manrent 1442-1603*. 1985: 20, 63, 289.

27. Fraser, W. 1892. I: 156-161; NLS Dep.313/32/41, 45.

28. Grimble, I. 1965: 44-45.

29. SRO GD84/1/11/4; Mackay, A. 1906: 108. This was not, as Mackay states, an outright disposition.

30. NLS Dep.313/35/101/1-11; Mackay, A. 1906: 122.

32. SRO DI63/3 ff.9v-10v; Grimble, I. 1993. 71-72, 94-95. GD84/2/128.

33. Mackay, A. 1906: 131; Grimble, I. 1993: 63-64, 78-79.

34. SRO GD84/1/8/12; GD84/1/12/1B, 12/2B, 12/4B. Sir Rorie soon afterwards assigned the bond to Alexander Corbat.

35. NLS Dep.313/35/101/6-8.

36. SRO RS37/3 f.290; RS37/6 ff.63-64; GD84/1/28/2B. This was a wadset right which subsisted until 1637 but Seaforth did not possess the lands: he was merely paid interest: SRO GD84/1/28/3B(2).

37. SRO RS37/3 ff.290-91.

38. SRO GD84/1/12/1; RS37/3 ff.291-92.

39. SRO GD84/1/9/1.
40. Grimble. I. 1993: 124.
41. NLS Dep.313/35/103.
42. SRO RS37/5 ff.171-72.
43. SRO GD84/1/12/1.
44. NLS Dep.313/35/105; Dep.313/40.
45. SC14/50/1 ff.25r-26r.
46. NLS Dep.313/50/273-278.
47. Grimble, I. 1993: 123.
48. SRO RS37/6 ff.85-86.
49. SRO GD84/2/6; NLS Dep.313/35/107 (1642). The lands of Invernaver and Borgiebeg, along with Embo's salmon fishings, appear to have been excepted.
50. SRO RS37/6 ff.63-64.
51. SRO RS37/6 ff.268-69.
52. His behaviour was evidence for the survival of what Sellar has termed Celtic secular marriage and which appears to have been practised by Mackay's forebears – although it must be said that extramarital sex was a pastime among the Mackay gentry well into the 18th century: Sellar, W.D.H. 'Marriage, Divorce and Concubinage in Gaelic Scotland', in *Transactions of the Gaelic Society of Inverness.* 1978. LI: 482-84.
53. Grimble, I. 1993: 124-27; SRO GD84/1/3/2-2B.
54. Stevenson, D. *Alasdair MacColla and the Highland Problem in the Seventeenth Century.* 1980: 269.
55. NLS Dep.313/36/papers associated with 115.
56. NLS Dep.313/35/102, 103, 106, 107; Dep.175/48/111 The Earl of Sutherlands Memorandum for Alexander Linton.
57. NLS Dep.313/36/papers associated with 115; GD84/1/9/3.
58. SRO GD84/1/17/1B, 7B. It is clear that this was a wadset and not, as Grimble states, an outright sale: Grimble, I. 1965: 144.
59. NLS MS3430 f.73.
60. Furgol, E.M. 'The Northern Highland Covenanter Clans', in *Northern Scotland* 7.1987: 123.
61. According to James Fraser, the minister of Wardlaw, Lord Reay and Mackenzie of Pluscarden were chosen joint leaders over the more experienced Colonel Hugh Fraser. 'The shame and dissaster of this defeat at Balvany filled most mens mouths with scorn, so that songs and satyres were vented up and down the country uppon that expedition': Mackay, W. (ed) *Chronicles of the Frasers* (Scottish History Society). 1950: 340.
62. SRO GD84/1/6/13.
63. NLS Dep.313/36/115-20.
64. SRO GD84/1/5/6.
65. Furgol, EM. 1987. 125.
66. NLS Acc.10824 box 1, bundle 1631-40, My Lord Sutherland Compt.
67. The apprising came into the hands of Sir Ludovick Gordon of Gordonstoun in 1673, who brought an action against the tenants. Captain William Mackay of Borley and others granted bond to Gordonstoun for 2,000 merks, and Gordon subsequently brought an action against them for non-payment. However, in 1680 Colonel Hugh Mackay bought back his right to the wadset lands from Skibo's son and Gordonstoun: SRO GD84/1/12/1B-14/4; NLS Dep.175/35/64.
68. Grimble, I. 1993: 156-62.
69. SRO GD84/1/5/10; NLS Dep.313/37/145 Ejection Gray v Lord Reay.
70. Dow, F.D. *Cromwellian Scotland 1651-1660.* 1979: 138-140; Grimble, I. 1993: 167-68.
71. NLS Dep.313/37/141, 142; Dep.313/38/154. The last major conflict was between the Mackays and the men of Caithness: Mackay, A. 1906: 154-55.
72. Grimble, I. 1993: 171-74.
73. Mackay, W. (ed) 1905: 450, 483.
74. SRO GD84/1/18/8B.
75. SRO GD84/1/10/9-10. Sir George assigned rights, for instance the apprising of Munro of Achness, to the Earl of Sutherland: SRO GD84/1/18/8B; NLS Dep.313/39/173.
76. SRO GD84/1/18/8B & 9B. Munro later assigned the wadset to Captain Hugh Mackay of Borley and moved to Rogart: SRO GD84/1/19/16; NLS Dep.313/49 wadset of Mudale 1694.
77. For the recovery in aristocratic building at this period: Brown, K.M. *Kingdom or Province? Scotland and the Regal Union 1603-1707.* 1992: 161.
78. SRO CS29/12 January 1773, 1764 proof p.116.

79. SRO RD2/86/1 Discharge Lord Reay to Munro 19 Jan 1702.
80. SRO GD84/1/14, GD84/1/16/1, 7.
81. Mackay, A. 1906: 176.
82. Lenman, B. *The Jacobite Clans of the Great Glen 1650-1784*. 1984: 76.
83. Kemp, D.W. (ed) *Tours in Scotland 1747, 1750, 1760 by Richard Pococke* (Scottish History Society). 1887: 128.
84. SRO GD84/1/32/6, 13, 16, GD84/1/33/5. In 1715 Lord Reay had entered into an agreement to sell the lands within 3 years.
85. Kemp, D.W. (ed) 1887: 130.
86. Maxwell, R. *Select Transactions of the Honourable The Society of Improvers In the Knowledge of Agriculture in Scotland*. 1743.
87. The succession to the estate between 1732 and 1767 may be traced in SRO CS26/579 28 November 1767; GD84/2/15A various memorials; RD15/182; Wilson, J. & Shaw, P. *Cases Decided in the House of Lords on Appeal from the Courts of Scotland 1825*. I: 306-314.
88. SRO RD2/152 17 July 1752 Disp. Lord Reay & to Lord Dromore.
89. SRO RD12/24 March 1749 Tack to Bighouse.
90. SRO GD84/2/26; Sedgewick, R. *The House of Commons 1715-1754*. 1970. II: 235; Namier, L. & Brooke, J. *The House of Commons 1754-1790*. 1964. III: 85.
91. Namier, L. & Brooke, J. 1964. III: 83-85.
92. SRO GD84/2/43.
93. SRO GD84/2/84 volume. This includes wadsets, heritable bonds and annuities.
94. Session Papers, Campbell Collection, March 1790.
95. SRO GD84/2/15A Copy View of the Situation of the Reay Estate 1792.
96. SRO GD84/2/53/14.
97. SRO CS238/R/5/27; GD84/2/53; Highland Council Library, Fraser Mackintosh Collection 1814.
98. SRO GD84/2/15A State of Debts due by Lord Reay 1816.
99. SRO GD84/2/101.
100. *SAS*. 1821-1830. no. 43.
101. Wilson, J. & Shaw, P. *Cases Decided in the House of Lords on Appeal from the Courts of Scotland 1825*. I: 306-314.
103. NLS Dep.313/462 Inventory; *RMS* VI 812; Mitchell, A. (ed) *Macfarlane's Geographical Collections* (Scottish History Society). 1906. II: 560. The purchase was completed in 1612: SRO GD214/486-88.
104. SRO DI63/3 ff.26v-27v.
105. In 1624 he was a party in a bond of relief and in 1626 he was cautioner for Sir Donald: SRO GD84/1/12/4B; GD84/1/9/1.
106. *RMS*. VIII. no. 2230; SRO SC14/50/1 ff.150r-150v where Angus and his mother are described as 'subtaxman and subtaxwoman' to Sir Donald Mackay of Strathnaver of the teinds of 'Strathhallowdell'.
107. Gordon, R. 1813: 451; SRO GD23/4/8; SRO GD214/489. Mackay appears to be mistaken as to William's wife: Mackay, A. 1906: 305.
108. SRO SC14/52/1 bundle 1632.
109. Gordon, R. 1813: 452.
110. NLS Dep.313/36/papers associated with 115; SRO GD84/1/9/3; NLS MS3430 f.73. See also Grimble, I. 1965: 144, 150.
111. Grimble, I. 1965: 157-58; Stevenson, D. *Revolution and Counter-Revolution in Scotland, 1644-1651*. 1977: 145-48; Mackay, A. 1906: 305; SRO GD214/489. It is possible that the Donald Mackay listed amongst those captured was Bighouse's son.
112. SRO GD84/1/6/13.
113. NLS Dep.313/36/115-20. This was on the strength of bonds granted in 1639 and 1644 and affecting both the Reay and Bighouse estates which had been acquired by Sir Robert Gordon of Embo and then handed on to the Earl of Sutherland.
114. NLS Dep.313/464.
115. NLS Dep.313/464/6; MS3430 f.74.
116. SRO GD84/2/219.
117. NLS Dep.313/463/12.
118. NLS Dep.175/60/166 The Rentall of Sutherland. The entries are rather cryptic.
119. NLS Dep.313/465/1-4.
120. NLS Dep.313/466/1.
121. SRO SC14/52/3 bundle 1665.
122. NLS Dep.313/466/1.
123. There is some uncertainty as to when Angus succeeded to the estate. He designed himself

'younger' of Bighouse in December 1673 and January 1674 but was 'of Bighouse' by March 1675: NLS Dep.313/465/5 & 6; Dep.313/464/11. However, there are references to Angus 'of Bighouse' from May 1673: NLS Dep.313/464/15; SRO SC14/50/3 17 June 1704. Ulbster acquired right to Gray's and part of Forbes' apprising in 1664 – the other part being acquired by Melness: NLS Dep.313/463/11; Dep.313/464/10, 13. The wadset of Torinver was redeemed in 1675 and that of Golval in 1679: NLS Dep.313/462 & 466/3. Mackay has followed the Blackcastle MS in erroneously taking Angus' retour (NLS Dep.313/467/1) to mark the death of Donald: SRO GD84/2/246; Mackay, A. 1906: 303-305.

124. Angus was alive in January 1688: SRO GD84/1/19/14.

125. NLS Dep.313/471/1; SRO GD87/2/20; SRO RT/1/6 ff.35v-38v. The entail was registered in 1722 and Elizabeth and Hugh's marriage contract was signed in July 1728.

126. SRO GD87/2/20.

127. Sage, D. *Memorabilia Domestica; A Parish Life in the North of Scotland.* 1889 (1975 edition): 27; Grimble, I. 1979: 5-7.

128. SRO GD87/2/20; NLS Dep.313/471/3. In 1765, Janet and her husband re-opened a legal action on the grounds that they had received nothing from her father's executry.

129. Firstly Janet's disposition was assigned to Clashneach who proceeded to obtain an adjudication against her on the grounds of non-performance. Secondly Clashneach obtained an adjudication against Elizabeth on a bond of £40,000 Scots (the bond was fictitious in that no actual debt existed). The two adjudications were assigned to Hugh in 1743, and the whole process was re-enacted in 1754-55: NLS Dep.313/471-72. An action was brought by Hugh of Bighouse's heirs against Clashneach's heir, Hugh Mackay in Durness (formerly of Jamaica) in 1773, to adjudge from him any title he might derive from his father: NLS Dep.313/445/8.

130. SRO CH1/2/75 f.125; SRO GD87/2/10. The agreement allowed Hugh to retain possession of Kirkton rent free, on condition that he relieved his mother-in-law of the public burdens of her lands and allowed her to cut 20 merks of hay in the 'Linn of Golval' [Lon of Golval?].

131. SRO GD87/2/13, 14. She also enjoyed some income from the estate of Giese in Caithness, in virtue of her second marriage to Robert Sinclair of Giese which lasted from 1712 until the latter's death in 1742. When her son, George Sinclair of Giese, engaged in the '45 Rebellion and was carried prisoner to London, his creditors attempted to seize the estate. Katherine, however, obtained an adjudication. When George and his wife heard that Katherine was dying, they battled through the snowstorms to Trantlemore and after sleeping with the corpse, broke into Katherine's sealed chest of papers. George later proceeded against his step-sisters for the balance owing to Katherine from the costs in bringing up her children and Hugh's funeral charges: SRO GD87/2/20; GD214/490/5. He also claimed for sums which his mother had uplifted but never accounted for during her second marriage: SRO RD4/185/2 12 June 1759 Discharge Sinclair to Mackay. Katherine's moveables were shared amongst the 5 daughters from her two marriages: she was owed £523 in rents and livestock at the time of her death: SRO RD4/185/2 8 June 1759 Mutual discharge.

132. HCA Sutherland 1/1/7 pp.19-20.

133. Grimble, I. 1979: 46.96-97.

134. MacLeod, R.H. 'The Independent Companies of the 1745 Rebellion', in *Transactions of the Gaelic Society of Inverness*. 1984. LIII: 336-38.

135. NLS MS1483 ff.234-35. Rob Donn's poem 'Bighouse's Farewell to the Forest' was probably composed after 1758, rather than as Grimble states in the early 1740s: Grimble, I. 1979: 53-56; Morrison, H. (ed) *Orain le Rob Donn: Songs and Poems in the Gaelic Language by Rob Donn.* 1899: 87-93.

136. SRO GD170/972 ff.74-75.

137. Janet's younger sister, known in the family as Mallie, spent a season in Edinburgh in 1750: GD170/972 f.48.

138. SRO GD170/391/8; Fraser, A.C. *The Book of Barcaldine.* 1936: 63, 145; MacDonald, C.M. 'Colin Campbell of Glenure, the Victim of the 'Appin' Murder', in *Transactions of the Gaelic Society of Inverness.* 1953-59. XLII: 352.

139. SRO GD87/1/38; GD170/972 f.30

140. 'ye Dr little Capt' Hugh died at Tongue of a 'Pleuresick fever' on 14 April 1751: SRO GD170/972 f.65; Morrison, H. (ed). 1899: 40-42. In a letter to his brother-in-law, William Baillie, Glenure wrote that 'Dr Hughies Death is a heavie stroke to us all, God pittie the father and mother their Load [letter torn] heavie to bear, whatever their outward appearance is [th]eir grief must be Immence': SRO SC34/28/50.

141. Session Papers, Campbell Collection, 44.
142. MacArthur, W. *The Appin Murder*. 1960. 16; Stewart, A. 'A memorial and opinion of 1762 given by Robert McQueen, later Lord Braxfield', in *Miscellany Three* (The Stair Society). 1992: 200-201. Janet and her daughters were named in the indictment of James Stewart as private prosecutors: Mackay, D.N. (ed) *Trial of James Stewart* (Notable British Trials). 1931: 41.
143. SRO GD170/1129/3. Grimble argued that the poem 'Oh! I sleep ...' was composed between 1742 and 1744, but this reference proves that it was composed ten years later: Grimble, I. 1979: 27, 40-41, 56 note; Morrison, H. (ed) 1899: 260-65.
144. SRO GD170/1313/4, 5. Both Mackay and Bulloch simply state that William Baillie married a daughter of Bighouse: he was in fact twice married. The marriage may not have been approved of, but Janet did not marry her nephew! Bulloch, J.G.B. *A History and Genealogy of the Family of Baillie of Dunain, Dochfour and Lamington*. 1898: 34-35; Mackay, A. 1906: 307. Janet, who received an annuity of 2,000 merks from her brother-in-law, and her young husband spent several years in Yorkshire until he was given a loan to raise a company in Colonel Simon Fraser's Regiment. Charles Baillie was killed at the siege of Louisburgh in 1758. Janet subsequently married ca 1760 Alexander Hart, a merchant in Edinburgh, and apparently resumed the upbringing of her children: SRO GD170/391/7; Session Papers, Campbell Collection, 44.
145. SRO GD170/1129/2, 3; GD170/1313/3, 6. Dr Sinclair, who had recently begun to inoculate for small pox, was married to Elizabeth's step-sister Barbara Sinclair: SRO RD4/185/2 8 June 1759 mutual discharge.
146. SRO GD170/1097/36, 39; GD170/1313/6-8. It was several years before Duncan Campbell registered an inventory of their estate. Even his relations cautioned him against disputing matters with Janet: Fraser, A.C. 1936: 101-102.
147. SRO GD84/2/15A Memoriall for Lord Reay 1762.
148. Henderson, D.M. & Dickson, J.H. (eds) *A Naturalist in the Highlands: James Robertson His Life and Travels in Scotland*. 1994: 50. It is probable that Bighouse was advised by Alexander Sangster, land surveyor and gardener in Ross-shire: SRO GD170/972 ff.69, 71.
149. NLS MS1485 f.168.
150. SRO GD84/2/53/4. The provisions included £500 to Mary, wife of William Baillie of Rosehall; £1,000 to Mackay Hugh Baillie, her eldest son; £500 to Katherine Baillie; and £200 each to remaining 5 children. Louisa and Colin Campbells each received £500.
151. *Caledonian Mercury* 22 April 1771.
152. SRO GD87/1/101. Her right was corroborated in 1788: *SAS*. 1781-1820. no. 64.
153. In 1774/75 George purchased the shares of the estate held by other members of the family: £1,376 to Mary, the wife of William Baillie of Rosehall who had a half-share of Lower Halladale and £688 to Colin or Colina, the wife of James Baillie, who held a quarter share of these lands: NLS Dep.313/445/8.
154. SRO RD14/105/9 Feb 1765 Tack Lord Reay to Lieut George Mackay; SRO GD84/2/53/26; NLS Dep.313/3326.
155. SRO GD87/1/103.
156. His accounts were not settled until 1829, when a payment of £271 was made to his widow: SRO GD84/2/53/25, GD84/2/84.
157. The headquarters of the Bighouse company, which was the first to be formed, were in the vicinity of Bighouse, near to the township of Melvich: Scobie, I.H.M. *An Old Highland Fencible Corps*. 1914.
158. NLS Dep.313/445/11-13; *Caledonian Mercury* 20 April 1799.
159. *SAS*. 1781-1820. no. 221; NLS Dep.313/445/13.
160. SRO GD84/2/246 p.98; *Caledonian Mercury* 15 March 1810; Henderson, J. *General View of the Agriculture of the County of Sutherland*. 1812: 40-41.
161. SRO GD87/2/31/1 & 2; TE19/182, 1 July 1795, Mackay of Bighouse. The figure of £1,076 quoted in a list of gross rentals for 1815 may refer to a few years earlier: NLS Dep.313/1469 p.106.
162. Scobie, I.H.M. 1914: 33-34.
163. NLS Dep.313/447/36; SAS, 1821-1830, nos. 78, 87. Bighouse had asked for £70,000: Dep.313/1196. The total price including furniture and stock amounted to £58,000: SRO GD268/251 p.87. The sale of the Reay estate enabled Lord Reay to pay off both the Bighouse family bond for £500 over Scourie and the wadset for £4,000 Scots over Torrisdale originally granted to Arthur Forbes in 1653: SAS, 1821-1830, nos. 72, 79.
164. In 1831 he bought the barony of Allanbank in the parish of Edrom, Berwickshire which, according to the disposition, was to be thereafter called Bighouse: *Berwickshire Abbreviated Sasines*. 1831-1840: no. 76.

165. SRO GD87/2/32/3. This was after the death of Eric, Lord Reay.
166. Grimble, I. 1993:71-72. 94-95; (see above).
167. SRO GD84/1/9/1; GD84/1/12/4B; GD84/1/28/1 & 3B; SC14/50/1 f.173r.
168. SRO SC14/52/1 bundle 1632.
169. SRO GD84/1/17/1B; GD84/2/128.
170. SRO GD84/2/130.
171. NLS Dep.175/box 25/bundle 28, minute of a contract 164[?]; Dep.175/box 66, no.496.
172. NLS MS3430 ff.73-74; Dep.175/60/166 The Rentall of Sutherland; SRO SC14/50/1 f.173r; SC14/52/3 bundle 1665.
173. The apprisings bought by Brims were led by William Dundas, advocate, James Sinclair, second son of David Sinclair of Southdun and Alexander McCulloch, merchant burgess of Tain: NLS Dep.313/41/192, 195, 203; SRO GD84/2/132, 141.
174. Gray, A.P. 'Some Gentlemen of Sutherland in Colonial Georgia', in *The Scottish Genealogist.* 1994. XLI: 15-19.
175. *SAS.* 1781-1820. no. 3.
176. Kemp, D.W. (ed) 1887: 132; Henderson, D.M. & Dickson, J.H. (eds.). 1994: 50.
177. Fereday, R.P. *The Orkney Balfours 1747-99.* 1990; NLS Adv.MS 37.2.4 f.137.
178. Although he took his title from his estate in Sutherland, he also bought property in the central Lowlands. The village of Armadale, near Bathgate, was a planned village which he established on the lands of Barbachlaw: *Linlithgow Abbreviated Registers of Sasines,* 1781-1820, nos. 952 and 1553; NLS Dep.313/41/209.
179. Henderson, J. 1812: 27.
180. Scobie, I.H.M. 1914: 32.
181. NLS Dep.313/41/209, 210, 214. The total cost of the purchase came to £25,690. Adam, R.J. (ed) *Papers on Sutherland Estate Management 1802-1816* (Scottish History Society). 1972. II: 160-61, 168, 174, 257.
182. NLS Adv.Ms 37.2.4 f.137; SRO GD84/2/246 f.115v-116r.
183. NLS Dep.313/36/121, 122, 133.
184. NLS Dep.313/36/123, 124, 128.
185. NLS Dep.313/37/140; Dep.313/38/163.
186. NLS Dep.313/36/130, 133 & 139.
187. NLS Dep.313/38/161, 162, 166. Lord Duffus subsequently acquired Rearquhar's wadset; NLS Dep.313/37/172.
188. NLS Dep.313/39/180; Dep.313/47.
189. NLS Dep.313/39/177, 181; Dep.313/67.
190. NLS Dep.313/50/278.
191. NLS Dep.313/37/147, Dep.313/38/148-153; Dep.313/39/169; Dep.313/51/281; SRO SC14/50/3 14 Feb 1680; Grimble, I. 1993: 177-78.
192. NLS Dep.313/67.
193. NLS Dep.313/67 execution of warning 1700. See also Grimble's comments: Grimble, I. 1993: 137-38.
194. Adam, R.J. (ed) 1972. I, xiii, II, 189.
195. NLS Dep.313/54.
196. NLS Dep.313/46 (Duffus), 52 (Erskine), 60 (Gilchrist/Fergusson).
197. NLS Dep.313/36/115.
198. Kemp, D.W. (ed) 1887. 121.
199. SRO RD2/135 22 April 1734; RD13/17 March 1737 Tack to Robert Mackay, tutor of Farr; RD14/9 Feb 1765 tack to George Mackay of Island Handa.
200. See for example SRO GD84/2/66/1; GD87/2/14; NLS Dep.313/53/286. The goat and sheep cheeses were delivered in 'creels crubands or casies': SRO GD84/2/52.
201. Richards, E. 1982: 143; NLS Dep.313/3477 p.68.
202. Mitchell, A. & Clark, J.T. (eds.) *Geographical Collections relating to Scotland made by Walter Macfarlane* (Scottish History Society). 1908. III: 108.
203. Mackay, M.M. "A Highland Minister's Diary', in *Cornhill Magazine.* 1935. 152: 572-73; Richards, E. 1982: 89-90; SRO CH2/508/1 pp.283-85, 288.
204. SRO CH2/509/3 p.8.
205. NLS Dep.313/37/145 contract 11 September 1634.
206. For a general account of livestock husbandry and the trade in cattle and horses in Ross and Cromarty and Sutherland, see Baldwin, J.R. 'The Long Trek: Agricultural Change and the Great Northern Drove', in Baldwin, J.R. (ed) *Firthlands of Ross and Sutherland.* 1986.
207. SRO CS234/Seqns/M/2/27; SC14/4/160 Writs in depositories of dec George Innes tacksman of Isauld; *Edinburgh Gazette* 17 April 1807.
208. *Caledonian Mercury* 12. 24 May 1792.

209. For the accounts of the Strathnaver fishings for 1558-59 when the Mackay lands were in the possession of the crown: Murray A.L. 'The Salmon Fishings of Strathnaver, 1558-1559', in *Review of Scottish Culture.* 1993. 8: 77-83.
210. SRO GD84/1/23/1B.
211. SRO SC14/52/2 bundle 1650.
212. SRO RD2/134 4 July 1733 Discharge Lord Reay & Falls.
213. Knox, J. *A Tour through the Highlands of Scotland and the Hebride Isles in 1786.* 1787 (reprinted 1975): 262.
214. Highland Council Library, Fraser-Mackintosh Collection FM 1814; NLS Dep.313/3326.
215. Session Papers, Campbell Collection, 10 July 1781.
216. SRO RD14/105/24 June 1765 Tack Lord Reay to Forbes.
217. SRO CS237/R/2/31/2.
218. Highland Council Library, Fraser-Mackintosh Collection FM1814; NLS Dep.313/3326.
219. Grimble, I. 1979: 8.
220. Gray, A.P. 1994: 7-21, 76-83.
221. SRO CH2/508/1 p.356; CS101/261; GD84/1/29/12; GD84/1/30/2, 3; GD84/2/26; Dep.313/470/2.
222. HCA Sutherland 1/1/7 pp. 17-18.
223. MacLeod, R.H. 1984. LIII: 336-38; Maclean, C.I. *The Highlands.* 1959: 176; Gibson, JS. *Ships of the '45.* 1967: 2-5.
224. SRO SC9/29/1 (1748-49). See SC9/29/2 (1750) for further agreement in 1750.
225. SAS, 1781-1820, no. 3.
226. SRO RH15/182/7, 1 2, 5; Grimble, I. 1979: 43.
227. SRO GD84/2/59; E326/1/120.
228. SRO SC9/29/1 (1769).
229. Morrison, H. 'Notices of the Ministers of the Presbytery of Tongue from 1726 to 1763', in *Transactions of the Gaelic Society of Inverness.* 1884-85. XI; Grimble, I. 1979: 42, 75.
230. Kennedy, J. *The Days of the Fathers In Ross-shire* [1861] quoted in Cowper, A.S. & Ross, I. (eds) *Pre-1855 Tombstone Inscriptions in Sutherland Burial Grounds.* 1989: 148, 201; Session 231. NLS MS1149 f.154.
232. Hunter, J. *A Dance called America.* 1994.
233. SRO GD84/2/65, 67, 70 & 71.
234. Morrison, H. (ed) *Parish Register of Durness, 1764-1814* (Scottish Record Society). 1911.
235. For this section see: Bangor-Jones, M. 'The Strathnaver Clearances', in *North Sutherland Studies* (Scottish Vernacular Buildings Working Group). 1987; Bangor-Jones, M. 'The coming of the great sheep', in *The Northern Times* 4 March 1988. For the essential background to the clearances on the Sutherland estate as a whole, see Richards, E. *A History of the Highland Clearances.* 1982. 284-362. For Patrick Sellar's background, trial and reputation see Richards, E. *A History of the Highland Clearances.* 1985. 373-408.
236. SRO GD87/2/31/1; Henderson, J. 1812: 28; *Caledonian Mercury,* 7 October 1802, 15 March 1810.
237. Richards, E. *The Leviathan of Wealth.* 1973: 237.
238. Richards, E 1982: 441-44; 1985: 323-325, 403; Mearns, A.B. 'The Durness Riots 1841', in *Am Bratach.* 37, November 1994.
239. Bangor-Jones, M. 1987.
240. Hunter, J. *The Making of the Crofting Community.* 1976.
241. Caird, J.B. 'The making of the North Sutherland crofting landscape in the Skerray district', in *North Sutherland Studies* (Scottish Vernacular Buildings Working Group). 1987; Bangor-Jones, M. 'The establishment of crofting in North West Sutherland', in *Am Bratach* 20-21, June-July 1993. Oldshoremore and Oldshorebeg were not reorganised into crofts until 1847.
242. There is some evidence that the lands of Glencoul lay in the parish of Lairg or even Creich.
243. The lands of Ribigill and Skail were churchlands: *OPS* II ii 708, 717. Pont's late 16th century map marks a number of chapels and many are listed by Pope: Pope, A. 1776: 341-49.
244. Cowan, I.B. *The Medieval Church in Scotland.* 1995: 92, 149.
245. Stuart, J. 'Articles by Robert, Bishop of Caithness, against George, Earl of Caithness', in *Proceedings of the Society of Antiquaries of Scotland.* 1876. XI: 87-102.
246. Donaldson, G. 1987: 53-67; Kirk, J. *Patterns of Reform.* 1989: particularly 312-18, 458, 462-65.
247. In the early 17th century, Caithness was divided into Wick and Dornoch presbyteries: Kirk, J. 1989: 483. The surviving minutes of the Presbytery of Caithness commence in 1654: SRO CH2/47/1.

248. *New Statistical Account.* XV: 102; *OPS* II ii 702; Kirk, J. 1989: 476.
250. SRO GD84/1/29/3. Kirk is misleading: Kirk, J. 1989: 475.
251. SRO CH2/47/1 pp.1, 20, 42, 51; Bangor-Jones, M. "'Abounding with people of dyvers languages": the Church and Gaelic in the Presbytery of Caithness in the second half of the 17th Century', in *Northern Studies.* 33. 1998.
252. Cowan, I.B. *The Scottish Covenanters 1660-1688.* 1976: 54, 85, 114.
253. Foster, W.R. *Bishop and Presbytery: The Church of Scotland 1661-1688.* 1958: 5.
254. For church discipline in general see Mitchison, R. & Leneman, L. *Sexuality and Social Control: Scotland 1660-1780.* 1989.
255. SRO CH2/47/1 pp.94, 97.
256. SRO CH2/47/1 p.173.
257. SRO CH2/47/2 p.32. The minister, Neil Beaton of Latheron, was only suspended for a time.
258. SRO CH2/47/2 p.68.
259. SRO CH2/47/2 ff.43v-54r.
260. SRO CH2/47/2; Mitchison, R. & Leneman, L. 1989: 224-25. It is noteworthy that the presbytery continued to call upon the sheriff for some years after the Toleration Act of 1712 deprived the church of that power.
261. Grimble, I. 1979: 22-23.
262. SRO CH1/2/25/3 f.291; CH1/2/26/2 f.151; CH1/2/66 ff.124-69; GD84/1/29/11, 12.
263. SRO CH1/2/75 ff.103, 127; CH2/47/2 p.189.
264. Grimble, I. 1979: 32-37, 182-85, 213-17.
265. SRO CH2/508/1 pp.167-70, 179, 190, 347-, 381. The proceedings take up a considerable proportion of the presbytery minutes during this period. Skeldoch had been forced to flee from Lochaber after he had outbid a local family for a farm: Macdonald, S. *Back to Lochaber.* 1994. 191.
266. SRO CH2/508/2 pp.27, 33-38, 43.
267. Beaton, D. 'Fast-Day and Friday Fellowship Meeting Controversy in the Synod of Sutherland and Caithness (1737-1758)', in *Transactions of the Gaelic Society of Inverness.* 1917. XXIX; Grimble, I. 1979: 35; Mackay, WR. 1996.
268. SRO CH2/509/3. Although the minutes start in 1744 there is only a single entry for that year. More extensive records commence in the 1780s. But even then it is noticeable that the account of the session's role in the famine of 1783 was not written up for 5 years.
269. SRO CH2/876/1 pp.13, 23.
270. SRO CH2/876/1 p.5.
271. SRO CH2/876/1 p.3.
272. SRO CH2/876/1 pp.39-40.
273. The case of Colonel Hugh Mackay at Balnakeil, who intimidated the kirk officer and witnesses executing the summons charging his maidservant to appear before the session, is a good example: SRO CH2/876/1 pp.24-33.
274. SRO CH2/508/2 p.49.
275. SRO CH2/876/2.
276. SRO CH2/867/2.
277. Withrington, D. 'Education in the 17th Century Highlands', in *The Seventeenth Century in the Highlands* (Inverness Field Club). 1986.
278. SRO SC14/50/1 f.26r. He was dead by July 1640: ff.50r-51v.
279. SRO SC14/52/3 bundle 1667 translation Margaret Macleod to William Manson reg 17 June.
280. SRO GD84/1/22/6B.
281. SRO GD84/1/27/5.
282. SRO GD95/11/5 section 22(1).
283. SRO GD95/9/1 pp.51-53, 218, 441.
284. See Withers' comments on the Society's advice to William Mackay, the teacher at Durness: Withers, C.W.J. *Gaelic in Scotland 1698-1981.* 1984: 122.
285. SRO GD84/2/140 letter Nicol Spence to Lord Reay 20 Sept 1729.
286. SRO CH2/508/1 pp.251-52, 257.
287. SRO CH1/2/78 ff.194-96, 212, 215; CH2/508/1 p.281. Withers, C.W.J. 1984: 171.
288. SRO CH2/508/2 pp.53, 55.
289. *Moral Statistics of the Highlands and Islands of Scotland* (Inverness Society for the Education of the Poor in the Highlands). 1826: Appendix p.vi.
290. An Account showing the State of the Establishment for Parochial Education in Scotland. *Parliamentary Papers.* 1826. XVIII: 952-53.
291. Inverness Society for the Education of the Poor in the Highlands. 1826: 56, Appendix pp. xi, xxiv.

292. SRO GD95/11/5 section 22(2).
293. SRO CH1/2/116 f.386; CH2/508/2 pp.12, 18.
294. SRO CH2/508/2 pp.161-64.
295. Gifford, J. *Buildings of Scotland: Highlands and Islands.* 1992. 579. By 1835 the building was in very bad repair. There were 'two square seats' belonging to the neighbouring tacksmen; the majority of the congregation (as many as 100 in summer) sat on planks: Fourth report by the Commissioners of Religious Instruction, Scotland. *Parliamentary Papers.* 1837-38. XXXIII: 516-17.
296. SRO CH2/508/2 pp.176-77.
297. Bardgett, F. *North Coast Parish: Strathy and Halladale.* 1990: 15-17. Although the Parliamentary churches and manses are often attributed to Thomas Telford, it appears that the main responsibility for the standard design belonged to William Thomson, one of Telford's surveyors: Gifford, J. 1992: 37, 127, 587.
298. *Parliamentary Papers.* 1837-38. XXXIII: 525.
299. *Parliamentary Papers.* 1837-38. XXXIII: 526-27. The average congregation was 550 out of a total population in Strath Halladale of 1125.
300. Grimble, I. *The Trial of Patrick Sellar.* 1993: 46-47; Prebble, J. *The Highland Clearances.* 1963: 81-86. This line has been followed by Temperley, A. *Tales of the North Coast.* 1977.
301. Richards, E. *The Leviathan of Wealth.* 1973: 189; Richards, E. 1982: 320-21; MacLeod, D. *Gloomy Memories.* 1892: 18.
302. Mearns, A.B. 'The Minister and the Bailiff: A Study of Presbyterian Clergy in the Northern Highlands During The Clearances', in *Records of the Scottish Church History Society.* 1990: 24. 53-75.
303. Sage, D. 1899 (1975 edition): 214-18. Temperley states that Sage 'supported people as he could during the clearances': Temperley, A. 1977: 214. See also Grimble, I. 1993: 126-140.
304. MacLeod, D. 1892: 21.
305. NLS Dep.313/1468 p.149 Suther to Sage 28 April 1818; Mearns, A.B. 1990: 60-61.
306. Logue, K.J. *Popular Disturbances in Scotland 1780-1815.* 1979: 173-74.
307. Paton, D.M.M. 'Brought to a Wilderness: The Rev. David Mackenzie of Farr and the Sutherland Clearances', in *Northern Scotland.* 1993. 13: 75-101.
308. Smith, D.C. *Passive Obedience and Prophetic Protest: Social Criticism in the Scottish Church 1830-1945.* 1987: 135.
309. Hillis, J. 'The Sociology of the Disruption', in Brown, S.J. & Fry, M. (eds) *Scotland in the Age of the Disruption.* 1993: 50.
310. Inverness Society for the Education of the Poor in the Highlands. 1826. Appendix p. xxiii; SRO GD136/524/252; MacLeod, D. 1892: 21, 37.
311. Inverness Society for the Education of the Poor in the Highlands. 1826. Appendix p. xxiii.
312. Hunter, J. 'The Emergence of the Crofting Community: The Religious Contribution 1798-1843', in *Scottish Studies* 18. 1974; Hunter, J. 1976: 94-103; Brown, C. *The Social History of Religion in Scotland since 1730.* 1987: 115-25; Macinnes, A. 'Evangelical Protestantism in the nineteenth-century Highlands', in Walker, G. & Gallagher, T. (eds) *Sermons and Battle Hymns: Protestant Popular Culture in Modern Scotland.* 1990; Devine, T.M. *Clanship to Crofters' War.* 1994: 100-109. A recent study of the Disruption on the Isle of Lewis stresses the leadership of the evangelicals and the lack of any sustainable alternative; Ansdell, D.B.A. 'The 1843 Disruption of the Church of Scotland in the Isle of Lewis', in *Records of the Scottish Church History Society.* 1991: XXIV.
313. Richards, E. 1985: 359.
314. Macrae, A. *Margaret Macdiarmid (Bean a Chreidimh Mhoir) or Mrs Mackay of Sheiggira and of Melness.* nd.
315. *Parliamentary Papers.* 1837-38. XXXIII: 508-29.
316. SRO CH2/509/3 p.42.
317. SRO CH2/508/2 pp.318-19, 324-28; CH2/508/3 pp.2, 7-8, 11, 13, 44-45, 55, 57-58.
318. SRO CH2/508/3 pp. 59-61, 80-81, 83-84, 86-88, 94-95, 111-113. Mackenzie was formally deposed by the presbytery in September 1833.
319. SRO CH2/508/3 p.8.
320. SRO CH2/508/3 pp.22-25, 27.
321. SRO CH2/508/3 pp.32-37; Bardgett, F. 1990: 17.
322. SRO CH2/508/3 pp.101-105, 107-111. For a revealing pen-portrait of the Rev Cook see Sage, D. 1899 (1975 edition): 324, 326-27.
323. Macrae, A. *Kinlochbervie: Being the story and traditions of a remote Highland parish and its people.* 1932: 51. Hillis has used the baptismal registers of various Scottish parishes, including Durness, to assess the completeness of the move into the Free Church: Hillis 1993.

324. For comparative accounts, see: Macinnes, A.I. 'The Impact of the Civil Wars and Interregnum: Political Disruption and Social Change within Scottish Gaeldom', in Mitchison, R. & Roebuck, P. (eds) *Economy and Society in Scotland and Ireland 1500-1939.* 1988; Bangor-Jones, M. 'Mackenzie Families of the Barony of Lochbroom', in Baldwin, J.R. (ed) *Peoples & Settlement in North-West Ross.* 1994.
325. Compare: Shaw, F.J. 1980: 43-46.
326. Donaldson, J.E. *Caithness in the 18th century.* 1938.
327. Brown, K.M. 1992: 38-39.
328. Dawson, J.E.A. 'The origins of the "Road to the Isles": Trade, Communications and Campbell Power in early Modern Scotland', in Mason, R. & Macdougall, N. (eds) *People and Power in Scotland.* 1992.
329. This is similar to what Macinnes has found for Argyllshire: Macinnes, A.I. 'Landownership, Land Use and Elite Enterprise in Scottish Gaeldom: from Clanship to Clearance in Argyllshire, 1688-1858', in Devine, T.M. (ed) *Scottish Elites.* 1994.
330. Further details of this extraordinary event are provided by Mackay who suggests that the 'shame' of Halmidary was an example of 'popular enthusiasm running far in advance of ministerial direction'. Mackay, W.R. 1996. 127-8.
331. Grimble, I. 1979: 2.

FEARCHAR LIGHICHE
AND THE TRADITIONAL MEDICINES
OF THE NORTH

Mary Beith

FEARCHAR BEATON: LEGEND & REALITY

On the 5 March 1823, one John Kelly sent a letter from Skye to South
Queensferry summarising three traditional Highland stories, the second of
which related to:

> Farquaar Bethune called in Gaelic Farquhar Leich [correctly: Fearchar
> Lighiche, Fearchar the Healer] which signifies the curer of every kind of
> diseases, and which knowledge he received from a book printed in red in
> which had descended in heritable succesion and is now in the posession of
> Kenneth Bethunne ... of Waterstane [Waterstein] in Glendale, and which
> they contain both secret and sacred; – what instructions are contained therein
> are descriptive of the virtues of certain herbs in particular which he denied
> having any equal, nor being produced by any other country by Skye, it has
> been examined by Botanists from London and elsewhere and its non-affinity
> to any other confirmed. He was gifted with prophecy, and held conf[erence]
> with the Brutal [natural] creation in that was quite a prodigy. This is only an
> outline of him.

What Kelly lacked in grammar and spelling is irrelevant; what is pertinent is
that his remarks about Fearchar Lighiche neatly encapsulate the tangle of
fact, legend and mystery in which the old Highland healers, official and
unofficial alike, were held in awe by their contemporaries and subsequent
generations.

The Fearchar of Kelly's note would have been a Beaton of Husabost in
Skye, a notable family of hereditary, trained physicians who practised in the
island from the 15th to the early 18th century, several of whom where named
Fearchar. However, many legends concerning this dynasty of doctors, which
also had branches in, among other places, Islay, Mull, Easter Ross and North
Sutherland, became all-purpose apocryphal yarns about a specific local
doctor – depending on where the tale was told.

The Fearchar Legend

The 'origin' story of how these medical men first acquired their 'secret and
sacred' gifts frequently pointed to a Fearchar of north Sutherland. We will
begin with the legend and see how it merges with the facts.

This Fearchar was a drover from the old Reay Country. One day, at a Lowland cattle tryst, he met a strange gentleman who, in the course of a warm and friendly chat, asked how he had come by his hazel staff. 'In Glen Golly, in the Reay Country', the drover replied, adding that if he were near it, he would certainly know the tree again.

'You'll get a rich reward from me if you return to the tree and see if there is a serpent's hole beneath it', the stranger said. 'If there is, you should wait a while and then you will see six brown serpents coming out of it. Let them be, and when they return a white serpent will be following them. Capture the white. Fearchar did as he was asked. Back at the hazel tree from which he had cut his stock, he found a hole as the man had described. After a while, six brown serpents crept out and slithered away across the grass. Shortly after this, they returned with a seventh, white snake. Fearchar put the creature into the bottle and made it fast with a cork.

When he met up again with the foreign gentleman, the man was delighted. He uncorked the bottle and shook the snake into a pot of broth that was simmering on a fire. Then the stranger instructed Fearchar to watch it didn't boil over until he himself returned. The man was not long gone when the liquid began to bubble fiercely and despite everything Fearchar did to dampen the fire, the broth looked set to lift the lid off the pot. As Fearchar tried to push the lid down, he burnt one of his fingers in the bree and thrust it into his mouth. In the Gaelic words of the Reay Country story:

Ann an tiota bha sùilean a thuigse air am fosgladh, agus fhuair èolais air dòigh leigheas air gach tinn is pian thainig riamh an car duine.

(In a flash the eyes of his understanding were opened, and he acquired the wisdom to heal every ache and pain that ever befell mortal beings.)

On his return, the stranger went straight to the pot, lifted the lid, dipped in a finger and sucked the bree. 'Aha,' he said to Fearchar, 'this is no use now. You didn't do as I told you, so you'll get no reward now.'

Just as the daughter in a Norse story of the Viper King deprived her father of gaining supernatural insight by taking the first mouthful of serpent's grease, so Fearchar's quick taste of the broth on his finger meant that he and not the mysterious stranger gained the wisdom. It could not be undone or altered. Fearchar returned home, and on his way healed all the sick people he met. At length he reached a town where he learned that the king was in agony from a sore leg. He was unable to walk and although the physicians had been most attentive, every remedy had been in vain.

When Fearchar heard of this he went to the castle gate and cried aloud: 'A' bhiast-dubh air a' chnàmh gheal!' ('The black beetle to the white bone!'). On hearing him, the king asked for the man to be brought to him. 'Are you a doctor?' asked the king. 'Indeed I am, sir,' replied Fearchar. 'If you heal me,' declared the king, 'I will give you what you ask, even to the half of my kingdom.'

Fearchar then revealed that instead of trying to cure him, the court physicians had been keeping the king's ulcers open by setting beetles to gnaw

at the flesh. After a proper poultice had been applied and the leg was healed,
the grateful king inquired as to Fearchar's fee.

'The fee', said Fearchar Lighiche, as he was to be known from then on,
'is every island in the sea between Stoer Head in Assynt and the red point in
Orkney.' 'Granted,' said the king, 'along with much land in your own country
besides.'

The Historical Record:
Hereditary Dynasties & Clan Patronage

Now for the historical record. A royal charter, dated 4 September 1379, confirms a grant of the lands of Melness and Hope in north Sutherland by Robert II and his son, Alexander Stewart (the Wolf of Badenoch), to 'Ffercado medico nostro'. In a further charter, dated 31 December 1386, Robert II grants 'our esteemed and faithful leech Fearchar' a number of islands from Stoer Point in Assynt to Armadale on the north coast 'for his service done and to be done to us'.

In the original charter, the first of the islands is called Jura but it is not the island known as Jura today. In Robert II's time, Jura was also the name of the one in Eddrachillis Bay now known as Oldaney. A note on the process by which the island's name was changed is included in a privately printed collection of Sutherland papers compiled by James Loch in 1859.

In 1511, Melness and Hope were resigned by a descendant of Fearchar to the chiefs of Mackay. Actual title to the islands must have been resigned somewhat earlier, as in 1504 they were gifted to Aodh Mackay by James IV. The 'red point in Orkney' of the legend may refer to Rubha Ruadh, an old Melness name given to the inshore Eilean Naoimh near Skerray, which looks from some view-points to be yet another rocky headland of a very irregular coastline. At the same time, the island stands out from its neighbours because of its pegmatite rock which glows a delightful rosy red in the sunlight. Eilean Naoimh is listed in the 1386 charter as 'Elaneuyofo', while the other islands (including the larger Eilean Roan) around the mouth of the Kyle of Tongue are simply referred to as 'et omnes insulas nostra jacentes inter'. From the mainland, the outline of Orkney may be seen across the Pentland Firth (weather permitting).

When the charters eventually arrived at Register House in Edinburgh they were accompanied by a letter (dated 13 April 1831) from James Loch, one of the more notorious of the first Duke of Sutherland's factors, to a John Mackay. Loch notes:

> In 1511 McKay obtained from McCorchie [Mac Mhurchaidh] the lands of Melness and Hoip [Hope] which Lands had been granted by King Robert to Farqhuar his Physician in 1376 [*sic*] and who in 1389 [*sic*] followed up this grant to the same person of all the Islands between Rhustore [Stoer Point] and Strathy point – are these the Charters alluded to by you under the date

of 1379 in the Charters in Lord Reay's possession? I think they must – Durness and Edderachyllis came still later into the family, indeed not till the 17th Century. In the Statistical Account of Edderachyllis Farqhuar [*sic*] is stated to have been a person of the name of Beton and a native of Isla.

Loch gives the wrong dates for the original charters (he gives the correct dates in his 1859 collection), and the assignee of 1511 was a Donald Mac Donnchadh of Melness, described in the document of 30 September 1511 as 'discendit fra Farquhar Leiche'. A Mackay history, written in 1832 by Alexander Mackay of Blackcastle, claims Fearchar Lighiche as a Mackay rather than a member of the Beaton medical kindred. The minister of Eddrachillis had noted in the *Old Statistical Account* for the parish:

> All these [Little Isles] from Roe-a-Stoir in Assint to Stroma in Orkney, were granted to one Ferchard Beton, a native of Isla, a famous physician, at his own request, by one of the Stewarts, kings of Scotland, whom he cured of a distemper. This Ferchard was a physician to the Mackays of Farr, who gave him in exchange for these islands, lands near Melness, opposite Tongue – the possession of which they recovered long since, yet it is said that some of his posterity remain still in the country under the name of Mackay.

Alexander Mackay conceded that the *Old Statistical Account* gives an inaccurate account of the transfer of land, but used the one mistake as 'proof' of another, adding: ' ... and presumably also inaccurate in saying that Ferchard was a Beaton, a native of Isla.' Mackay was concerned to show that Fearchar was a Mackay, citing the 'clear and unanimous testimony of the Reay charter chests'. This testimony relates to:

1. a genealogical manuscript found among the Reay papers in 1829, in which, says Alexander, 'a Ferchard is represented as being the son of Iye [Aodh], chief of Mackay who was killed at Dingwall ca 1370'.
2. a supposition that Mariota – a hand-fasted wife of Alexander Stewart, Wolf of Badenoch, whose original grant of Melness to Fearchar was confirmed by his father, Robert II, in 1379 – was a daughter of Iye Mackay and, if so, was a sister of Ferchard'. Alexander Mackay's argument for making Mariota a daughter of Iye is that in the *Moray Registrum* (No. 271) she is described as a daughter of Athyn, and Mackay asserts that 'Athyn is a Latinised form of Iye' or Aodh.
3. the existence of the above-mentioned charters of land.

That 'some of [Fearchar's] posterity remain still in the country under the name of Mackay' is highly likely; but Alexander Mackay's 'testimony' needs more stringent investigation. There might well be a case for suggesting that the royal patronage of Fearchar was linked with the Wolf and Mariota – if she was genuinely a Mackay (other sources claim she was a Ross). However, Mackay simply assumes that the Fearchar son of Aodh is one-and-the-same as Fearchar Lighiche. Fearchar was not, however, an uncommon forename.

Alexander Stewart's lawful wife, Euphemia, Countess of Ross, complained to the Church over her husband's poor treatment of her and his relationship with Mariota. In November 1398 the Bishops of Moray and Ross pronounced his excommunication. Pope Clement VII had been made aware of the situation and it appears that the medieval 'latinisation' of Mariota's Gaelic patronymic in the contemporary correspondence was not from *Nic Aoidh* but from *Nic Eachainn* – daughter of Hector, as Eachann is usually anglicised. Athyn/Eachann certainly makes more sense than Athyn/Aodh. A 'Latin' Odo or Hugo might have been a more likely contemporary adaptation of Aodh which was often anglicised as Iye.

According to Mr Hugh Macdonald of Skinnet, Melness, local oral tradition also maintains that Fearchar was a Beaton (or MacBeath) and that, while some of his descendants took on the Mackay identity, and may also have served as physicians to the Mackay chiefs in the north, the main line of Fearchar's descendants became hereditary physicians to the Munros of Foulis. The *Munro Writs* record the names of Beaton doctors (under such variations as McVey and McBeyth) from the early 16th century, although they claimed to have held lands in the area as far back as the 13th century.

It might be argued that the historical occurrence of numerous hereditary medical families of the same name in disparate parts of the islands and mainland – eg Islay, Mull, North Uist, Skye, Melness, Delny, Glenconvinth – points to a 'trade-name' rather than one signifying blood relationship, though there may have been inter-marriages. Certainly patronage by the well-to-do meant that in the middle ages, and especially in the hey-day of the Lordship of the Isles, native Gaelic-speaking doctors could afford the best official medical training of their time – whether in Salerno, Montpellier, Bologna, Padua or Leiden. On returning home, they combined this professional education with their native custom, giving rise to a unique healing tradition. They also left a fascinating legacy of Gaelic medical manuscripts which form the bulk of pre-18th century Gaelic manuscripts in the National Library of Scotland.

In his rigorously researched work on the Beaton medical kindred, Dr John Bannerman is in no doubt that Fearchar of Melness was a member of that professional dynasty. In addition to the charters, this Fearchar is named in late-14th century *Exchequer Rolls* as 'Ferchardus Leche' or 'Ferchardus medicus' for receiving gifts of money in 1381, 1390 and 1397. Bannerman also points out:

> Fearchar's attribution to Islay [noted in the *Old Statistical Account*] is further confirmation for the ongoing tradition that all medical Beatons derive ultimately from there no matter their eventual location ... . The contemporary official records suggest that Fearchar originally hailed from the neighbourhood of Inverness, and this would be a more likely centre if he was an ancestor of later Beaton medical families of the mainland division.

A Non-Fearchar Legend

Special knowledge of healing in North Sutherland has another 'origin' legend, however, which makes no mention of Fearchars or Beatons, and is very similar to one told of the renowned Welsh medieval Physicians of Myddfai. As such, the link may suggest an earlier Celtic, perhaps pre-Gaelic, line of healers. Here is the gist of the tale:

As an elderly widow came out of her cottage on a slope of the Carrach, above Swordly Mill near Bettyhill, to fetch water, she heard high-pitched cries from the top of the fairy knoll. The woman, who was friendly with the fairies, hurried up the wee hill where she found a tiny girl lying in the grass with a raging fever and an equally small boy standing beside her. The boy chattered frantically and, though the woman could not make out a word he was saying, she understood the meaning exactly. She was to take the girl back to her house and care for her since there was nothing more the fairies could do and they feared she would die.

Taking a fresh handkerchief from her pocket, the woman placed the girl gently in it and took her into the cottage where she nursed her constantly for seven days until the fever broke. After a week of convalescence, the old lady returned the child to the top of the Carrach where a crowd of grateful fairies was waiting. The tiny boy who had called for her help gave her a bunch of beautifully scented miniature flowers which, so long as the woman lived, never lost their bloom.

Then the little girl spoke and while the woman could not make out the strange words, she knew exactly what the fairy was saying. She was promised that her daughters and all their descendants until the end of time would be splendid nurses.

The similarity of this story with the fairy gift of knowledge to the healers of Myddfai is undeniable.

There would undoubtedly have been practitioners of medicine in the north before the rise of the medieval physicians, and it is likely that many, if not most of them would have been women. Female healers again came into their own between the demise of the old medical kindreds and the early 20th-century implementation of the Highlands and Islands Medical Scheme.

Fearchar in Surviving Oral Tradition

More of the 'unofficial' healers later. We have not yet done with Fearchar. The 14th-century doctor is still strong in the memories of some present-day Melness people. Hugh Macdonald, Alec George Mackay and Joseph Mackay can identify three sites in Strathan Melness which belonged, they were told in their younger days, to a school of medicine that had been endowed by a king of Scots. This school, tradition has it, was founded for the training of surgeons for the Scottish army.

Of particular interest is a remark made to me by Hugh Macdonald that 'Fearchar was a specialist in eye diseases'. Robert II, who gifted Melness to Fearchar, had, among other chronic health problems, much trouble with his eyes. The ground occupied by the school itself (just above the west side of

Achininver Bay), was ploughed over some years ago and no remains are visible. The second site, known as the ruin of the doctors' house (presumably where the students were accommodated), is by the burn which flows towards the Strathan Melness road, just to the south of Dalnafree. The third, known in Gaelic as *An Larach Taigh Fhearchair* ('the ruin of Fearchar's house'), is situated in a field just across the road from Dun Buidhe and is by far the most interesting. Although it no longer stands – its stones were used for a nearby byre and dykes – it was situated on what is probably an Iron Age mound overlying a possible souterrain. Stories abound of 'underground houses' and a network of underground passages in Strathan Melness – a place ripe for sensitive archaeological exploration.

There is a story about the poisoning of a medieval Sutherland doctor named Fearchar. This is the gist of it:

A doctor named Fearchar was called to attend to an Earl of Sutherland who was dying of poisoning at his castle on the east coast, but on his return home by boat to the north (Fearchar Lighiche's territory), the doctor himself became seriously ill by poisoning and was put into an island where he was attended by monks who failed to save his life, as indeed, the doctor had failed to save the life of the earl.

Robert Gordon recounts the fatal poisoning of several people, including an Earl of Sutherland at Helmsdale in 1567. This is obviously far too late a date for Fearchar Lighiche, but if the scenario fits in with the traditional story of a poisoned Dr Fearchar, the latter may have been a descendant of the former. It is a macabre tale on a par with the last scene of Hamlet.

In 1567 Isobel Sinclair, wife of Gilbert Gordon of Garty and daughter of William Sinclair of Dunbeath, hatched a plot with her brother, William, and the Earl of Caithness, to do away with the Earl of Sutherland, with his pregnant second wife and with the Earl's only heir and son of his first marriage, Alexander. The idea was to give Lord Caithness control of Sutherland. The story runs thus:

At a hunting lodge near the river Helmsdale, the conniving Isobel gave poison to the earl and countess of Sutherland which killed them after a lingering agony of eight days. However, the young Alexander, whose death was crucial to the conspiracy, escaped supper when he returned late from a hunting trip in Kildonan. When he arrived at the lodge, the already stricken earl – apparently unable to speak a warning – swept the cloth from the table, thereby spilling the poisoned wine and causing the 15 year-old boy to flee to Dunrobin where the earl and countess were also taken.

Meantime, and with uncanny dramatic irony, John Gordon, Isobel's eldest son, chanced to call at the Helmsdale lodge and, being thirsty after his journey, asked a servant for a drink. The servant, in all innocence, handed him some of the poisoned wine. John Gordon died two days later. Isobel Sinclair was tried and condemned in Edinburgh, and is said to have committed suicide hours before she was due to be executed.

It is feasible that an astute Highland doctor correctly diagnosed the victims' condition and the particular poison that had been administered, and was similarly despatched in order to silence him.

TRADITIONAL FOLK HEALERS AND THEIR CURES

Just under a century and a half later, an end also came to the system of medicine and training of native Gaelic-speaking doctors under clan patronage. Through the inspiration of the great Hermann Boerhaave of Leiden (1688-1738), official European medicine abandoned its previous reliance on increasingly complex potions and turned to a simpler, more clinical approach to healing the sick. The Edinburgh Medical School was to become pre-eminent in the new medicine; and the hereditary medical kindreds of the Gaels, whose own ancient social order was in decline, either chose to practise outwith their own region, or pursued careers in teaching or the church.

The Role of Women

This change coincided in the Highlands with the turbulent years of the 18th century. Few trained physicians were tempted into the area, and those who were usually charged fees well beyond the means of ordinary people. It was during this time, and throughout the following century with its clearances, poverty and hardships, that folk healers, especially women, came into their own.

Unlike other parts of Scotland, the Gaelic-speaking areas remained largely free of the witchcraft persecutions of the 16th and 17th centuries. Throughout that time there were only 89 indictments in the then more populous Highlands and western islands, most of them relating to the isle of Bute, the east coasts of Ross and Sutherland and the largely non-Gaelic county of Caithness.

In terms of traditional healing this meant that, where Gaelic culture still held sway, there was a freedom to perpetuate the old knowledge in a way unparalleled in the rest of Britain or much of mainland Europe – where peasant and feminine lore were perceived as a threat to orthodoxy. In Gaeldom the old ways survived, not as the province of the outcast or through the whim of genteel enthusiasts, but in the natural context of a pre-industrial society.

Perhaps because of this acceptance, the healers themselves tended to be generous and caring. A woman known as Sandy Skipper's wife, who lived in Latheronwheel, Caithness, in the middle of the 19th century, was typical. She was believed to have exceptional healing powers and her speciality was children's ailments. She used only incantations and mystic rites, and no one seems to have taken her to task for this. A Caithness minister, the Revd

George Sutherland said: 'Her services were willingly and cheerfully rendered without money and without price to all who sought them. The belief that she was benefiting her fellow human beings was her sufficient reward'.

Use of Natural Materials

Bogbean

Although charms and rituals were widely used – and many had a psychological benefit – most remedies employed herbs and other practical means. Of all the many herbs that were used in the north, there were some which were especially popular. One of these was the bogbean, and it certainly cannot have been celebrated for its taste which is extremely bitter and somewhat nauseous. Sugar or a proprietary sweet drink was sometimes used to disguise the cascara-like flavour.

The dried or fresh roots and stem were chopped and boiled in water until the liquid was the colour of dark rum. This liquid was then strained off, cooled and stored until required for healing gastric complaints, particularly ulcers. In the form of a homemade beer (in which bogbean took the place of hops), it was taken in small amounts as a tonic before meals to create an appetite and strengthen weak stomachs. The fresh juice of the roots was taken for tuberculosis; a poultice of bogbean leaves was applied to boils and skin eruptions, followed by a drink of juice to clear the blood; and right across the Highlands and Islands the plant was used for a variety of problems: jaundice, constipation, chills, colds and coughs, asthma, dropsy, heart troubles, rheumatism, for healing wounds, for worming, as a chest rub and as a general tonic in all cases of convalescence and debility. The dried leaves were sometimes even used as a substitute for tobacco. In all events, it had to be used with discretion. Too much of it causes vomiting and diarrhoea.

In Melness, it was used successfully to treat ulcers. One such cure that is still remembered 100 years later, involved a soldier who was pensioned out of the army on account of chronically bad stomach ulcers. Army doctors in India, where he was stationed, could do nothing for him. Edinburgh doctors declared him incurable. Back home in Melness, he went to an elderly relative, Giorsail, who was noted for her cures. She took him in and treated him with regular infusions of bogbean, which grows profusely in the area. He made a complete recovery and lived in good health for many years.

Seaweeds

Giorsail (Grace) also used seaweeds in her cures. In this she was following an ancient Gaelic tradition. A large rock jutting out of the sea below the cliffs to the west of Achininver Bay, and only accessible by boat, is known as Fearchar's rock since it was there, local tradition has it, that the famous 14th-century Melness healer collected his supplies of carrageen, a valuable food for invalids.

Dulse soup was not only a nourishing addition to anyone's diet, it was said to be an excellent remedy for skin disorders caused by general ill-health if taken several times a week. Sometimes a dish of boiled dulse was simply prepared with butter. Dulse soup, *càl duilisg*, was also believed to be very good for indigestion and other stomach disorders.

Other plants

The use of heather for promoting refreshing sleep lingers on, though now it tends simply to be in the form of a sprig under the pillow. In 1582, the Scots historian George Buchanan remarked on the healthy Highland custom of using heather shoots for bedding:

> In this manner they form a bed so pleasant, that it may vie in softness with the finest down, while in salubrity it far exceeds it; for heath, naturally possessing the powers of absorption, drinks up the superfluous moisture, and restores strength to the fatigued nerves, so that those who lie down languid and weary in the evening, arise in the morning vigorous and sprightly.

A spring tonic of nettle broth or tea continues to be taken by some people as a continuation of an old custom, rather than as a born-again interest in herbs prompted by current fashions. And in the Reay Country Gaelic of north-west Sutherland, the blaeberry – known as *fiagag* – was highly rated in the area for dissolving kidney stones.

Some treatments survived into our own times because of their cosmetic value, especially for toning or softening the skin. An infusion of fir club moss, once used as a powerful purge, was still being used in the first half of this century as a moisturiser by women and girls in north-west Sutherland. The moss was collected in quite large quantities, boiled and then the liquid was strained off, cooled and applied to the skin.

Traditional medicine was always open to new ideas and materials, and the humble tattie is proof of that adaptability. Within only a few decades of its introduction to the Highlands, it had established itself as an 'old remedy'. In Brora, on the east coast, a piece of raw potato was strapped to a rheumatic hip.

Use of Manufactured Materials

In post-Clearance times, remedies often involved industrial, domestic and veterinary materials, rather than natural ones.

Brora miners had an unusual cure for toothache: a small piece of dynamite was placed in the offending cavity, the active constituent being nitroglycerine which, dissolved under the tongue in the form of glyceryl trinitrate tablets, is an orthodox remedy for the pains of angina and the paroxysms of severe asthma attacks. The miners would also suck on a small piece of coal in order to relieve heartburn. (Pregnant women are prone to heartburn and quite a number have a craving for chewing coal, usually without knowing why, since instinct is very much to the fore during pregnancy. Did miners learn of this remedy from their womenfolk, or vice versa?)

Carbolic soap was mixed with a sprinkling of sugar to draw a boil, with the mixture being held in place with a bandage. Sugar was also a remedy for sore throats: one dessertspoonful was soaked in as much vinegar as it could absorb and then taken before going to bed. Another cure for a boil was to add boiling water to a lump of bread, slap it over the part and tie it down. This was repeated as often as necessary. It was also used for drawing poison from cuts.

Shepherds would use the balsam formerly used for treating the cuts made to neuter lambs (before the days of rubber rings), to paint any accidental cuts to human limbs. Before chemical dipping came in, sheep were smeared with a mixture of Archangel tar and butter, and this proved an effective preservative from the parasites and skin diseases to which stock are liable. The tar was also applied to some human ailments. For rheumatic pains in the back, a little Archangel tar, mixed with a bit of new-made butter the size of a hen's egg, was boiled in a pot, spread on a piece of paper and applied to the affected part.

Purging and Blood-Letting

Writing of north coast remedies in the 1930s, the Revd George Sutherland said: 'A course of purgatives was gone through every autumn and every spring so as to adapt the body to the change of season. At an earlier date it was bleeding, not purgatives, that were in use at those seasons.' When a purgative was needed, the cheapest and most effective was sea water, but Epsom salts dissolved in a decoction of senna leaves was also largely used.

Long after bleeding as a way of 'purifying the body' had been discounted by mainstream medicine, it was still carried out in the Highlands (and by the British army for troops stationed in hot countries, especially India) well into the 19th century. A North Uist doctor recalled in 1896, 'I remember when lancets were a part of the equipment of the manse, and my father, till later years, bled his parishioners when he or they thought it beneficial.' The Revd Donald Sage wrote of one of his father's tenants in the Strath of Kildonan, 'Mr Donald Macleod, parochial schoolmaster ... was very useful in the parish, for he could let blood ... '.

The Highlands do not seem to have suffered from the obsessive and debilitating (and sometimes fatal) enthusiasm for blood-letting that pervaded most of medieval Europe. The official Gaelic physicians themselves laid down rigid rules for the prudent employment of bleeding.

It was claimed that Murdo Macpherson of Melness who died ca 1880 was 'bred from Fearchar Lighiche's breed'. Murdo used the horse leech, *gearrach-dall*, to bleed people with fevers. His son Donald lived to the ripe age of 93 (another son, Robert, lived to be 97), and claimed that his longevity was due to never having put salt on his food. No salt was used in cooking by the family. 'If anyone wanted salt, they'd add it later at table,' Hugh Macdonald of Skinnet said. Long daily walks were another of this family's prescriptions for a healthy life. Such practices are certainly reminiscent of the advice given by the Beatons.

Ways with Warts, Corns and Snakebites

Cures for warts are mysterious and abundant – everyone remembers at least one 'miracle cure' from childhood days – but then warts themselves are quirky, and can literally disappear overnight for no apparent reason. Clinical tests have verified that they can indeed be responsive to hypnosis.

However, one Highland remedy for warts also had a fine reputation for removing corns and, as most people know to their regret, corns are not at all receptive to 'magicking' away, let alone easily got rid of by practical means. In Gaelic, the slug and the black snail are known by the same name *seilcheag*, and they were used in the same way for removing warts and even corns. A few years ago, an eight year old boy in Kinlochbervie was cured of a mass of warts on his hands when his grandmother treated them with slime from a black slug.

As elsewhere in Gaeldom, the traditional north Sutherland remedy for a snakebite was to wash the wound with water in which a dried adder's head had been steeped. It was perhaps a homely forerunner of the use of snake venom extract in official medicine.

Charms and Rituals

Although a belief in the touch of a seventh son of a seventh son appears to have disappeared earlier in the north – though it was still the custom in the Southern Isles of Barra and Uist but sixty years ago – the area once included the feminine 'touch' in this respect. In Caithness and Sutherland, it was claimed that a seventh son could cure the King's Evil (*scrofula*) in a woman, while a seventh daughter could do the same for a man.

Another belief was in the power of the caul, the membrane which sometimes covers the head of a newly-born infant. It was greatly prized by the Gaels, and particularly by seafarers, and once had a considerable market value owing to the belief that it offered protection against drowning. The caul of a child was of special value, but those of animals were also treasured. In the 1970s, a woman on the east coast of Sutherland was known to carry her own caul about in a special purse which she always kept in her handbag.

Beliefs about the evil eye – in Gaelic, the *droch shùil* – were much the same in Highland tradition as elsewhere in the world, the possessor of the 'eye' being perceived as not necessarily consciously responsible for any ill befalling the victim. The 'evil eye' was believed to stem from jealousy, therefore those who incurred it were considered to have brought it on themselves by inciting envy or resentment. 'Antidotes', however, were plentiful.

A preparation of water in which gold, silver and copper – usually coins or rings – were placed, formed the basis of the cure for the 'evil eye'; and doubtless it worked on a psychological level. The water was fetched from a place 'where the living and dead passed by' – that is near, or under a bridge which served as a common path for daily travel and the route bearing of coffins to the cemetery. The cure consisted in sprinkling handfuls of the water on the affected person or animal while invoking the Trinity. Any remaining water was poured on a fire or taken outside and spilled on a rock in front of the house.

In Strathhalladale, the water was given to the human or animal victim to drink. Sometimes water from a special spring might be used without adding gold and silver. The water from *Fuaran Deòraidh* (Spring of the Afflicted) was in great demand for curing bewitched animals in the Durness area.

Loch Mo Nàire, in Strathnaver, was famous in the north for its healing water which was supposed to be resorted to on the first Monday of a quarter – the May and August ones being the most popular, probably because the weather was better. Most patients came from Caithness, but many came from Ross-shire, Inverness-shire and Orkney, as well as other districts of Sutherland, since it was believed a more certain cure was to be had from waters outwith one's own parish. Severely mentally-afflicted invalids arrived the day before taking the cure, and were kept tied up and fed sparingly until sunset. At around midnight, they were unbound and assembled near the loch where they were stripped naked. As the first streak of dawn appeared, their attendants directed them to walk backwards into the dark, cold waters of the loch until they were fully immersed. While this was done, coins were thrown into the water. The patients were then pulled out, dressed in silence and walked sunwise around the loch's edge. Then they had to walk away, without once turning their heads, until they were out of sight of the water before the sun rose.

Many of the people who underwent this stringent ritual were suffering some form of mental distress, in varying degrees of severity from mild depression to outright mania, and it is possible that the sheer drama of the setting and events, and the trauma of the immersion acted as a shock treatment. The long-lived popularity of the proceedings suggests there must have been the occasional cure. Coachloads of Caithness people visited the loch until at least the late 1930s.

A Neat Prescription

The water of life, whisky, was rather more frequently relied on for an instant cure that is unlikely to go out of fashion. On the north coast, there was a saying to advise on the quantity of whisky that might be drunk at a sitting with safety and benefit:

Aona ghloin', chan fheàirrd' 's cha mhisd'.
Dà ghloin' 's fheàirrd' 's cha mhisd'.
Trì gloineachan 's misd' 's chan fheàirrd'.

(One glass, not the better of it or the worse of it.
Two glasses, the better of them, and not the worse of them.
Three glasses, the worse of them and not the better.)

A variation of this was:

Aon ghloin' chan fheàirrd' 's cha mhisd' mo chorp no m'anam e.
Dà ghloin', 's fheàirrd' mo chorp e, 's cha mhisd' m'anam e.
Trì gloineachan 's misd' m'anam e, 's chan fheàirrd' mo chorp e.

(One glass, neither my body nor my soul is the better or the worse of it.
Two glasses, my body is the better of them, and my soul is not the worse
  of them.
Three glasses, my soul is the worse for them, and my body is not the better
  of them.)

'May the Lord preserve us from the disease whisky cannot cure!' was a popular Highland saying. In their time, there was also very little the hereditary physicians of Highland Scotland, Fearchar among them, could not cope with through their unique blend of traditional and academic knowledge.

Acknowledgment

My thanks to all the people of the area, especially Hugh Macdonald, Skinnet, Melness, who have given information relating to old remedies; to Ronald Black for his constant advice and encouragement throughout my researches into the traditional medicines of the Gaels; to John Bannerman for permission to quote from *The Beatons: A Medical Kindred in the Classical Gaelic Tradition*; to the late Kirsty Larner for her insights into the ways of folk healers; to Olive Geddes and Roger Miket for tracing the charters and John Kelly's letter; to Morfydd Owen for help with the Swordly/Myddfai legend; and to Elizabeth Sutherland for comments that Mariota was most likely a Ross (possibly a cook's daughter) from her research for *The Five Euphemias: Women in Medieval Scotland, 1200-1420*. Special thanks to Alasdair Mearns for checking the quotations in Reay Country Gaelic.

References

Manuscript:

National Library of Scotland:

MS 874 ff xxvi, 275-6: Letter to I. Train, Supervision of Excise, South Queensferry, Edinburgh,
  from John Kelly, in Dunvegan.
Blackcastle MS (Signet Library).
Black, R. *Catalogue of the Classical Gaelic MSS. in the National Library of Scotland.*
  (Publication forthcoming.)

Scottish Record Office:

Cal. Charters: RH 6/772.
Reay Papers: RH 6 1/74, RH 6 1/86, GD 84.2.2.
Munro Writs: GD 93

Printed:

Banks, M.M. *British Calendar Customs: Scotland.* vol. I. 1937.
Bannerman, J. *The Beatons: A Medical Kindred in the Classical Gaelic Tradition.* 1986.
Beith, M. 'Deanamh a' Leighis: Gaelic Medical Tradition', in *West Highland Free Press.* July 1989 onwards: *passim.*
Beith, M. *Healing Threads: Traditional Medicines of the Highlands and Islands.* 1995.
Buchanan, G. *Rerum Scoticarum Historia* (1582), trans. James. Aikman, *The History of Scotland.* 1827.
Caledonian Medical Journal. Edinburgh. 1883-1968. (The early volumes, 1890-1910, contain many papers on Highland remedies.)
Cameron, J. *Gaelic Names of Plants.* 1900.
Comrie, J.D. *History of Scottish Medicine.* 1932.
Dewar Report. *Report of the Committee on the Highlands and Islands Medical Services.* (Cmnd 6559). 1912.
Gordon, R. *A Genealogical History of the Earldom of Sutherland.* 1813.
Hamilton, D. *The Healers.* 1981.
Hand, W.D. 'The Folk-Healer: Calling and Endowment', in *Journal of the History of Medicine.* vol.26. 1971.
Henderson, G. *The Norse Influence on Celtic Scotland.* 1910.
Larner, C. *The Thinking Peasant: Popular and Educated Belief in Pre-Industrial Culture.* 1982.
Larner, C., Lee, C.H. & McLachlan, H.V. *A Source-Book of Scottish Witchcraft.* 1977.
Lightfoot, J. *Flora Scotica.* 1777.
Loch, J. *Dates and Documents relating to the Family and Property of Sutherland extracted chiefly from the Originals in the Charter Room at Dunrobin.* 1859.
McCutcheon, A. 'Some Highland Household Remedies', in *Pharmaceutical Journal & Pharmacist.* 19 April 1919.
MacFarlane, A. 'Gaelic Names of Plants: Study of their Uses and Lore', in *TGSI.* 32. 1924-5.
Old Statistical Account: Caithness & Sutherland. 1793.
Owen, M.E. 'A Preliminary Survey of Some Medieval Medical Writing in Wales', in *Studia Celtica.* X-II. 1975-6.
Sage, D. *Memorabilia Domestica.* 1899.
Scottish Home & Health Department: *General Medical Services in the Highlands & Islands.* HMSO (Cmnd 3257). 1967.
Sutherland, G. *Folklore Gleanings and Character Sketches from the Far North.* 1937.
Temperley, A. *Tales of the North Coast.* 1977.
Thomson, D. 'Gaelic Learned Orders and Literati in Medieval Scotland', in *Scottish Studies.* 12. pt 1. 1968.
Wood, J. 'The Fairy Bride of Legend in Wales', in *Folklore.* 103. 1992.

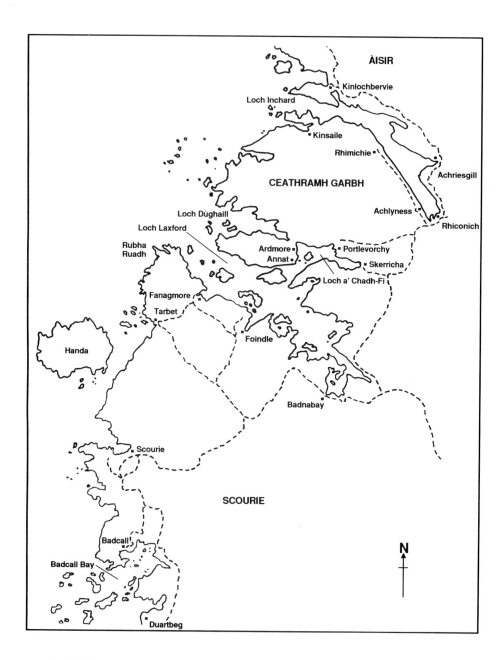

Fig. 6.1 Settlements and coastline around Loch Inchard, Loch Laxford, Scourie and Badcall Bay.

WORKING WITH SEAWEED
IN NORTH-WEST SUTHERLAND

John R. Baldwin

Seaweeds have been exploited in many parts of the world and over considerable periods of time. Given that the North Atlantic is well-endowed with such resources, it is hardly surprising that they have long been gathered coastally around the Highlands and Islands, and for many varied purposes, not least:

* as a manure or fertilizer
* as a food, medicine and preservative
* for making kelp.

In recent decades harvesting has continued in a number of places around the northern mainland and the islands, mainly for the alginate industry but occasionally still for enriching the land or supplementing diet. Traditional uses are generally little more than a lingering memory, however, and the economics of the modern alginate industry has meant that traditional techniques for gathering the raw material are now seen as largely uneconomic, particularly when linked to high costs of drying and transport – too expensive when set alongside crops imported from elsewhere, harvested increasingly by machine.

This paper concentrates, therefore, on field evidence for traditional seaweed-gathering in north-west Sutherland, along with a short summary of the crofting and commercial frameworks within which these practices survived. It forms part of a wider historical review of working with seaweed in north-west Sutherland and the Western Isles.

EXPLOITING SEAWEED AROUND LOCH LAXFORD:
1960s-1970s

The *Ceathramh Garbh*

Once fleetingly part of the far-flung 'province' or 'country' of Strathnaver, in 1724 the parish of Edderachillis, like that of Tongue, was carved out of the vast parish of Durness. It was traditionally divided into three districts [Fig. 6.1], each bounded by great sea lochs:

* *Ashare* or *Àisir*: bordering on the parish of Durness, lay mainly to the north of Loch Inchard, Lochbervie and Loch Clash, and included the corn lands of Oldshore Mor and Oldshore Beg
* *Ceathramh Garbh*: the 'rough quarter', and formerly the southern

Fig. 6.2 West across Loch Laxford from Sgeir a'Chadh. Fanagmore (top, far side of loch), Rubh na h-Airde Bige (centre), Eilean an Eireannaich and Loch a'Chadh-Fi (upper right). Traces of former settlement cluster around the bay (foreground). 1973.

Fig. 6.3 Badcall Bay, ca 1886. Seaweed is plentiful around its shores (Erskine Beveridge).

part of the 'Davoch of Ashir', covered that desolate and rocky landscape between Loch Inchard and Loch Laxford where settlement was always scarce and scanty
* *Scourie* or *Sgobhairigh*: barely less rugged, but with a scatter of generally small pockets of more fertile land, stretched south from Loch Laxford to Loch a' Chairn Bhàin and Loch Glendhu on the marches with Assynt.

The lands around Loch Laxford (ON *lax-fjorðr*, salmon fiord) are mainly Lewisian gneiss, either side of a band of granite running inland along the southern flank of the loch. Continual pounding of the waves has created an extremely varied, indented and complex coastline slashed by deep and narrow geos and by glacially-deepened fiords stretching along fault lines some considerable way inland. Numerous small islands and skerries lie scattered across these sea lochs, notably within Loch Laxford and in the mouth of Badcall Bay [Figs. 6.2; 6.3], whilst storm-driven seas have cut deep caves, rock arches, sea stacks and often spectacular sea cliffs. The underlying geology has resulted in numerous low, rounded and bare rocky hillocks and ridges, streaked with cracks and fissures and interspersed with vast numbers of small lochans; and most of the moorland is badly-drained peat – whether blanket bog or peat-filled hollows. The sourness of this landscape is extended by prolonged and heavy rainfall carried on the prevailing south-westerly and westerly winds, particularly in autumn and early winter. Only very occasionally do small and sometimes sandy bays provide more attractive anchorages and patches of land better-suited to localised agriculture than the largely stony and acid soils characteristic of the widespread glacial deposits (Ross et al 1982. 42 et seq).

The Crofting Background

It is hardly surprising that in recent decades crofting has declined to such a degree that most holdings have reverted to grass – greener patches in an apparently chaotic wilderness of rock, water and peat bog. Where traditional communities have not collapsed, and the young moved away, those indigenous families that remain depend primarily upon their livestock (mainly sheep) and a modest tourist industry. They may still put down a few drills of potatoes for personal use, or pasture a few caravans; by and large, however, they no longer toil on the scraps of land that were so precious to their forebears.

By the early 1970s, Fanagmore and Foindle were in long-term decline as traditional crofting townships, and Tarbet appeared little better off. There were some seven inhabited houses in Tarbet, two in Fanagmore and two (out of five) in Foindle – the Ross family having recently moved from Foindle to Tain for the sake of their children's education. (The east coast boarding hostels which removed children from family life and influence were far from universally welcomed, and the establishment of a secondary school at Kinlochbervie in 1995 came too late to undo the effects of earlier, long-term 'educational emigration'.) In the Ceathramh Garbh, and apart from Achlyness and Rhiconich at the head of Loch Inchard, there were perhaps four people still in Ardmore, one man at Rhimichie, one man at Skerricha, and a shepherd at Portlevorchy (Mrs Mackenzie 1974). This represented the fragmentary remains of a post-clearance settlement pattern which had once included such abandoned townships as Foindle Beg and Weavers' Bay on the south side of Loch Laxford. A grandmother of Alick McAskill (Fanagmore) had been cleared in turn from Kinsaile, Rhimichie, Achlyness and Scourie – clearances initiated by the Reay estates between 1801 and the 1820s. But although the Ceathramh Garbh formed part of these clearances, sheep losses there were subsequently deemed too high, and it was resettled in 1831 (Bangor-Jones 1993. vol 21. 21.)

By way of contrast, just a few years before the land was redivided following the Crofters Commission Report and the Crofters' Holdings

Fig. 6.4   The former school and schoolhouse at Fanagmore stand beside the jetty. Beyond: Rubh na h-Airde Bige and the ridge of Foinaven. 1973.

(Scotland) Act of 1886, one of Mr McAskill's grandfathers had moved to Fanagmore from Tarbet in 1881, to a bigger holding with a better harbour [Fig. 6.4]. And it was this grandfather who was the first to improve Fanagmore with closed drains. It was not an old settlement, however, and there were only ever two crofts – one amounting with rough pasture to 53.5 acres (21.7 ha), including 6.5 acres (2.6 ha) arable land; the other, 22 acres with 3 acres arable (9 ha; 1.2 ha). The name means simply 'big rig, piece of ground' (*feannag mòr*), and local tradition says that people were first put into Fanagmore because of ships wrecked on Ruabha Ruadh (Red Point): with no help to hand, survivors had died on the shore (A. McAskill 1974). This may well explain why the common grazings for Tarbet and Fanagmore run together, but are separate from those of Foindle (D. Mackenzie 1974): Fanagmore was maybe an outset, pendicle or perhaps shieling on the earlier farm of Tarbet? Certainly the *tairbeart*, isthmus, runs directly between the two places, and although it would have been an energetic 'carry', it would certainly have allowed boats to avoid the tempestuous seas around Rubha Ruadh and Sgeir Ruadh.

Donald MacLeod, on the other hand, had come to Foindle at the time of World War I, to where uncles of his father lived. (He had been born at Melness on the eastern shore of the Kyle of Tongue.) Whilst the name may suggest a Gaelic/Norse hybrid (Gaelic *fionn* + ON *dalr*, white/pale/fair

Fig. 6.5   The crofting/fishing settlement at Badnaban, south of Lochinver, Assynt, ca 1886 (Erskine Beveridge).

valley), it was most likely coined by Gaelic speakers at some point after ON *dalr*, valley, had entered Gaelic as a loan word. When it first became a settlement remains unclear: Donald MacLeod simply recalled that the 'old houses' all disappeared around the 1920s – houses with hangin' lums linked to a hole high up in the gable wall leading to a gable chimney. They were thatched either with rushes or bent grass from Handa or from islands within Loch Laxford, or with barley straw; and they were secured with stone-weighted twisted heather ropes [Fig. 6.5]. In Tarbet too, all the houses were thatched in Mrs Mackenzie's childhood there in the 1910s: most of today's 'older' houses [Fig. 6.6] were built in the late 1930s – wood-panelled inside because plaster was not easily available.

Until the coming of the road, transport and communications between the settlements depended upon the boat, the pack-pony and back creels. To go to the cattle sales, therefore, people walked from Tarbet and Fanagmore to Foindle to get a boat to Ardmore; then walked on over the moorland to Rhiconich (Mrs Mackenzie 1974). Provisions would come twice a year from Glasgow, organised by 'Hamilton Murray of 548 Argyll Street'. The boat stopped at both Foindle and Fanagmore with supplies of meal, flour, oatmeal, groceries, furniture and clothes. According to Mr McAskill, a branch from the Scourie-Durness road reached Foindle in 1903-4. It was extended to Fanagmore in 1927, and in 1937-8 a second branch reached Tarbet. Only in 1960, however, was the steep, tortuous link between Tarbet and Fanagmore completed. As for the upper reaches of Loch a'Chadh-Fi, although there was an unmetalled track into Skerricha, only in the mid 1970s did a short branch road (as opposed to a bridle path) reach Portlevorchy, and there is still no road to Ardmore.

Between them, Alick McAskill (Fanagmore), Danny MacKenzie and Donald MacLeod (Foindle), and Mrs MacKenzie (Tarbet/Scourie), all from traditional crofting backgrounds, have helped provide a detailed insight into the seasonal round of crofting activities [Fig. 6.7] – cultivation, harvesting and the processing of oats, barley and potatoes; peat cutting; livestock husbandry, soumings, shielings and grazing rights; fishing and fishing marks; transport, creels and carts; sea-bird fowling and the trapping of land birds; hunting for land mammals and otters; whisky smuggling and language. Sadly, their own north-west Sutherland Gaelic was far more under threat than what they light-heartedly termed the *Gaidhleag nan ceardean* of Lewis. Not surprisingly, the nature and practice of these activities parallels closely that recorded by the writer in Coigach, some 50 or 60 miles (80-95 kms) south along the coast (Baldwin 1994. 290 et seq).

Coastlines around Loch Laxford

In terms of their potential for human exploitation, seaweeds are conveniently divided between those that grow on the shore or are washed up there by winter storms, and those that are permanently submerged. The former

Fig. 6.6   Crofts at Tarbet. Little heaps of seaweed await spreading on the land. 1973.

Fig. 6.7   Farming landscape at Scourie, ca 1886 (Erskine Beveridge).

include the greenish-brown wracks (generally Fucoids), some red weeds and storm-driven tangles (mainly Laminaria). The latter are primarily the golden brown/reddish tangles and oarweeds, with certain red weeds growing in amongst them.

As far as the coasts of north-west Sutherland are concerned, the thick-stemmed tangles have certainly been gathered and used historically, even though densities are of no great contemporary economic significance. Littoral seaweeds, however, are another matter. These intertidal species require sheltered conditions if they are to grow luxuriantly, and when the Scottish Seaweed Research Association surveyed some 158 miles (254 kms) of Sutherland coast in the 1940s, they recorded substantial densities in virtually all the main sea lochs, principally Ascophyllum nodosum or knotted wrack. They concluded that the shores around Loch Laxford and Loch Inchard, as also around Lochinver, would yield up to 38 ton(ne)s per acre of seaweeds growing between the high and low water marks (Jackson 1948, 138-9) [Fig. 6.8].

SEAWEED DENSITIES IN
NORTH-WEST SUTHERLAND

Location	Tons per Acre (range)
Kyle of Tongue	27/28
Loch Eriboll	26/29
Loch Clash/Loch Bervie	
/Loch Inchard	28/38
Loch Laxford	
/Loch a'Chadh-Fi	37/38
Badcaul Bay	
/Calva	28/34
Loch Glendhu	35
Lochinver	38

Fig. 6.8   Distribution of littoral seaweeds in north-west Sutherland taken from surveys by the Scottish Seaweed Research Association, 1945-6 (Jackson 1948).

After parts of the Uists, this north-west corner of the mainland, particularly around the Ceathramh Garbh and Assynt, has more potential for modern commercial exploitation than almost any other significant concentration of intertidal seaweeds around Scotland's northern and western shores. The figures help reinforce, therefore, the significant role that seaweeds must have played in north-west Sutherland in earlier times, whether commercially (kelp) or at a domestic, subsistence level (food, medicine, fertilizer).

That seaweeds grow so well in the area is due in no small way to the configuration of the coastline and seabed, in particular to the sinuous and sheltered nature of the sea lochs and to their many promontories, islands, skerries and other relatively shallow rocky outcrops. Many of these features also figure prominently as fishing marks or medes for some eleven inshore fishing grounds (and two great-lines grounds):

* promontories such as Rubha Ruadh, Rubha na Mhinistear
* channels such as Caolis na Glasneich
* rocks and skerries such as Sgeir Ruadh, Sgeir Dubh, Bogha na Cudaigean, Bogha Mór (Handa)
* islands such as Eilean Ard, Eilean a'Mhadaidh, Eilean Port a'Choit, Eilean an t-Sithein, Eilean Saille, Eilean Loch an Roin, Glas Eilean, Eilean Buigach.

And it is yet another such small island that features in local tradition. A smuggler bringing whisky from Ireland was seen and chased up Loch Laxford by a revenue cutter; he turned into Loch a'Chadh-Fi, past what is now called Eilean an Eireannaich (Paddy's [the Irishman's] Island), and then doubled back behind the island. By the time the revenue cutter realised that it was not a backwater, but a narrow channel, the smuggler was off and away.

The islands were also divided between the townships both sides of the loch for grazing:

Fanagmore	: Eilean Ard and the small one next to it
	Eilean an t-Sithein
	Eilean Dubh na Fionndalach Bige
	Eilean Port a'Choit
Foindle	: Sgeir Iosal
	Eilean a'Mhadaidh
Ardmore	: Eilean an Eireannaich
	Eileanan Dubha
	islands in Loch a'Chadh-Fi
Skerricha	: Eilean Meall a'Chaorainn

Tarbet, by contrast, had islands in the Sound of Handa; Scourie Beg had Calva Beg and Calva Mór – with a turf/feal dyke dividing their onshore, mainland grazings (A. McAskill 1974).

Using Seaweed in Recent Times

When it comes to seaweed, no great detail survives of agreements that formerly obtained between crofters regarding collection rights, though when the Fanagmore lands were redivided in the 1880s, a newly-erected iron fence divided both the two crofts and their foreshores; and not surprisingly, the school and schoolhouse had no shore rights. Meantime, Kinlochbervie men used to come across and take drift ware from Loch Laxford, which was shared out once all the other seaweed had been allocated (A. McAskill 1974).

Three kinds of seaweed were gathered for the land – *feamainn dubh*, a 'black' seaweed, mainly Ascophyllum nodosum or knotted wrack; and

125

Fig. 6.9   Seaweed carried from the shore and heaped up for use as manure. Tarbet, 1973.

Fig. 6.10   J.G. Ross's potato patch at Badcall was manured with seaweed. 1973.

liadhag and *stamh*, respectively the fronds and stems of tangles, probably mainly L. digitata. For use as a fertilizer, rock weed was cut at low tide with a *corran*, a sickle or hook; sometimes with a toothed or serrated edge, but commonly smooth-bladed and kept sharp with a whetstone. About five tons a day could be cut, put in creels and carried clear of the high water mark at Foindle (D. MacLeod 1974). Alternatively it could be loaded into a boat and brought round to the harbour (at Fanagmore), where it was also left above the high tide mark. Alick McAskill used some 40 ton(ne)s a year, brought back by boat three ton(ne)s at a time. By the 1970s, far more modest amounts were simply brought up in old polythene fertilizer bags. Formerly, a willow creel or *cliabh* carried on a person's back would take about one hundredweight (51 kg) of peat, potatoes or seaweed; and it could be heightened by adding extra ribs (always hazel) to the completed creel, thereby adding perhaps half a hundredweight (25 kg) to the overall load (A. McAskill 1974).

Once clear of the sea, Donald MacLeod left the seaweed for about three weeks to rot. It was then brought up from the shore in cart loads or in creels, and put in piles about 6ft (1.8 m) apart on the rigs to heat up, before being spread over the ground and dug in [Fig. 6.9]. Bringing the seaweed up from the shore was 'very heavy work', and 'the old folks used to shake it on the ground' (C. MacLeod 1999). Donald MacLeod used bladderwrack for oats, and 'seaweeds from the lowest part of the tide' (ie tangles) for potatoes – though potatoes fertilized by seaweed were generally soft [Fig. 6.10]. For Alick McAskill, red weed (tangle) was used only for turnips and had to be ploughed in; black weed (bladderwrack, which he still used on his blackcurrants) was also ploughed in, or simply spread on land left in grass. One man would plough (he had a pair of horses; the other Fanagmore croft had none), and three people would 'sow' the seaweed. In other words, the seaweed was not ploughed in direct for it would have caught around the coulter and soc; rather was it placed in a freshly-turned furrow and then covered by the next furrow turned. For potatoes (fomerly *tat dubh*, black potatoes; later Champion, Kerr's Pink and British Queen), seaweed was never placed directly above or below the tubers, but always to one side, in adjacent furrows. For barley (last grown in the 1920s) and oats (formerly black oats, with just a few ordinary oats still grown in the early 1970s), it was simply laid in every furrow and left for about a month to rot and to allow the land to dry out before the seed was sown. It then gave 'extraordinary crops'!

Many considered 'natural manure' to be better than seaweed, however, since although seaweed proved fine for a few years, it then left the soil exhausted (J.G. Ross 1974). That said, different fertilizers were not uncommonly applied to different crops, largely depending on their availability. Cow dung alone might be given to oats, potatoes and hay ground; otherwise seaweed alone, or a mixture of seaweed and dung: and in 1916 slag was first imported as a dressing, normally for hay ground.

Quite apart from its use as a fertilizer, seaweed continued to be exploited as a foodstuff, albeit incidentally. Fragmentary evidence confirmed that sheep grazing on such seaweeds as dulse were always in very good condition, and that the curly crispy channelled wrack, *feamainn chìreadh* (Chrondrus crispus), found high up on the shore, was also gathered for cattle (see Baldwin 1994. 317-20, 324). For human consumption, meantime, *an cairgean*, carrageen, was found only on a very low tide (and there was said to be a lot on Skye!), whilst short reddish-brown *duileasg*, dulse, was picked and chewed raw (A. McAskill 1974).

Commercial Cutting of Seaweed

These traditional uses of seaweed have now largely died out in the north-west mainland and the Western Isles. Over the past half century or so, however, there have been moves to develop a more commercially-sustainable seaweed industry, based in part on traditional techniques and practices. For one man in Foindle (and for a handful of others along the north-west coast) the harvesting of seaweed became a regular part-time occupation and the account that follows is based on observation, discussions and the crofter's own description of the practices he adopted. The data was gathered some 25 years ago, and applies to circumstances at that time.

Assigned Areas and Rotations

According to Danny MacKenzie, it was an activity begun in the islands (Hebrides) some 20-30 years previously, but much more recently in north-west Sutherland. It was coordinated by Alginate Industries whose Inverness office assigned or allocated areas to be cut, and other teams worked for instance at Kylesku and at Stoer. He began cutting in 1971; two men worked together until 1973; from 1974 he was on his own, covering the coastline from Badcall south of Scourie and north to Loch Laxford and Loch Inchard. The cut weed would be collected by boat from Lewis, and partly dried at Keose on the east coast of Lewis. At the factory, it was first spread on the ground to dry in the sun, although some was dried by electricity. Factory-drying would take about four hours: thereafter it was crushed, bagged and sent south to what he termed the ICI plant at Ayr, where it was graded. He understood that good quality weed was subsequently used for medicines; poorer quality for manures.

Mr MacKenzie's 'cutting year' had to be carefully managed, for it depended primarily on the tides and the weather. For about 12 days each month – every second week – it was not possible to work because the tides were not low enough. Thus, in March 1974, there was a new moon on the 23rd, with cutting possible either side of the critical date. Cutting started on the 20th at about 7.30 am, on the 21st at about 8.15 am and so on – about three-quarters of an hour later each day until 26th March. In winter he worked six days per cycle; in summer, seven days, with lighter evenings allowing cutting up until 10 or 11pm. To maximise 'dead' time and make best use of daylight, Mr. MacKenzie would start at Foindle and cut Loch Laxford during the winter months; he then moved further afield and cut Loch Inchard and Badcall Bay in the summer, when he would leave his boat in the far-off sea lochs and drive home each night. However, he did not visit these more distant shores every year, alternating Badcall Bay and Loch Inchard (he had not yet considered cutting Loch Dùghaill, just north of Loch Laxford). His timetable, therefore, was:

Loch Laxford	:	1971-2	(May, through winter, to May)
Badcall Bay	:	1972	(May to November)
Loch Laxford	:	1972-3	(November to May)
Loch Inchard	:	1973	(May to November)
Loch Laxford	:	1973-4	(November to May/June)
Badcall Bay	:	1974	(May/June to November)

In 1971, his first year, he started cutting Loch Laxford in May rather than November; in 1974, his first year cutting without a partner, he was unsure in March whether he would have finished his winter cut of Loch Laxford in time to start in Badcall Bay in May.

Within this broadly-based geographical and tidal timetable, he had also to integrate rotational cutting of the shore. The stumps of the weed left on the rocks stay black for about a month after cutting; after four to six weeks they begin to grow brown again, and it takes about four years for them to re-grow to cuttable length. This varies, however, depending on location, for he confirmed that seaweeds grow faster where the tide is stronger – to about 4ft (1.2 m) long.

Cutting and Roping the Weed

Danny MacKenzie would cut any weed that floated – any of the bladderwracks, in other words: mainly knotted wrack (A. nodosum), but likely mixed with the 'true' bladderwrack (F. vesiculosus).

Starting about halfway down the shore on an ebbing tide, and following it out, he would normally use a *corran* – a small and light hook, preferably serrated, though sharpness was more important than teeth [Fig. 6.11]. At the lowest part of the tide, however, and in his waders, he would use a scythe in up to roughly 2 ft (60 cm) of water – but only over small stones: otherwise still the sickle [Figs. 6.12; 6.13]. Scythe blades (bought in Dornoch) had to be small and short-bladed, about 18ins (46 cm) long, so as to be easily manageable and not to catch on the rocks. The weed would be floating upright, and the scythe blade did not go very low. This was no significant disadvantage, however, for it ensured that the seed was left – an important factor in ensuring a sustainable industry, and an environmental implication of which he was not only aware but also respectful.

Before cutting began, up to 14 ropes, each 10 fathoms long by one inch in circumference (18.3 m x 25 mm) were knotted together and laid around the area to be cut – in all perhaps 840 ft of rope (256 m). As cutting

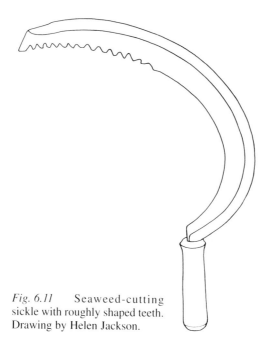

Fig. 6.11   Seaweed-cutting sickle with roughly shaped teeth. Drawing by Helen Jackson.

progressed, seaweed from about three-quarters of the area would be wound around the rope, the rest being left loose [Fig. 6.14]. As rope and weed later floated on the incoming tide, however, there were dangers that the cut weed might float off. Particularly with a strong wind, the weed tended to ride over the rope (the reason why so much was wound around it) and pile up at the top of the beach, making it difficult to gather. As the rope was tightened, therefore, the weed was repeatedly pushed hard against the rope with a semi-circular piece of hard plastic foam attached to the end of a long wooden pole. The head-piece, perhaps 18 ins wide x 6 ins (46 cms x 15 cms), was fixed at right-angles to the shaft and secured further with two wire stays. The pole itself, according to Mr. Mackenzie, should ideally have been 1-2 ft (30-60 cm) longer than his 10 ft (3 m) shaft – which had broken in two that very day [Fig. 6.15]!

As operations progressed, the rope around the cut weed was regularly tightened to compress the weed into a ball, better able to withstand wind, weather and tides. Up to 11 individual ten-fathom ropes (660 ft; 201 m) were untied in turn as the circle was increasingly tightened and closed, leaving the equivalent of perhaps two to two and a half ropes' length (120 ft/150 ft; 36.5 m/45.7 m) to secure the day's work – fairly dense growth cut from a 30 ft (9.2 m) band between high and low water marks, along some 90 - 100 ft (27-30 m) of shore. This would represent an average of five ton(ne)s of wet weed – around four ton(ne)s in the smallest circles, six ton(ne)s in the largest.

Fig. 6.12   Cutting seaweed with a sickle. Loch a'Chadh-Fi, 1973.

Fig. 6.13   Danny Mackenzie cutting seaweed in shallow water with a scythe. Loch a'Chadh-Fi, 1973.

Fig. 6.14 Twisting cut weed over the encircling rope to help discourage it from overriding in strong winds. Loch a'Chadh-Fi, 1973.

Fig. 6.15 Consolidating weed against the rope to help prevent it scattering. Loch a'Chadh-Fi, 1973.

Fig. 6.16 A cluster of some five rafts of cut seaweed anchored in Loch a'Chadh-Fi awaiting shipment to Keose, Lewis. 1973.

Fig. 6.17 Checking buoyancy and ropes around the rafts of seaweed. Loch a'Chadh-Fi, 1973.

Once fully-tightened and secured, the floating circles would be towed to a sheltered spot and anchored. Though no name was given, *claighe* has been recorded a little to the south, around Kylesku (NMAS RHS 1985). It signifies something round – *claigean, claigionn,* variously a skull, the headstall of a bridle, the round wooden head of a fishing buoy and the bowl of a pipe (Dwelly; McDonald 1958). Elsewhere, this circle or raft was a *ràth* (Lewis), a *maois(-feamann)* (Argyll, Uist) or *ball* (Uist), towed with a *fasda* (rope: Uist and Eriskay, where at one time it was made from twisted heather). Unsurprisingly, *fasda* could refer also to the raft itself and *ball* to the rope, whilst *maois* – cognate with Shetland/Orkney *maise, maishie* and descended from Old Norse *meiss,* basket – might otherwise denote a given number of fish, commonly 500 herring, or the large basket or container that held them. (Dwelly; Macdonald 1934; MacDonald 1958; Macdonald 1978. 90; Fenton 1968. 76).

For towing, Mr. MacKenzie used a two-year old 17 ft (5.2 m) Orkney-built boat fitted with an outboard. In such circumstances, the rudder was of no practical use, however; it was the 'float' that steered the boat, and pulling the tow rope to one side or the other determined a change in direction. The first day's float was anchored off-shore; then a line put to the shore and secured. For the second and subsequent days, further circles were attached to the buoyed anchor rope and tied also to the shore-rope [Figs. 6.16; 6.17].

Seaweed cut over no more than six consecutive days could be kept in this way without further attention. If not collected by the Lewis boat within this time, however, it became necessary to put nets around the ropes to keep all of the weed intact: indeed, there were some operators who only ever used nets, never ropes. Nets were specially made of 0.5 in (12.7 mm) nylon mesh, so small that the weed would not tangle with it. Each was about 25 ft long by some 3 ft deep (7.6 m x 90 cm), with floats placed 8 ins (20 cm) apart along the top edge, and lead weights some 3 ft (90 cm) apart at the bottom. These were packed more tightly on the windward side of the circle, where there was a greater danger of the weed being taken away; and the longer the period before the weed was collected, the more necessary the nets. For after a month or more in seawater, normally about six weeks, the weed would become saturated and sink just below the surface. This would be hastened if fresh water seeped into the bubbles or bladders, thereby making the weed that bit heavier so that it would not float.

Transferring the Weed

Normally, however, the weed would be collected before that happened. Loading was a delicate operation in its own right if the seaweed were not to disperse before it could be lifted, so only one float or circle was dealt with at a time.

Since each circle had several ropes around its circumference, at first one knot only was undone and the end of the rope fastened to the ship, the other end being kept tight in alongside. Then a second knot was undone at the 'loose' end and a single length of rope pulled through, thereby releasing the weed wound around it. It was critical to release at one time only as much weed as could speedily be taken up and lifted by the ship's grab – a requirement that had determined the 10 fathom (18.3 m) lengths of rope in the first place. It was also critical for the remaining ropes to be kept tight in order to keep the remaining weed hard up against the side of the ship. They were subsequently unknotted in turn, one at a time.

Once aboard, the seaweed was no longer the crofter's concern. It was now in the hands of a fully-industrialised modern business, and the crofter was simply paid for what he had collected. Up to the point of transfer, however, the scale and techniques of cutting and collection were those of the age-old traditions of a localised subsistence activity – a remarkable juxtaposition of the old and the new, and one that has so far proved particularly difficult to change.

Cutting for the Alginate Industry: The Wider Context

The alginate industry gradually emerged out of E.C.C. Stanford's discovery of alginic acid in 1884, and his development of a process to extract it from seaweed (Major 1977. 80). Alginates have come to be used in a wide range of industrial applications, not least in the manufacture of foods, pharmaceuticals, toiletries, cosmetics, drugs, textiles, plastics, paints, detergents, inks, agricultural products and in engineering. By the early 1950s, the food industry took roughly 50% of the output, drugs and cosmetics 40%, other industrial applications 10%. Further development of the industry in Scotland is not limited so much by any shortage of weed or difficulty in extracting alginates, rather by the economics of harvesting, drying and transportation, and by the still relatively limited number of known uses for seaweed derivatives (Moncrieff 1953. 74; Jertson 1953. 70).

In Scotland, the industry began in a small way in Kintyre in the 1930s. An English company Cefoil Ltd was established in 1934, and prior to 1939 its work was essentially experimental. During World War II it produced a crude alginate used in making camouflage material for the Ministry of Supply (and explosives?: A. Miller 1999), and it was for this purpose that the Ministry established factories at Balcardine (Benderloch) and Girvan (Ayrshire). Towards the end of the war, the company had taken on a more overtly commercial complexion; the South Boisdale and Orasay (South Uist) plants opened in 1944; in 1945, Cefoil Ltd became Alginate Industries Ltd (AIL); and from the early 1950s, home sales and export networks were developed along with the more extensive collection of unprocessed seaweeds, mainly from the old Hebridean kelping shores. Further small factories were opened at eg Sponish in North Uist (1955), as well as seaweed collecting stations at eg Loch Torridon, Loch Carron, Loch Eil and Tiree (and three locations in Orkney). By 1964, AIL was continuing to expand its operations, particularly in Lewis and Ireland (with additional trial collections of tangle 'rods' in Shetland); and in 1965 it opened a further drying facility at Keose on the east coast of Lochs in Lewis, which had a modest through-put of around 100 ton(ne)s a week in its first year (ISR 1954. 11 Fig 1; *Weekly Scotsman* 30 September 1965; *Scotsman* 21 October 1965; NMAS RHS 1977). In its final Report, the Institute for Seaweed Research was positive, recalling that whilst the Scottish alginate industry had been but very small in the 1950s, by 1968 it was producing some 15,000 tons a year (15,240 tonnes) and anticipated continued expansion (ISR 1954. 11 Fig 1; 1964. 7, 10; 1965. 10; 1967. 10; 1968. 8).

During these years everything had gone reasonably well. In the early 1960s, year-round cutting was available for 'Asco' collectors in the islands (those cutting bladderwrack, Ascophyllum nodosum, to supply the North and South Uist factories) – although 'tangle' collectors could only be employed seasonally, October to March, when the tangles were cast up on the shores. Even then, however, the Orasay and South Boisdale factories were only kept operational all-year-round by ferrying in supplies from elsewhere – notably from Tiree and Orkney. Indeed, according to R Cambell-Preston, Managing Director of AIL, some two-thirds of the tangle stipes processed at Orasay had to be brought in (*Glasgow Herald* 22 August 1962; 25 September 1962; *Scotsman* 16 July 1962).

The site for the new drying facility at Keose (1965) was chosen for easy access by puffers – the coastal cargo boats that could be beached following high tide to allow for loading and unloading as the tide receded. After drying, milling and bagging, some 120 wet ton(ne)s per week reduced to 30 bagged ton(ne)s, and the puffer could carry 200 ton(ne) loads south to Girvan on the Aryshire coast. In the early days, around 12 crofters were gathering seaweed (mainly bladderwracks) around the shores of East Loch Roag and Bernera (west Lewis), Husinish and Scarp (north-west Harris), Loch Erisort (east Lewis) and Loch Seaforth (east Lewis/Harris). Where there was good access, the cut weed was loaded onto a lorry and taken direct by road to Keose; otherwise, it was towed in rafts behind a motor-boat. And as the industry developed, mainland crofters such as Danny MacKenzie at Foindle were brought into the scheme.

In 1973, just a few years after cutting and collection had begun on north-west mainland coasts, Alginate Industries Ltd went public, and a new plant was opened at Balcardine in 1976. In 1979, however, AIL (which had dominated the British seaweed and alginates market) was taken over by Merck, the US pharmaceuticals giant that already owned other major alginate businesses worldwide. Gathering seaweed by hand continued to be a problem, restricting the amount of weed available for processing and (unless it were particularly plentiful) adding to the cost of collection. Moreover, in the words of John Sanderson, manager in Girvan for Kelco International (part of the multinational Merck Corporation): 'All the coal had to be shipped out there, and it would take something like half a tonne of coal to dry a tonne of seaweed' (*Scotsman* 11 November 1991).

In other words, a sound beginning did not progess sufficiently strongly; in 1980 Merck pulled out of the Western Isles (*Scotsman* 6 January 1982); and Brian Wilson, subsequently a minister in the U.K. Labour government, wrote in the *Glasgow Herald* (15 December 1983):

> For Alginate Industries, the economics of the Keose factory had always been problematic. There was a supply problem in getting enough weed from Lewis to keep the plant going at full volume. The further afield they went with boats and lorries to collect it, the more costs rose. ... Alginate Industries were buying weed from places like Chile and Iceland, yet the Keose weed was costing them £30 per ton more than from anywhere else.

Since the primary problem was cost, the idea of a workers' cooperative at Keose was mooted; and because a monopolies ruling in America meant that Merck was not allowed to sell the factory before the end of 1984, the company agreed to the facilities being used by such a cooperative to supply it with weed at a competitive price. This move reflects the 'needs must' tendency on the part of local communities in the north and west, as developers (often in receipt of substantial subsidies) first move into remote areas, and then move out again after discovering that profits (in large part not reinvested locally) are not as substantial as anticipated. Out of a workforce of 13, the six longest-serving employees formed the cooperative in 1981, 'following a trend which is becoming a feature of island life' (MacSween [1982] 1987. 408). It expanded into mussel cultivation, salmon farming and a car repair service; and was unique at the time amongst other multifunctional community cooperatives in the Western Isles, in that it was established in response to a specific threat of closure.

A new problem, of course, was that AIL/Merck was its sole customer for the dried weed, and although the cooperative was able to cut costs by reducing staff and other overheads, it was far from secure, even though its finances were sound. For where the reason for low or reduced profit is cheaper supplies elsewhere, what proves uneconomic for large multinational companies tends eventually to prove uneconomic for local cooperatives, however much the latter may be prepared to accept lower wages and profit margins. This is particularly so where the cooperative depends on that very same monopolistic multinational for the sale of its product.

By 1991, Kelco's operation in the Western Isles was becoming increasingly marginal, and according to Sanderson, it was partly only tradition that encouraged the company to continue taking island weed: 'We are happy to accept material from such a place, where it has been cut for generations' (*Scotsman* 11 November 1991). Seven years later, however, in 1998, and with the Keose drying factory closed, Nutrasweet-Kelco (now a subsidiary of the global bio-technology conglomerate, Monsanto) stopped taking weed from the Western Isles, with the loss of some 40 jobs (and almost 100 more at Girvan). Richard Searle, the current manager, explained (*Eòrpa*, 17 December 1998):

> One of the problems was the variable quality. The quality of the weed arriving wet at this factory, and the price of carrying a lot of water to this factory, made it no longer viable as a source to match the new requirements of this factory. ... The facilities around the world are not subsidised to any significant extent. We have to buy our raw material where it's competitive, and that is a fact of economic life. We have to look to the survival of this factory [Girvan]. Without the survival of this factory, then we're not going to be talking about seaweed from the Uists or anywhere else.

International competition and international recession meant that it was cheaper for Girvan to bring in weed from Iceland than from the Hebrides. The company might be willing, it said, to buy good quality dry weed from the Uists at a future date, but this would not be for some time. Given the market downturn, it reckoned it would be buying less in 1999 in any case – perhaps 50% less from Iceland (where it owned two-thirds of the factory) and from Ireland (where it owned nearly half). Furthermore, good quality dried weed would require investment in new drying facilities in Uist. Kelco had pulled out of Keose in 1980 and was not inclined to reinvest, so the matter was referred to such public agencies as Highlands and Islands Enterprise, the Local Enterprise Companies, the Western Isles Council and the emerging new Scottish Parliament, as well as to the UK Government. Unless new uses and buyers were to be found for Hebridean seaweed, however, Kelco could ultimately be accepting public subsidies whilst setting competing communities in all three countries off against each other – in two of which, but not Scotland, it part-owned the facilities.

The difficulties lie in more than drying facilities and outlets, however. Searle continued:

> Traditionally, and today, I think hand cutting can compete. I think it's going to be more difficult over the years, and that the move towards mechanical harvesting will certainly have to be investigated.

It is ironic that in Iceland's Breiðafjörður, not only is the company Thorverk able to make use of highly economical geothermal power to dry the seaweed in just two hours, but it uses a harvesting machine (originally designed to remove seaweed from the Great Lakes in North America) that was tried out in Scotland some 20 years ago. This machine, capable of cutting 30 ton(ne)s per low tide, was not successful in Scotland, however, since – unlike most suitable locations in Iceland – the seabed was too rough and rocky.

As things stand, therefore, Kelco's decision would seem to have put an effective end both to environmentally-friendly harvesting methods in the Uists and elsewhere, and to the major market for Scottish-sourced bladderwracks. It has also removed a critical part-time employment for what in the early 1990s amounted to some 60-70 'Asco' crofters on the sheltered, mainly eastern coasts of the Western Isles (and for those once working similarly sheltered coasts on the west mainland); and it has ended a shore-based tangle-gathering and drying operation which employed up to 30 and

150 people, mainly in the Outer Isles/Tiree and Orkney respectively. A ton(ne) of stipes fetching around £150 was a not insubstantial supplement to a family's income (Briand 1991. 259 et seq; Munford & Donnan 1994. 233-4) – even if the price for wrack, largely unchanged for many years on account of strong international competition (the company's view), was considerably lower and causing discontent: 'At £14 per tonne, some islanders are hanging up their scythes, picking up their buckets and turning to the despised winkles. At £40 a hundredweight [50.8 kg], it sounds a better deal' (*Scotsman* 11 November 1991).

CONCLUSION

For most of the 18th to mid/late 20th centuries, as no doubt earlier, seaweed continued to be recognised coastally in Sutherland as a valuable and locally-available resource. And where seaweed maintained this direct local value, there was long-term stability of techniques and terminology.

Much yet remains unclear, however, whether for Sutherland or more widely across Gaelic Scotland – particularly the directions and nature of cultural diffusion, and more specifically localised terminologies, practices and experiences of working with seaweed. That a not insignificant number of Gaelic names for seaweeds are Norse in origin would point to a surviving substratum of Norse cultural influence, particularly in certain of the western isles. Meantime, structural features of 18th and 19th century Highland kelp kilns suggest links with both lowland Scotland and Ireland. Whilst much of the evidence comes from the Outer Isles and Skye, there is no reason to suppose that the importance of seaweed and associated practices and traditions were hugely different on suitably-endowed coasts elsewhere in the west.

What has survived in documentary sources and orally would seem, even so, to represent the last strains of 'an auld sang'; and Kelco's decision to switch exclusively to foreign supplies for its Girvan alginates factory puts under greater threat not only the continuing viability of a number of peripheral communities, but also the survival of environmentally-friendly methods of gathering seaweed and a centuries-old cultural tradition. Traditional collection of uprooted, storm-driven tangles, just as the carefully-rotated cutting of rock weeds, has had no obviously deleterious effect on the marine environment. Mechanised harvesting, however, if introduced without careful controls and monitoring, could put underwater seaweed forests and food sources for fish and other marine life at significant ecological risk. It could also increase significantly the dangers of erosion, especially for fragile western machairs, most particularly in the Uists. For dense offshore tangle forests soak up considerable amounts of wave energy, protecting vulnerable shorelines from the full force of the Atlantic (Munford & Donnan 1994. 233-4).

As for present-day communities, patterns of crofting are maybe evolving in such a way as to provide a partial living for a much-reduced population, but reasonably secure part-time employment – the key to maintaining a local working population in remote townships – remains scanty. People such as Danny MacKenzie on the shores of Loch Laxford, typical of those who sought to make their way in a harsh environment, within their own cultural tradition, are the ones who have most to lose by the disappearance of industries and activities that are small-scale at local level, can be followed on a supplementary part-time basis, and are founded on renewable natural resources. Indigenous communities, languages and cultures are as diverse and valuable as indigenous landscapes and wildlife, and in just as much need of nurturing. The likes of fish-farming, forestry, estate work, information technology, conservation and tourism can help in their own modest ways, particularly when associated with a more direct, long-term stake in the land and its resources. And at Breasclete, Loch Roag, Lewis, the pharmaceutical development of specialised seaweed dressings contributes to such diversification. Vigorously pursuing new uses and outlets for seaweeds, rediscovering their value locally and extending sustainable practices, would be an attractive way of helping secure the survival of coastal communities, cultures and environments.

Acknowledgement

This paper is based largely on fieldwork carried out in the spring of 1974. I am much endebted to Alick MacAskill (Fanagmore), Donald MacLeod (Foindle), John George Ross (Badcall) and Mrs MacKenzie (Scourie, formerly Tarbet) for their willingness to discuss life in and around Badcall Bay, Scourie, Tarbet and Loch Laxford in the earlier part of this century; and in particular to Danny MacKenzie (Foindle) for introducing me to the practice of cutting and gathering seaweed in Loch Laxford. At Easter 1999, it fell to Chrissie MacLeod (Foindle, late Tarbet) to confirm the deaths of earlier contacts as well as of the industry itself; and Sandy Miller (Coigach) began to reminisce about life in the Balcardine alginate factory during the World War 2. For comparative material from the Uists, I am equally grateful to John MacDonald (Malaclete, North Uist, 1970), and to Norman MacCormick (Lochboisdale), Allan McIntyre (Loch Eynort), Mrs MacMillan (Iochdar) and Donald Walker (Daliburgh) (all South Uist, 1971).

Sincere thanks go also to William P.L. Thomson (Burray, Orkney) for invaluable comments and suggestions on the paper as a whole; to Professor Donald Meek (Aberdeen) and Jonathan MacDonald (Duntulm, Skye) for helping clarify Gaelic terms for seaweeds; and to BBC Alba for material from their current affairs programme, *Eòrpa*, and from Thorverk HF, Iceland.

Figures 6.3, 6.5 and 6.7 are Crown copyright, courtesy of the Royal Commission on the Ancient and Historical Monuments of Scotland; Figure 6.1 was computer-generated by David Baldwin; all other illustrations form part of the writer's fieldwork collection and are reproduced courtesy of the Scottish Life Archive (SLA), National Museums of Scotland.

References

Baldwin, J.R. 'At the Back of the Great Rock: Crofting and Settlement in Coigach, Loch Broom', in J.R. Baldwin (ed) *Peoples and Settlement in North-West Ross*. Edinburgh. 1994.

Bangor-Jones, M. 'The Establishment of Crofting in North-West Sutherland', in *Am Bratach*: 20-21. Strathnaver. June-July 1993.

Baxter, J.M. & Usher, M.B. *The Islands of Scotland: A Living Marine Heritage*. Edinburgh. 1994.

Briand, X. 'Seaweed harvesting in Europe', in N.D. Guiry & G. Blunden (eds) *Seaweed Resources in Europe*. Chichester. 1991.

Cameron, J. *Gaelic Names of Plants*. Edinburgh/London. 1883.

Chapman, V.J. & D.J. *Seaweeds and their Uses*. London/New York. 1980.

Conway, E. 'Clyde Seaweeds and their Economic Uses', in *Proc. Royal Philosophical Society of Glasgow*. LXVII, pt v. Glasgow. 1942.

Darling, F.F. (ed). *West Highland Survey: An Essay in Human Ecology*. Oxford. 1955.

Dickinson, C.I. *British Seaweeds*. London. 1963.

Dwelly, E. 1971. *The Illustrated Gaelic-English Dictionary* [1901-11]. 7th ed. Glasgow. 1971.

Eòrpa: BBC Alba, BBC 2 Television. 17 December 1998. Glasgow.

Fenton, A. 'Seaweed Manure', in *The Shape of the Past 2: Essays in Scottish Ethnology*. Edinburgh. 1986.

(The) Glasgow Herald: 22 August 1962; 25 September 1962; 15 December 1983. Glasgow.

Grant, I.F. *Highland Folk Ways*. London. 1961.

ISR: Institute of Seaweed Research (Inveresk): *Annual Reports* 1957, 1964, 1965, 1967, 1968.

Jackson, P. 'Scottish Seaweed Resources', in *Scottish Geographical Magazine*. vol 64. no 3. Edinburgh. 1945.

Jertson, E.C. 'The Potential Utilisation of Seaweed Extractives in the United States', in *Proc. First International Seaweed Symposium*. [1952]. Edinburgh. 1953.

Macdonald, A. 'Some Rare Gaelic Words and Phrases', in *Trans. Gael. Soc. Inv.* XXIX. [1915]. Inverness. 1922.

McDonald, A. *Gaelic Words and Expressions from South Uist and Eriskay* [1886-99 +]. Dublin. 1958.

MacDonald, D. 'Some Rare Words and Phrases', in *Trans. Gael. Soc. Inv.* XXXVII. Inverness. 1934.

MacFarlane, A. 'Gaelic Names of Plants: Study of their Uses and Lore', in *Trans. Gael. Soc. Inv.* XXXII [1924]. Inverness. 1929.

Mackenzie, G.S. *A General Survey of the Counties of Ross and Sutherland*. London. 1810.

MacKenzie, J. *An English-Gaelic Dictionary*. Glasgow. 1936.

MacSween, N. 'Parish of Lochs', in *Third Stat. Acc.* vol XIII [1982]. Edinburgh. 1987.

Major, J. *The Book of Seaweed*. London. 1977.

Moncrieff, R.W. 'The Uses of Alginates', in *Proc. First International Seaweed Symposium*. [1952]. Edinburgh. 1953.

Munford, J.G. & Donnan, D.W. 'The Sustainable Use of the Renewable Marine Resources of the Scottish Islands', in J.M. Baxter & M.B. Usher (eds). 1994. qv.

NMAS RHS. 1977: National Museum of Antiquities of Scotland, Royal Highland Show label. Scottish Life Archive. National Museums of Scotland, Edinburgh.

New Statistical Account [NSA]: Vol XIV. Inverness, Ross and Cromarty. Edinburgh/London. 1845; Vol XV. Sutherland, Caithness, Orkney, Shetland. Edinburgh/London. 1845.

Newton, L. *Seaweed Utilisation*. 1951.

Old Statistical Account [OSA] (1790s): Vol XVII. Inverness-shire, Ross and Cromarty. Wakefield. 1981; Vol XVIII. Caithness and Sutherland. Wakefield. 1979.

Omand, D. *The Sutherland Book*. Golspie. 1982.

O'Neill, T.P. 'Some Irish Techniques of Collecting Seaweed', in *Folk Life* 8. 1970.

Ross, S. et al. 'The Landscape', in D. Omand (ed) *The Sutherland Book*. Golspie. 1982.

(The) Scotsman: 16 July 1962; 13 July 1964; 21 September 1965; 6 January 1982; 11 November 1991. Edinburgh.

SND: *Scottish National Dictionary*. Edinburgh. 1927-76.

Stephenson, W.A. *Seaweed in Agriculture and Horticulture*. London. 1968.

Thomson, W.P.L. *Kelp-Making in Orkney*. Kirkwall. 1983.

Walker, F.T. 'Summary of Seaweed Resources in Great Britain', in *Proc. First International Seaweed Symposium*. [1952]. Edinburgh. 1953.

(The) Weekly Scotsman: 30 September 1965. Edinburgh.

Durness, ca 1886.

BIGHOUSE AND STRATH HALLADALE, SUTHERLAND

Elizabeth Beaton

INTRODUCTION

Bighouse (NH 891648) [Fig. 7.1] is a group of 18th- and 19th-century buildings sited on the east bank of the Halladale River close to its confluence with the sea: within the group Bighouse Lodge is paramount. The estuarine site has not always been called Bighouse, though this anglicised title is well-suited to the location dominated by a mansion-house.

From the 16th century until sold in 1830 to the Marquis of Stafford and his wife, the Countess of Sutherland, Strath Halladale belonged to the Mackays of Bighouse, originally domiciled further up the strath. North-west Sutherland was dominated by various branches of the Mackay family, headed by the Lords of Reay at Tongue, of which the Bighouse branch was a principal cadet line (see Bangor-Jones, this volume).

This paper seeks to set the buildings at Bighouse in their architectural and historical context, the background material drawn from a variety of sources.

PLACE-NAMES

The anglicised name Bighouse immediately conjures up a mansion or substantial dwelling, Bighouse Lodge fitting neatly into this classification. Confusingly *Bighouse* or *Beghous* is derived from *bygdh-hús*, a settlement name of Norse origin meaning 'village house', combining the ON element -*byr*, farm, with *hus*, house (Omand 1982. 282). Timothy Pont (1560 – ca 1625/30), cartographer and Minister of Dunnet, Caithness (1601-14) spells the name *Begos* (Blaeu 113. 1654) [Fig. 7.2], while *Beghous* and *Bighous* also make their appearance. Locally the pronunciation 'Begus' prevails.[1]

However, Pont's *Begos* is not sited at Bighouse! *Begos* was further up-stream, at or near Upper Bighouse (NC 887573), between six and seven miles up the Halladale River from the mansion-house. The present Bighouse was originally Tor, castle (Owen nd.). It appears as *The Tor* in a farm rental of 1819 (Mackay 1906. 480; Bardgett 1990. 18), *Tor* in 1823 (Thompson. 1823) and optional as *Torr* or *Bighouse* in 1885 (*OGS* vi. 420). The name survives in *Rubha an-Tuir*, headland of the castle, to the north-east of Bighouse.

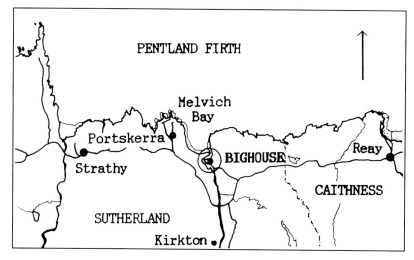

Fig. 7.1   Pentland Firth and Bighouse. 1994.

STRATH HALLADALE

Strath Halladale runs north/south from Melvich Bay (formerly Bighouse Bay) to Forsinard, sheltered east and west by low but often rugged hills. It is settled with scattered farms principally devoted to sheep and cattle, with pasture land flanking the winding river. Historically, the salmon fishings of the Halladale River were an important source of wealth. In 1726, the river 'runs North towards the sea where it has salmond fishing with nets and cruives'[2] (MacFarlane 1906. i. 186): there is still some commercial salmon fishing at Bighouse.

Though always in Sutherland, Strath Halladale formed part of Reay Parish, Caithness, from the 13th century until 1892 (*OPS* 1885. 742; Smith 1988. 148), but was *erected* as a *Quoad Sacra* parish with Strathy in 1846 (*FES* 1928. vii. 109). The Mackay Lords of Reay took their name from Reay parish, where the shell of their 16th-century castle still stands within, and has given its name to, the Dounreay Nuclear Power Development Establishment.

It is recorded that 'In 1274 and 1275 ... the church at "Halludal" or "Helwedale" contributed around 9sh.4d. towards the expenses of the Crusades' (Bardgett 1990. 8). This was probably the predecessor of the chapel at Balnaheglish (various spellings, all meaning 'place of the chapel'), otherwise Kirkton, mentioned in 1574 and 1576 and existing in 1726 when the Minister of Reay 'was bound to preach in it eight times a year' (*OPS* 1855. 743). Six 18th-century tombstones from Kirkton are in the Strathnaver Museum, Bettyhill. None record principal members of the Mackay of Bighouse family, some of whom are commemorated in the Bighouse aisle at old Reay burial ground.

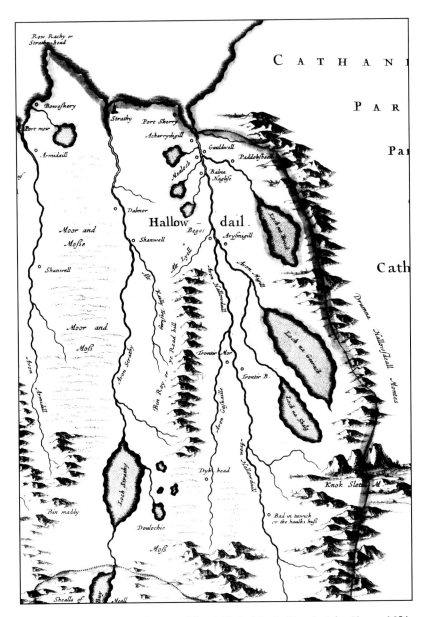

Fig. 7.2 Timothy Pont's map of Strath Halladale, in Blaeu's *Atlas Novus*, 1654. Note 'Balna Haglise' (Kirkton) and 'Begos', the latter sited at the present Upper Bighouse.

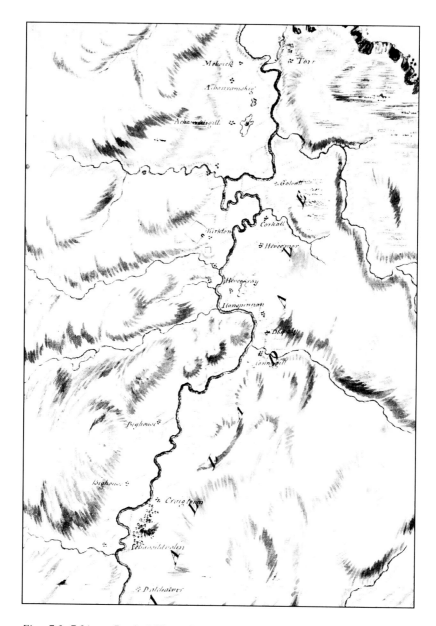

Figs. 7.3; 7.3A   Roy's *Military Survey of Scotland*, 1747-55. Note hatching of run-rig cultivation. The square enclosure at Kirkton is the former 'dwelling house of the laird of Bighouse' (revealed as U-plan, when enlarged as Fig. 7.3A). The smaller square is the burial ground. Note two settlements named Bighouse, the spelling anglicised, presumably by English-speaking military surveyors: also Torr at the river-mouth.

146

Fig. 7.3A

Though Kirkton seems to have been the principal ecclesiastical site in the strath, there were others. At Craigtown, the present church of 1910 is a successor to 'the meeting house where', also in 1726 'the people conveen, when the minr [*sic*] comes to preach to them which is every Lords day' (MacFarlane 1906. i. 186). Recent excavations revealed a T-plan church of ca 1800 at Deasphollag ('Dispolly' in Bardgett 1993. 10-11). Here, in 1840 'a missionary preaches every third Sabbath', the church 'supported partly by the Royal Bounty and partly by the people' (*NSA* 1840. xv. 20).

The mansion of Bighouse Lodge, together with ancillary buildings and garden, occupies low-lying land on the east bank of the river, close to where it joins the sea in Melvich Bay. Here, the fast-flowing river forms a pronounced 'S' bend, encompassing within its sinuous curves both the mansion site and the higher sand dune mound opposite on the seaward side – both sites obviously naturally defensive. Eastwards, the land rises gently to 314 ft (100 m), culminating in the headland of Rubha an-Tuir. The former presence of a stronghold is re-enforced by place-name evidence quoted above. Whether this stronghold was a fort, broch or tower-house must remain conjectural. Timothy Pont indicated no building nor settlement here on either of his maps of the area, surveyed between 1584-1596 (Blaeu 1654): nor, more pertinent to this paper, do any buildings appear on Roy's *Military Survey of Scotland*, executed between 1747-55, except for three small settlements on the headland slopes to the east [Fig. 7.3]. It is worth noting that there are two places named The Borg (which could be construed as fortified or enclosed) at the upper and lower limit of inhabited Strath Halladale (NC 890635; NC 899509), and four ruinous brochs. The brochs, at least, indicate settlement from around the beginning of the Christian era, and subsequent townships and farms are associated continuously with local names such as Trantlemore and Golval.

Strath Halladale has a varied history of ownership. At least by the 16th century, *Bighouse* was implied as neighbouring Trantlemore and Trantlebeg when, in 1527, King James V 'granted anew' these lands to Gavin Murray, son of Roderic Murray of Spinningdale. The strath, or portions of it, was owned or argued over by the Sutherlands of Duffus and the Mackays, besides branches of other northern landowners (*OPS* 1855. 744).

KIRKTON

Though the principal A 897 road northwards through Strath Halladale is on the east bank of the Halladale River from just north of Forsinard, there is a parallel track or secondary road on the west bank commencing south of Trantlemore. This road passes north through Kirkton, reflecting the importance of that site and communication between townships on the west bank. That Kirkton was a settlement in its own right, is clearly stated in 1726 in a description of the strath in which 'the places inhabited are ... Bighouse, Kirkton, Golwake, Melvik ... ' (MacFarlane 1906. i. 186).

Other than an empty cottage, there are now no buildings near the Kirkton burial ground [Figs. 7.3A; 7.4]. Kirkton farm, with modern bungalow and outbuildings of 19th- and 20th-century date, is half a mile north. Yet in 1726:

Fig. 7.4   Burial ground, Kirkton, looking north up strath. This was Balnahaglis (also Balna Haglise), place of the chapel. Pediment dated 1630 mounted immediately left of gateway in foreground. 1994.

Fig. 7.5   Dormer window pediment dated 1630 mounted on Kirkton burial ground wall. 1994.

> Four miles west of the church of Rae [*sic*] is the house of Kirktoun standing clos on the west side of the river Halladale (upon which is Strath-Halladale) which is the dwelling house of the laird of Bighouse proprietor of the said Strath' (MacFarlane 1906. i. 182).

– indicating that the 'laird of Bighouse' was domiciled at Kirkton at least by 1726. The existence of a house of standing is confirmed both by Roy in the mid 18th century and in *The Ancient Parochial Map* (*OPS* 1855).

Mounted on the burial ground wall, close to the lower, south-west entrance, is a dormer window pediment dated 1630 with Mackay armorial and monogram AMK for Angus Mackay, almost certainly Angus 1st of Bighouse, who died in 1634. The pediment is a typical early 17th-century upper storey window gablet, triangular in shape, the outer edges decorated with cable moulding and naive scrolls [Figs. 7.5; 7.6]. It is supported by a stone block bearing the following worn inscription:

> Found on church site by D. Macaskill Kirkton 1894.
> Erected by [?R?S] Macdonald M[?D], Dunedin NZ 1895

This pediment of 1630 is the earliest fragment of the 'dwelling house of the laird' at Kirkton. Another datestone of 1738, now at Bighouse, is discussed below. It is of interest to note that Kirkton formed part of the Bighouse estate until the early 1980s.[3]

Fig. 7.6   Pediment with AMK (Angus Mackay) above Mackay armorial; dated
16 (left) and 30 (right) at base. 1994.

At Kirkton, Roy's *Military Survey of Scotland*, surveyed between 1747-55, clearly reveals a U-plan house flanked either side by the walls of an enclosed yard or garden extending to the rear. The site is approximately that of the ruined cottage slightly to the north-west of the burial ground, standing on a terrace (?man-made) overlooking the valley. The same map names Bighouse as being two settlements near the present Upper Bighouse, further up-stream. Presumably the surveyors were English, for the anglicised spelling Bighouse is used.

THE MACKAYS OF BIGHOUSE

The genealogy of the Mackay family of Bighouse has been adequately covered elsewhere (Bangor-Jones, this volume; Mackay 1906. 303). Sufficient for this paper that '[Rory] Murray [of Bighouse] alienated these lands to William Mackay for 1000 merks on 15 July, 1597', the deal finalised 'by charter of confirmation under Great Seal 18 December, 1598' (Mackay 1906. 304). William Mackay, second son of 'IYe Du xii' of Strathnaver, was thereafter 'of Bighouse'. These formalities may have confirmed the *status quo* established some years earlier when:

> on 20 September 1587 William Mackay with certain brokin heiland men ...
> came to the lands of Bighouse or Strath Halladale (Mackay 1906. 334).

William probably lived near what is now Upper Bighouse: he died in 1612 and was succeeded by his son Angus, whose first wife, Jane Elphinston, died in 1630 and was buried at Kirkton. In 1631, Angus extended his holdings by purchasing from the 1st Lord Reay 'the church lands of Belnaheglis and Goval with the salmon fishings of Halladale' (Mackay 1906. 304). This early 17th-century acquisition suggests that Angus was responsible for building the family house at Belnaheglis (Kirkton), of which the 1630 armorial is a surviving fragment. Though this armorial is dated a year earlier than the formalities of purchase, these may have regularised a previous *status quo*. Angus died in 1634, his death 'was much lamented, being a very active and able Gentleman' (Mackay 1829. 273).

By 1681, the estate had passed to Angus' great-nephew, also Angus, who with his wife Jane Sinclair is buried in the Mackay aisle in the old burial ground at Reay.

In 1722, Angus' grand-daughter Elizabeth succeeded to the estate. Six years later, in 1728, she married Hon. Hugh Mackay, brother of the 4th Lord of Reay, a prosperous factor and cattle trader. They acquired Kirkton in 1737, probably building the U-plan house (now The Barracks, Bighouse?) at Kirkton, even though they did not settle there permanently until the winter of 1758/59. They subsequently moved to Tor, where they built the mansion-house, both dying in 1770. The property passed to their daughter, Janet, who had married Colin Campbell of Glenure, Argyll, in May 1749, and in turn to

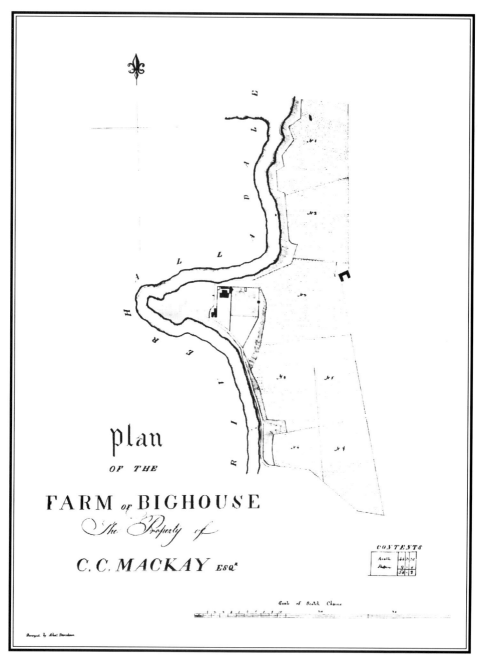

plan

OF THE

FARM OF BIGHOUSE

The Property of

C. C. MACKAY ESQ.

Fig. 7.7 Plan of the Farm of Bighouse, undated but drawn between 1819-30 (NLS Dept. 313/3590/24).

her daughter Louisa Campbell, wife of George Mackay of Handa and Sandwood, by whom she had twenty-one children.

George was was a military man and 'a gentleman of great worth and probity' (Mackay 1829. 454). A portrait by Raeburn reveals Louisa as a matronly figure with strong features, wearing a turban decorated with a crescent brooch and a ruffle about her neck to relieve the darkness of her gown (Mackay 1906. 333). George died in 1798 and is commemorated in the Mackay aisle, old Reay burial ground. Their eldest son, Hugh, a merchant in Antigua died in 1818 and was succeeded by Louisa's third son, Colin Campbell Mackay, though it was not until 1829 that his mother (died 1834) finally settled the estate on him. It was he who commissioned three estate maps[4] in the 1820s, selling the Bighouse estate to the Marquis of Stafford and his Countess of Sutherland in 1830. [Fig. 7.7]

THE BUILDINGS AT BIGHOUSE

The buildings at Bighouse are a remarkable group. As with three other important north-coast 'Lairds' houses' – namely Balnakeil, Tongue and Sandside – all are sited close to reasonably sheltered bays or sea lochs on the stormy but major sea route of the Pentland Firth, a reminder that this Sutherland/Caithness coastline was the hub of the northern Scottish mainland. All these properties were enlarged or rebuilt during the 18th century: Balnakeil in 1744, Tongue House apparently heightened in 1750, and Sandside House built in 1751.[5]

Bighouse Lodge appears to have joined this coastal group of mansions in the early 1760s, for the 'genteel dwelling house, adorned by a garden' was noted in 1767 by the naturalist James Robertson (see Bangor-Jones); while in 1774, the Rev Alexander Pope of Reay described it as a 'modern house' (Pennant 1774. 323). Alexander Broune 'made alterations' in 1763; whether these were connected with Bighouse Lodge or The Barracks (at Kirkton or Tor) is unclear (Gifford 1992. 106).

Bighouse is sited on a spit of level land projecting into the Halladale River by which it is enclosed on three sides [Figs. 7.8; 7.9]. Screened and protected from the open sea at the north by a high mounded dune, the general impression is that of an 18th-century complex, though subsequent alterations to Bighouse Lodge (the suffix Lodge was added in 1984) give it, at first glance, a 19th-century appearance.

The principal buildings are Bighouse Lodge, The Barracks, the walled garden with its garden pavilion and the icehouse. At the rear of Bighouse Lodge is a low irregular 2-storey, L-plan range of service buildings, which with The Barracks, are incorporated in the walls enclosing house and garden. The main house and The Barracks, facing south up the Halladale River, are sheltered at the east by rising ground and overlooked on the west by the township of Melvich strung out along the A 836 road.

Fig. 7.8   Bighouse Lodge (right) and The Barracks (left), fronted by the curve of the Halladale River. 1994.

Fig. 7.9   Site plan of Bighouse Lodge:
1. Bighouse Lodge   4. Former farm buildings
2. The Barracks   with kiln-barn
3. Garden Pavilion   5. Icehouse

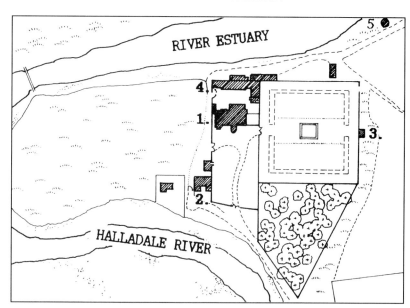

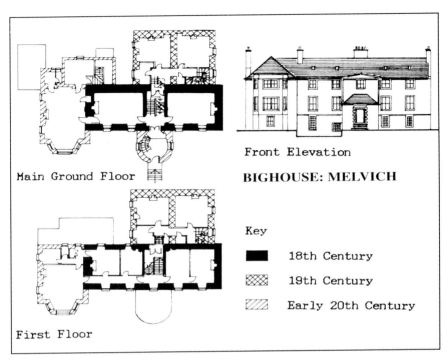

Front Elevation

BIGHOUSE: MELVICH

Main Ground Floor

First Floor

Key

■ 18th Century

▨ 19th Century

▨ Early 20th Century

Fig. 7.10   Plan and elevation, Bighouse Lodge. ca 1980.

Fig. 7.11   Bighouse Lodge: Edwardian wing at left. Entry to walled garden just visible between trees at right. 1994.

Bighouse Lodge

Exterior

Bighouse Lodge, ca 1761-65, is an austere 3-storey house [Figs. 7.10; 7.11]. The centre bay is slightly advanced and rises above the wallhead as a shallow pediment, while the central doorway is masked by an Edwardian porch approached by steps. The projecting wide single-bay west wing, with canted windows rising full height, was also added in the early 20th century, but after the porch.[6] At the rear, a massive double-gabled 3-storey and attic wing projects to form a T-plan. A rear wing appears on a plan of Bighouse drawn before 1830: this may be incorporated in, or have been replaced by the present very large rear extension – which seems of two builds, divided longitudinally down the centre by a thick (?former outside) wall.

The house is of harled rubble, the window margins of sandstone ashlar and chamfered.[7] This chamfering is repeated on the window margins of the Edwardian west addition, but not on the tooled margins of the rear wing. The

Fig. 7.12 Bighouse Lodge: narrow raised basement window with scarcement (ledge) and wider window above. 1994.

156

Fig. 7.13 Bighouse Lodge: stone
scale and platt staircase. Note centre
spine wall rounded at landing face, with
square base and capital. Also moulded
risers to stone stairs. 1982.

Fig. 7.14 Bighouse Lodge: first
floor landing and staircase spine wall.
1982.

substantial panelled chimney stacks all have flaired copes, stylistically dating
from the early 20th-century alterations.

The projecting porch, ca 1900, has a bowed front, the rusticated and
corniced doorpiece surmounted by a cornice enriched by a pulvinated
(convex) frieze. Within the porch, the stone staircase rising to the raised
ground-floor entrance is constructed of re-used stone treads, apparently the
former outside stairs that originally oversailed the basement well to the main
door. The bottom tread of the stairs has a scroll terminal where the final
handrail baluster is mounted, a characteristic of 18th- and early 19th-century
splayed outside stairs. Over the main inner doorway (original main door) is
an 18th-century semicircular fanlight with intersecting astragals.

The lower ground floor, in effect a raised basement lit by the well (which
only survives left of the front entrance), has very narrow windows in the
south elevation. Three remain: one lighting the present family kitchen left of
the entrance porch [Fig. 7.12] and two to the east (right). Furthermore, a
narrow scarcement (ledge) runs horizontally across the frontage above these
windows, indicating slightly thicker lower external walls. The narrowness of
the windows suggests an earlier build and that there was some change of
fenestration breadth by the time the main part of the house was constructed.

Fig. 7.15 Bighouse Lodge with The Barracks (left). Note contemporary store immediately to rear of The Barracks, with modern glazed bay window. 1992.

Fig. 7.16 The Barracks. The inserted window dated 1738 just visible set back at centre first floor. 1994.

Interior

Internally, the only original feature to survive the Edwardian alterations is the central scale-and-platt staircase[8] [Figs. 7.13; 7.14]. This substantial stone staircase fills the centre of the house, the stone treads with moulded risers bedded in the central masonry spine wall which is rounded at each landing face. The type is consistent with a mid 18th-century date for Bighouse Lodge, found elsewhere in Scotland and particularly appropriate in treeless northern Sutherland and Caithness, where timber for staircases with decorative turned balusters was at a premium. The staircase, a massive integral part of the house, is an important piece in the architectural jig-saw of Bighouse Lodge, a vital clue in the dating of the building to the 18th century.

Otherwise, the internal features of the house, the chimney-pieces and carpentry such as window shutters and doors, are of early 20th-century style.

Building Date

The architectural evidence suggests that the lower ground floor of Bighouse Lodge may have been commenced a little before 1760. If so, either the foundations were of no importance to Roy's military surveyors at work in the area ca 1750, since they are not entered on the finished map, or there was nothing there for them to note. Elizabeth Mackay of Bighouse and Hugh Mackay of Reay, a dominant Mackay of his generation, were married in 1728 but apparently did not settle at Kirkton until 1758/59. Perhaps they planned to build at Tor rather earlier, but either Hugh's health, business affairs, or the 1745 up-rising delayed the project. Bishop Pococke travelled from Tongue to Sandside in June, 1760. It is not clear whether he passed near Tor or Kirkton, but he makes no mention of a new mansion, only that:

Fig. 7.17   Plan and elevation, The Barracks. Courtesy of G. Leet, 1994.

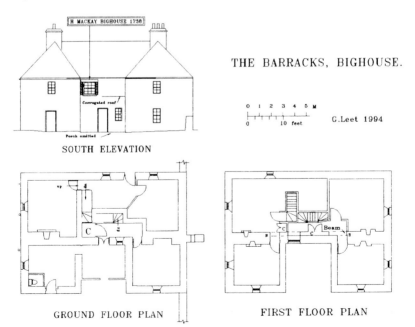

[we] crossed upon Avon Hallowdale ... and passed by Bighouse, another apenage of the house of Reay that discended [*sic*] to the present Lord's brother by his marriage of the sole heiress. This is a beautiful vale of considerable extent (Pococke 1887.132).

Had there been a new mansion, surely Pococke would have noted it? A building date of 1761-65 seems a reasonable assumption.

The Barracks

The name of this small U-plan dwellinghouse, sited in front of and slightly to the west of the main house [Fig. 7.15], is enigmatic. Local tradition has it that, during the 1745 rebellion, troops were quartered there and arms kept in the contemporary square store to the rear. The complete absence of any building on Roy's map, however, suggests this is legend rather than fact. The name could have come about if the house was relegated to servants: in north-east Scotland servants' quarters were termed 'barracks', and no doubt there was a need for considerable domestic and outdoor staff during the tenure of Louisa and George Mackay with their large family of twenty-one children.

The Barracks [Figs. 7.16; 7.17] is a modest neat U-plan, 2-storey rubble structure, with small regularly-disposed windows, those in the first floor tucked closed under the eaves. Two advanced wings, each with 2-bay long elevations facing east and west, are linked by a narrow recessed bay with centre entrance (now masked by a corrugated iron lean-to). A further entrance was slapped in the front gable of the west wing when the house was divided into two dwellings. Each wing has a piended (hipped) slated roof with a central ridge chimney, the stacks with simple cornice and high cope chamfered along the upper edge in early 18th-century style.[9] Nothing of interest survives internally except a massive timber ridge beam.[10]

In the first floor of the narrow centre bay of The Barracks, there is an awkwardly-placed window, larger and squarer than the other symmetrically-arranged fenestration. This window is obviously a later intrusion, the jambs moulded in 17th-century manner (re-used from the 17th-century dwelling?), but the lintel inscribed 'H Mackay Bighouse 1738'.

To the rear of this interesting little house is a contemporary, free-standing store with similar gable end chimney stack to those on the The Barracks.

Stylistically, The Barracks dates from the first half of the 18th century, probably 1738: assuming the correctness of Roy's map, it could not have been on this site before 1755. Yet that same map reveals a small U-plan dwelling at Kirkton. Was The Barracks moved *in toto* to the present site? It has already been suggested that Hugh Mackay built this house at Kirkton after he and Elizabeth acquired possession in 1737, and that Louisa and George may have moved the building after they took over in 1770? As it stands now, slightly to the west of Bighouse Lodge and outside the walled perimeter of mansion and gardens, The Barracks lacks a premier or even

Fig. 7.18   Garden pavilion. 1994.

Fig. 7.19   Garden pavilion. 1994.

Fig. 7.20 Garden pavilion from rear with forestair leading to first floor room. 1994.

Fig. 7.21 Garden pavilion roof with chimney-head and salmon silhouette windvane. 1994.

logical position in the complex. The re-used lintel, dated 1738 and bearing Hugh Mackay's name, must also have come from Kirkton, perhaps rescued and installed after the house was re-built at Tor.

Walled Garden and Garden Pavilion

The high walled garden, immediately east of the Lodge, measures approximately 263 ft x 263 ft (80 m x 80 m). In the centre of the east wall, aligned with the entrance at the west, is a small two-storey garden pavilion [Figs. 7.18; 7.19]. By 1767, this was the centre-piece of the 'garden, which, for it's size, is the best and most elegant ... in the North' (Henderson & Dickson 1994. 50). The only other garden pavilion of this type in northern Scotland is at Dunrobin Castle, Golspie, the seat of the Earls of Sutherland, constructed by Lord William Strathnaver (heir to the 17th Earl) in 1732. At Bighouse in 1780:

> The appearance of the gardens was unexpectedly pleasing. In a spot enclosed by such barren ridges of rocky hills, one does not look for such a display of luxuriance; the borders decked with variety of the richest flowers, plenty of wall-fruits; apples, pears, plums, cherries, which are often as early ripe as at Edinburgh; beds of melons and cucumbers; and whatever can give variety, or grace the entertainments of the table. (Cordiner 1780. 93)

Fig. 7.22 Garden pavilion: blocked hearth in ground floor with bolection moulded surround. 1994.

Fig. 7.23   West entrance, Bighouse Lodge. The flanking walls have been raised.
1994.

Fig. 7.24   Looking up Halladale River from Bighouse Lodge; later gatepiers,
possibly replacing those now flanking west entrance. 1994.

The pavilion is of harled rubble with ashlar dressings and quoins, the front wallhead angles each crowned with a ball finial supported by a stout, attenuated stalk rising from a fluted rectangular base. The centre front wallhead chimney, with a cope similar to those on The Barracks, is matched at the rear. The garden walls abut the pavilion in the centre of the north and south gables: against the latter is a forestair serving the first floor, reached via a doorway in the garden wall [Fig. 7.20]. The slated pyramidal roof is crowned by a weathervane with a salmon silhouette, a usual feature on buildings associated with the salmon industry – from which Bighouse traditionally gained wealth [Fig. 7.21]. Internally there is now no ceiling; the floor is paved with stone slabs, and the chimney-piece in the rear wall is of early 18th-century type with bolection moulded frame [Fig. 7.22]. That serving the first floor is later, of plain tooled ashlar and possibly a replacement. The longer windows in the first floor suggest that this was the more important of the two rooms and worthy of an elegant chimney-piece.

The west side of the walled garden flanks both the court at the rear of Bighouse Lodge and the lawn in front. A further wall encloses the west side of the front lawn, the entrance aligned to the present footbridge and perhaps previous ferry crossing of the Halladale River. The gate-piers are very similar to those of the walled garden [Fig. 7.23]. That these piers are not in their original position is suggested by the heightening of the masonry west wall each side of the gateway. No entrance is shown here on Surveyor Alex. Davidson's *Plan of the Farm of Bighouse* – but neither does he indicate any entrance, anywhere, to the walled garden on this plan! However, on the evidence of the west wall being altered to accommodate the piers, and as the entry centred on the front of the house lacks emphasis, it is suggested that these west entrance piers may once have flanked the short south drive between the shore and the house, leading directly to the front door [Fig. 7.24].

Former Farm Buildings

The *Plan of the Farm of Bighouse, The Property of C C Mackay Esq.* was prepared by surveyor Alex. Davidson during the period of joint ownership of Bighouse by Colin Campbell Mackay, 1818-30, with his mother [Fig. 7.7]. It is mainly devoted to the field layout of Bighouse – large fields superseding the run-rig of the three former settlements on the slopes of Rubha an-Tuir indicated in the mid-18th century by Roy. The plan reveals a U-plan steading to the east, but no farmhouse. From this it appears that whoever farmed the property lived in the main house, with the rear detached L-plan range as farm and service buildings [Fig. 7.25]. The mid 18th-century kiln-barn and barn at Sandside are so disposed, and a similar layout is shown on Wm. Aberdeen's plan of Castlehill, Castletown, Caithness, prepared in 1772.

At Bighouse, the two rectangular buildings shown on the plan at right angles to one another are still there, though altered. Sufficient evidence

Fig. 7.25   Bighouse: ?former kiln-barn; note vent immediately below eaves and another in gable end. 1994.

Fig. 7.26   Sandside, kiln-barn: the kiln occupied the left hand section, the upper floor reached by staircase in canted stairwell fronting gable end. 1992.

survives to suggest that they were in fact, kiln-barn and barn similar to those at Sandside and Castletown, probably of late 18th-century date. The ridge stack, small circular vents below the eaves and 18th-century chamfers to a very small window in the west gable, all suggest that the west end of the block running parallel to the river was the original kiln of the kiln barn. This was later gutted and altered to accommodate gig-house and saddle room, the latter heated by a hearth utilising the former kiln flue, with chimney stack re-built and capped with a 19th-century cope.

Farm kilns were usual in the north, to dry the grain before grinding: they took various forms, sometimes quite small, but substantial on the larger properties. They required mural ventilation to the upper floor where the grain was spread to dry, and a flue to carry warmth upwards and to draw off smoke. While most Caithness farm kilns are bow-end, that at neighbouring Sandside, like Bighouse, is also square (Beaton 1988), the kiln-barn and barn laid out at right angles to each other with barely passage room between [Fig. 7.26]. In 1772, there was the same arrangement at Castlehill, Castletown, east of Thurso [Fig. 7.27]. Based on similar buildings of this type sited on the

Fig. 7.27 Kiln-barn, Castlehill, Caithness, by Wm. Aberdeen, ca 1772. Note L-plan layout of paired buildings, similar to those at Sandside and Bighouse (SRO RHP 1221).

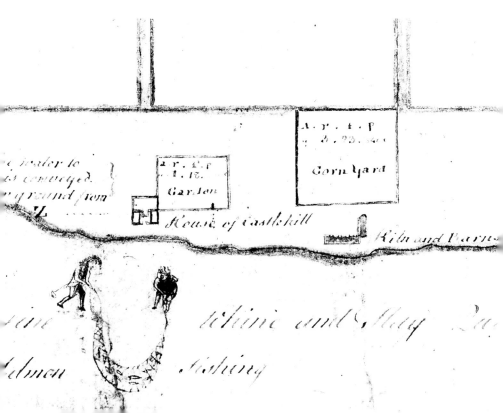

more substantial farms of the Pentland Firth coast, and the requirements of 18th- and early 19th-century farming, one can be confident of the origin of this building.

These improved farm offices would have contributed to the rental paid for the farm. In 1819, the annual rental paid by Gabriel Reid (Louisa's son-in-law) for the farms at 'North Golval and Tor' (Bighouse) was £160. The only higher rental of that year was for Forsinain, possibly used also as a sporting estate, where 'Mr. Robson' paid £550 pa (Mackay 1906. 480).[11] The rents at Bighouse (presumably Upper Bighouse) varied between £1.11s.6d to £10.10s.0d pa (Mackay 1906. 480).

Fig. 7.28 Icehouse. Bowed ante-chamber fronts lower portion: chute to rear of turf conical roof. 1992.

Icehouse

As elsewhere in Scotland, commercial salmon fishing was a source of wealth, peaking during the early 19th century when the growth of urban centres provided ready markets for the fish. The importance of the salmon fishings was always emphasised throughout the history of Strath Halladale. This perishable commodity was transported by sea, at first salted and in barrels. From ca 1800, in order that the fish remained (reasonably) fresh, they were par-boiled in brine and packed in ice collected during the winter and retained in semi-subterranean stores called icehouses.

Commercial icehouses were masonry vaults with rear chutes down which the ice was thrown, and a doorway at the front – sometimes preceded by an ante-chamber, or dead-room, leading into the ice store. The icehouse at Bighouse is of a less usual cylindrical form with conical roof, the rear chute approached by a track, and the entrance fronted by a semi-circular ante-chamber [Fig. 7.28]. It was used until the early 1980s, when the ice, instead of being collected from river or pond and transported thither by cart, was delivered from the ice factory by lorry (pers. comm. ca 1983).

This icehouse is not revealed on the undated *Plan of the Farm of Bighouse*. Given that the plan probably dates from the mid 1820s, the icehouse and neighbouring salmon fishers' bothy must have been built after the survey, perhaps before Bighouse was sold to the Marquis of Stafford in 1830. It is less likely to have been built by the Sutherland estates, whose icehouses followed an estate pattern, vaulted with curved, gabled front – as at Bettyhill, Brora, Helmsdale (Bridge) and Littleferry.

It is interesting that the rent paid for the commercial salmon fishings at Bighouse in 1819 was £150 pa, the third highest rental on the estate. The gross rental for that year was £1,566.18s.8d.

The 18th/early 19th-Century Bighouse Buildings: A Summary

Much of Bighouse remains an enigma and will continue so until more detailed research is carried out in both Reay and Sutherland estate papers. Meantime, archival and published sources, maps and architectural evidence encourage assessment of this fascinating complex. Recapitulating all that has been outlined above, we know that the Mackays of Bighouse were established in Strath Halladale at the end of the 16th century. They may at first have been domiciled in the Upper Bighouse area, but certainly by 1630 had built their home, probably a small tower-house, at Kirkton, near the chapel and burial ground. A new house, revealed as U-plan on Roy's *Military Survey*, 1747-55, was built there ca 1738, probably what is now The Barracks, Bighouse. Elizabeth and Hugh Mackay relocated their principal residence to Tor in the early 1760s, from then called Bighouse. Perhaps they also re-built their former house at Kirkton as The Barracks or, more likely, left that task to their daughter Louisa and her husband George Mackay with their twenty-one children.

Alex. Davidson's *Plan of the Farm of Bighouse*, apparently dating from the 1820s, reveals the extent of the farm, the disappearance of the settlements at Tor, large enclosed fields and a U-plan steading some distance from the house – perhaps the first stage of removing farming activities from the mansion to the Mains farm (home farm). The L-plan layout of the rear offices at Bighouse, similar to others on 'Laird's' estates on the Pentland Firth coast, coupled with some building evidence, suggests that this range was originally the kiln-barn and barn.

The importance of the salmon fishings on the Halladale River, and the wealth they generated, was apparent throughout the Mackay tenure. Had the icehouse been built before Alex. Davidson surveyed the farm in the 1820s, it would certainly have been included on his plan. Maybe until the mid 1820s the fishings were centred further up-stream, or the fish caught were salted before export rather than packed in ice. Be that as it may, the icehouse does not appear and it is suggested it was built after survey but before Bighouse was sold to the Marquis of Stafford in 1830.

Fig. 7.29   Halladale River between Kirkton and Bighouse (in distance): note embankments flanking river and meadowland at left with grass cut for hay or silage. 1994.

BIGHOUSE AFTER 1830

Bighouse was run as a sheep farm after it was sold by Colin Campbell Mackay and his mother, Louisa, in 1830. The Marquis of Stafford (from 1833 the Duke of Sutherland), together with the 2nd Duke, made 'great improvement[s]' in Strath Halladale. By 1840:

> a new chanel [*sic*], at a vast expense, has been dug for water and a high and strong embankment raised to confine the river from flooding and extensive meadow of very excellent pasture, thought to be worth upward of £200 per annum (*NSA* 1840. xv. 19) [Fig. 7.29].

These embankments were long anticipated, for in 1795 Sir John Sinclair of Ulbster, that great agricultural 'improver', wrote:

> On the estate of Bighouse there is a meadow of immense extent, the value of which would be greatly augmented by carrying the river Halladale in a straight line to the sea, and embanking it for greater security. This is an improvement which it is to be hoped, the present intelligent possessor of that property [Lieut. Col. Mackay], when peace is restored, will soon have it in his power to attend to and to execute. (Sinclair 1795. 153).

The banks built to contain floods are still clearly visible, and still help to 'confine the river'. A chain ferry over the Halladale River, similar to that at Loch Hope, was installed as part of the development of the road along the north coast, constructed by the Marquis in 1830, immediately after he had purchased the Bighouse and neighbouring Reay estates.

The Bighouse estate was sold by the 4th Duke of Sutherland in 1919, after when it served, under various owners, as a shooting lodge. That role has ceased, and it is now the home of a family with local connections.

Louisa and George Mackay's large family scattered in Scotland and overseas, some of them naming their new homes Bighouse. One member established a farm in Australia, also Bighouse. A descendant of this family, Louisa's great, great, great, grand-daughter, has returned to Sutherland from Australia, making her home at Strathy, not far from Bighouse.

Acknowledgement

I am most grateful to Mr & Mrs Wares for welcoming me at Bighouse Lodge, for their help and interest and for lending architectural drawings of the Lodge. These were prepared for publication by Mrs. Louise Crossman. The Leet-Rodgers Partnership, Thurso, loaned drawings of The Barracks, prepared for publication by Mr. Geoff Leet. Dr. Malcolm Bangor-Jones has generously shared material researched for his chapter in this volume. I have also received help from Mr Elliot and Mrs Pat Rudie, Bettyhill; Miss Primrose Richards, Strathy; Miss Margaret Wilkes and the staff of the Map Department, National Library of Scotland; Mr Robert Steward, Archivist, Highland Regional Archives, Inverness; Ms. Jane Brown, Scottish Record Office.
Figures 7.3 & 7.3A, Roy's *Military Survey of Scotland*, are reproduced by permission of The British Library; Lord Strathnaver has kindly given permission to reproduce Figure 7.7 from

the Sutherland Papers (National Library of Scotland, Dept. 313/3590/24); and Brodies WS, permission to reproduce Figure 7.27 (SRO RHP1221). Figures 7.13 & 7.14 are reproduced by courtesy of Historic Scotland and are Crown Copyright. Mr Les Hester, Forres, helped with photography.

Notes

1. *Pers. Comm.* Mrs. Kathleen Wares. Miss Priscilla Richards, Louisa Mackay's great, great, great, grand-daughter, recalls her grandmother in Australia emphasising 'Begus' as the correct pronunciation of the Sutherland family home.
2. Cruives were fish traps made of osiers and timber, staked in the river to catch salmon.
3. Pers. comm. Mrs. Wares.
4. National Library of Scotland: Dept.313/3590/24, 27, 28.
5. Neighbouring Sandside House, Reay, Caithness, appears on Roy's *Military Survey of Scotland*. This seems to be the house dated 1751, suggesting an approximate date of the Roy survey of the area to 1751-5.
6. A picture postcard of Bighouse (posted 1908) reveals porch but no west wing: Richards, C. (ed) *Postcards from Caithness.* 1992. 136.
7. *Ashlar*, finely tooled and squared facing stone. *Chamfer*, an arris or angle splay.
8. *Scale and platt stair*, a staircase with landings and straight flights of stone stairs, bedded into a central masonry spine wall.
9. The Barracks resembles Ardmaddy Castle, Argyll, as re-built in 1737 by Colin Campbell of Carwhin, Chamberlain of the Breadalbane Estate. Colin Campbell of Glenure, who married Janet Mackay of Bighouse in 1749, held land in feu from this estate. The likeness between contemporary Ardmaddy and The Barracks suggests that the Campbells, both of Glenure and Ardmaddy, and the Mackays of Bighouse, were acquaintances some years before formal links were established by marriage, perhaps through cattle-dealing as suggested by Bangor-Jones (this volume). I am grateful to Ian Fisher, Royal Commission on the Ancient and Historical Monuments of Scotland, for drawing my attention to Ardmaddy. (See RCAHMS *Argyll* 1975. ii. 248-52.)
10. *Pers. comm.* Geoff & Lyndall Leet, Thurso.
11. This tenant is the only one entitled 'Mr.' in the rent roll.

References

Bardgett, F. 'Deasphollag', in *Am Bratach*. No. 16. February 1993.
Bardgett, F. *North Coast Parish: Strathy and Halladale.* 1990.
Beaton, E. 'The Sandside Kiln Barn, Caithness', in *Caithness Field Club Bulletin.* Spring 1988.
Blaeu, J. *Atlas Novus.* 1654.
Cordiner, C. *Antiquities and Scenery of the North of Scotland.* 1780.
FES : Fasti Ecclesae Scotticanae. vol vii. 1928.
Gifford, J. *The Buildings of Scotland, The Highlands and Islands.* 1992.
Henderson, D.M. & Dickson, J. H. (eds) *A Naturalist in the Highlands:James Robertson His Life and Travels in Scotland.* 1994.
MacFarlane's Geographical Collections. vol i. 1906.
Mackay, A. *Book of Mackay.* 1906.
Mackay, R. *History of the House and Clan of Mackay.* 1829.
NSA : New Statistical Account. vol xv. 1840-45.
Omand, D. (ed) *The Sutherland Book.* 1982.
OGS : Ordnance Gazetteer of Scotland. vol vi. 1885.
OPS : Origines Parochiales Scotae. pt ii. 1855.
Owen, W. *Understanding Highland Place-Names.* nd.
Pennant, T. *A Tour in Scotland.* 3rd ed. 1774.
Pococke's Tours in Scotland, 1747, 1750, 1760. Scottish History Society, 1887.
Roy's *Military Survey of Scotland.* ca 1747-55.
Sinclair, Sir J. *General View of the Agriculture of the Northern Counties and Islands.* 1795.
Thomson, J. *Map of Scotland* (Sutherland sheet). 1823.

THE EXCAVATION OF A
TURF LONG-HOUSE
AT LAIRG, SUTHERLAND

R.P.J. McCullagh

INTRODUCTION

This paper concentrates on just one aspect of a large-scale archaeological project funded jointly by Highland Regional Council and Historic Scotland and centred upon a series of excavations near Lairg, Sutherland [Fig. 8.1]. The project was instigated by a proposal to upgrade, and in places re-route the road between Bonar Bridge and Lairg as part of a general programme of infrastructure improvements throughout the then Highland Region. As part of the preparations for these works, archaeologists were consulted on the best means of mitigating the impact of road construction. Surveys by the Ordnance Survey and the Royal Commission for Ancient and Historical Monuments of Scotland had listed a substantial number of individual and groups of archaeological sites, but their precise nature extent and significance was poorly understood. The road planners (the then Highland Regional Roads Authority) had defined a zone of interest within which the improvements would be contained, and it was within that zone that the Lairg Project has subsequently operated. The zone of interest comprises of a corridor of land some 3.5 km long by 0.3 km wide, centred on the existing roadline. Within that corridor a large scale programme of archaeological survey, prospection and excavation has sought to mitigate against the anticipated loss of archaeological information. From a very large and diverse assemblage of recorded monuments, well-preserved examples of potentially threatened monument types were then excavated under optimum conditions and, wherever possible, well in advance of the actual construction of the new road.

In 1988, in the course of the survey, some 32 rectangular structures were identified. Trial trenching in 1989 provided some 20 profiles through randomly selected examples and as part of the analysis programme three radiocarbon dates from rectangular buildings or associated monuments were obtained. In 1991, Sites 1103 and 1099 were fully excavated [Fig. 8.2] and in 1994 a much smaller scale investigation took place within Site 966, a similar sized structure some 600 m to the south of Site 1103. In 1996, the site of House 1103 became a quarry for road stone. The quarry eventually consumed both the whole site and some of the adjacent field boundaries, and from the new road no hint of this former dwelling is visible. In the excavation report,[1] the site nomenclature has been simplified and Site 1103 is referred to as House 9. It is so referenced in this text.

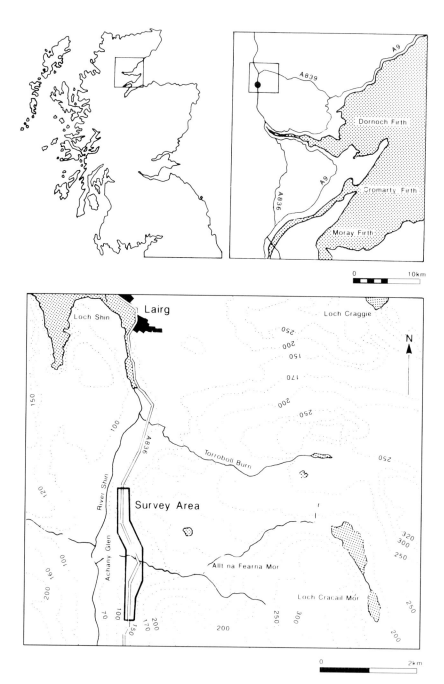

Fig. 8.1   The survey transect encompassed all possible routes for the upgraded road.

House 9 was initially interpreted as an example of the class of housing that typified pre-Clearance settlement in the Highlands. As work progressed, it became apparent that the site contained far more archaeological information than is ever likely to be gleaned from a prehistoric structure, yet it represented a form of architecture and a way of life that remain largely unnoticed within Scottish archaeological literature. In turn, this wealth of detail has drawn attention to some inadequacies in our techniques and to the continuing lack of familiarity with the potential benefits from joint historical and archaeological research. It is also hoped that House 9 may demonstrate that those untapped benefits can accrue mutually to archaeologists and historians.

THE EXCAVATIONS

Aims & Objectives

The excavation's aims were to:
* establish the form of each component in the structural sequence
* establish the duration and date of occupation
* acquire evidence for the relationship of the structure to its contemporary local landscape
* establish the function or functions of the site throughout its period of use
* place these diverse fragments of the site history within a dynamic model of social and landscape change.

Before excavation began, a radiocarbon date obtained in 1989 provided a good indication of the approximate cultural horizon from which the structure originated, and from the outset the site was assumed to represent the type of dwelling that had preceded the revolutions in Highland estate management in the early 19th century. One of the main attractions of such a site was that it might offer up sediments, ecofacts and artifacts whose origin, function and mode of deposition were in some way referenced within the ethno-historical literature of that period. Such monuments hold the potential to elucidate many of the interpretational problems that beset or lie hidden within the investigations of much older sites.

A detailed account of the excavation methods and results can be found within the project archive and an extended summary is included within the main project report. This paper highlights those findings, and those inferences that have a particular relevance to studies in post-medieval northern Scotland.

Location

The site was first recorded in 1988, in the course of a topographic survey along the prospective route of the upgraded A836, 1.5 km south of Lairg

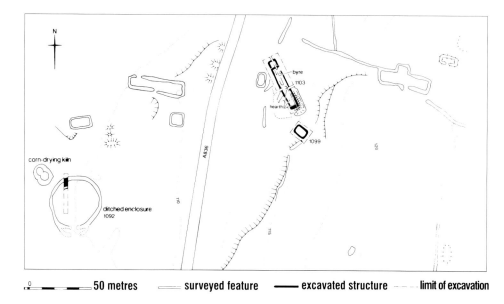

N

byre
1103

hearth

1099

120

corn-drying kiln

A836

110

ditched enclosure
1092

115

0
50 metres   ⟺ surveyed feature   —— excavated structure   ---- limit of excavation

Fig. 8.2   Surveyed sites and excavation areas at the northern end of the survey.

station [Fig. 8.1]. This rectangular monument (the original survey code was Site 1103) is located on a short terrace (113 m OD) within a generally steep (gradient: 19%) slope [Fig. 8.2]. The site lies towards the northern end of the surveyed area and at the northern end of a large enclosed area of improved pasture (30 ha). All the extant maps refer to the general area as Achumor, Achimor or, as in the current Ordnance Survey maps, Achiemore. It is overlooked from the east by Cnoc an Achaidh Mhoir. These various names can be translated as 'big field', and it is not improbable that this name may be contemporary with and derive from the establishment of the large enclosure. Documentary evidence suggests that this enclosure was in existence from at least the late 18th century.

A second rectangular structure (survey code: Site 1069) lies 8 m back up the slope (at a height of 120 m OD), and a third such site (survey code: Site 1082) is situated some 40 m downslope (110 m OD). Although not identical, these three sites appear to be so similar that it is reasonable to presume their approximate contemporaneity. Numerous other field monuments were recorded in the immediate vicinity, including field banks, cairns, smaller rectangular structures (?barns) and a certain grain drying kiln, seemingly incorporated into a small turf building. The large circular enclosure (Site 1092 and entitled Ditched Enclosure 1 in the published report) was identified by excavation as a 1st millennium BC ditched and palisaded site. It may also have functioned as an enclosure (eg a kale yard) within the much later complex of buildings. Limited excavation on the interior in 1989 revealed marks in the subsoil surface which may have resulted from recent tillage.

All of the rectangular buildings, and most of the smaller monuments, were examined in 1989 as part of a more detailed analysis of the field monuments in this area. The results of this work point to a building tradition based on the use of turf as the main building material. A small assemblage of artifacts pointed towards a late, perhaps 19th century site-use.

A series of radiocarbon dates were obtained in 1989 from charcoal extracted from wall or sub-wall soil samples (see 'Chronology', below). The resulting medieval or early post-medieval dates therefore do not date construction, they merely provide a *terminus post quem* for the inclusion of the charcoal into the turf.

In 1991, House 9 was selected for excavation. This site was chosen as it appeared to be typical of its class of monument and also to be relatively well-preserved. It was selected in preference to the more substantial site, 1082, because the latter appeared to suffer from impeded drainage that could reasonably be assumed to affect the progress of excavation and to cause problems at the interpretation and analysis stages. From the outset it was assumed that the site represented a class of dwelling that would have been typical for the majority of the rural population until the late 18th or early 19th centuries. Fairly detailed descriptions[2] and illustrations[3] of such structures abound, characterised by a remarkable degree of conformity through time. This is illustrated by the similarities between the house in the Lairg area described by Bishop Pococke in 1760,[4] and Hugh Miller's description of his aunt's home at Gruids, which he visited in the 1820s.[5] The common appearance of such dwellings, and the apparent and almost uniform use of space internally, indicates an architectural tradition deeply embedded within the social and cultural structure of the native population. The excavation of House 9 at Lairg thus offered the prospect of excavating the remains of independently identifiable activities contained within a readily reconstructed architecture.

Stratigraphy & House Layout

The archaeological remains of House 9 were generally well-preserved and the recorded relationships suggest that the building process was more of a complex continuum than a single event or series of separate events. The interpretation combines the evidence from field work with a suite of insights drawn from other data, especially various soil analyses.

The structure consists of four composite soil and stone walls forming an elongated rectangular building aligned across the contours. The upslope, short wall measured 4.5 m wide externally [Fig. 8.3]. This gable wall was almost entirely built in dry stone masonry and was keyed-in at its base to the more sparse stonework of the long walls. The inner face of the gable retained small fragments of clay bonding or cladding. The basal layers of both long walls, but especially the downslope half of the northern wall, contained stone; but the uppermost elements throughout were soil. It is probable that the source of these wall sediments was cut turves that have decayed in situ. Soil analyses (particle size analysis) indicated that the turf originated from a single location, although this was not in the immediate vicinity of House 9. The maximum length of the building was uncertain but it had clearly undergone a complex series of re-builds and various vestigial wall lines for the downslope gable were identified up to a maximum of 24 m downslope from the upper gable. The building narrows slightly towards its lower end and one gable position measured just 3 m wide externally. No substantial internal partition walls were identified. The total declination of the ground surface over the length of this structure was 1.7 m.

Prior to excavation, the low broad profile of the walls gave no clue to their original width. In the excavation, the long walls revealed in each case a series of compacted deposits and occasional large blocks of stone forming an axial ridge. These were initially interpreted as the remains from a series of rebuilding phases. Away from the centre of the ridge, the layers became indistinct and it was assumed that each wall had in time slumped to form the flattened profile observed in the initial survey. In several places, sections cut through this ridge revealed a basal layer that was clearly narrower than the overlying vestiges of the wall fabric. Soil thin-sections of the putative wall layers indicated that in fact the lowest layer was probably a compacted vestige of the original turf surviving in situ. The overlying wall material was also shown to be turf, but containing mineral components that were similar but not identical to the subsoil on site. It is probable, therefore, that these were obtained from ground in the vicinity of the building but the site itself was not stripped of turf prior to construction. To judge from the width of the *in situ* turf layer recorded in excavation, the wall base varied from 0.8 m and 1.0 m wide, although, in one transect profile, the width of this preserved topsoil measured 1.2 m wide.

Along the inner face of the northern wall, especially along the downslope half, a series of small post- and stake-sockets were identified. These are interpreted as the sockets for structural timbers, though presumably not crucks, and for smaller timbers such as the sails in wattle panels. Two of the larger holes had been cut at the same location in sequence and must indicate a phase of full or partial re-building, refurbishment or repair. Only one certain post-hole was found on the southern long wall and none on either gable walls. Both long walls contained a few large stone blocks which could have served as pads for crucks (an interpretation suggested by Dr Bruce Walker), but no regular setting was apparent. In both long walls there was a slight but distinct distortion northwards giving a slightly bowed ground plan, as if the whole building had been pulled slightly off its true line. The apparent stronger or more elaborate build of the north wall may either reflect extra stresses that were anticipated in the design or were extra elements made

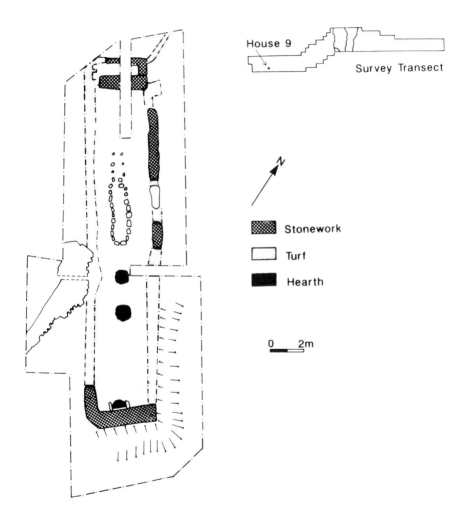

House 9

Survey Transect

Stonework

Turf

Hearth

0   2m

Fig. 8.3   Simplified plan of House 9:   dark stipples = stonework
                                             grey stipples = turf

179

necessary by the outcome of those stresses. The source of these unequal stresses could possibly be either the tethering of livestock against the inner face of the north wall, or unequal moisture within the fabric of the opposing walls resulting from differential exposure to weather conditions. These may not be the only explanations, but whether or not either alternative is credible in this case, it should be noted that the uneven and often flimsy nature of some structures was a frequent object of comment by travellers in northern Scotland in the 18th century.[6]

Access to the building was by way of a well-laid stone path leading to the entrance on the south side, some 7 m from the upper gable. Inside, the building was split into two unequal parts, separated by a slight scarp. The upper half was dominated by a substantial hearth set almost at the centre and some 4.5 m downslope from the upslope gable. The hearth survived as a few fire-cracked slabs, small deposits of ash and a large, dished area of intensely reddened sub-soil. In the lower half, a stone-lined gully or drain had been laid parallel to, but slightly off from the central long axis of the building and stopped short of the lower gable wall. Post-excavation analyses, such as soil phosphates, pollen and fungal spores, failed to identify any evidence of a specific function but, at some risk of circularity, this feature was interpreted as a byre drain and provided the primary evidence for the use of the lower half of the building as stalling for cattle.

External drainage also appears to have been of importance. Around the upslope gable, on its northern and eastern sides, a broad gully had been cut. During excavation the gully served to drain away surface water from the marked lynchet directly upslope from the building and it is likely that this was its original function. A second external drain had been laid beneath the stone pathway leading to the doorway in the southern wall.

Prior to excavation, the low broad walls gave no clue to the original wall width. In sections cut through the long walls in several places, the basal sediment was clearly narrower than the overlying and supposedly slumped wall fabric. Particle size analysis has demonstrated that this sediment probably represents the topsoil on to which the turf walls were directly laid. To judge from the width of this sediment, recorded in excavation, the wall base varied from 0.8 m and 1.0 m wide, although in one transect profile the width of this preserved topsoil measured 1.2 m wide.

In cross-section the interior surface of the structure was slightly concave, though this was less apparent in the longitudinal section. At several places where there were large stones at the base of the wall, for instance at the base of the upslope gable, a slight scarp had formed, accentuating the dished or hollowed profile of the interior. These features were only revealed with the excavation and removal of a series of highly variable sediments that formed a sparse and uneven capping to the irregular and clearly worn surface of the glacial till. The removal of these sediments had revealed the central hearth in the upslope half of the building and on this basis those overlying the hearth, at least, were interpreted as originating in some later phase of use.

Traditionally, such sediments would be interpreted as 'occupation deposits' and treated by the more sophisticated archaeologist with great reverence; these layers might possibly retain direct evidence of the every-day use of space within the structure. A less optimistic explanation could be proposed, that these sediments merely represented the residue of the collapsed building fabric. In fact neither explanation is supported by the evidence drawn form soil analysis. In thin-section, the vestigial wall fabric was shown to contain very little organic material, and low phosphate readings emphasise this trait. In contrast, the internal sediments contained relatively high levels of phosphate and the thin-sections contained abundant burnt and unburnt peat fragments. One further trait was noted in soil thin-section of some of the interior sediments, these contained microscopic slivers which were identified as minute fragments of some form of calcareous rock. None of the constituents of the local till was calcareous and the nearest source of such material is almost 20 km away. Perhaps the best explanation for the presence of such material on site was that it was derived from a lime wash or render applied to the wall surfaces. Although not proven, this explanation would then imply that the slivers and fragments became detached from the rendered surface as it decayed. If correct, then the internal sediments formed when the walls were still standing but in the initial stages of neglect.

Thus organic sediments, rich in fuel residues, had accumulated after the main hearth had ceased to function and when the wall surfaces were weathering. Far from describing an 'habitation' use of the building, these so-called occupation deposits can be best provenanced to a period of neglect, when refuse was accumulating in the building. Perhaps the best analogy is one that is a familiar sight in the Highlands, a dwelling that has passed from human habitation to a shelter for sheep.

One further corollary of this interpretation is that the marked dissimilarities between wall fabric and the internal sediments probably means that in situ slumping of the wall mass did not occur and instead all but the basal vestiges of wall fabric were removed after abandonment. It is worth noting that no trace of burning of the building fabric, so often mentioned in accounts of evictions, was identified in this case.

Prior to this abandonment, it seems likely that the building was temporally re-occupied despite its now poor condition. Two sets of hearth deposits, one set located almost centrally in the building (ie downslope from the abandoned primary hearth) and the second set lying upon a stone hearth built into the upslope gable, had been superimposed on the internal sediments and point very definitely to a late phase of re-use of the building. Downslope from this secondary, central hearth, one particular deposit was marked by such an abrupt downslope boundary that the excavator interpreted it as abutting a, now, otherwise undetectable screen or partition wall. This putative screen, which would have lain over the primary deposits within the upper end of the axial drain, indicates that this late occupation was not without some sophistication but partition walls seem to have been features of even the meanest hovels.[7]

DATING EVIDENCE & CHRONOLOGY

Three sources of dating evidence are available for House 9:[8] radiocarbon dating, artifacts and historical references and analogies.

Radiocarbon Dates

A single radiocarbon date was obtained from a sample of the wall fabric from House 9:[8]

GU-2848 350 ± 50 BP
    AD 1450 - AD 1595 (70%)
    AD 1445 - AD 1660 (96.17%).

Two other sites in the vicinity of House 9 have also produced dates:

GU-2856 430 ± 50 BP
    AD 1420 - AD 1475 (68.71%)
    AD 1405 - AD 1660 (95.9%).

GU-2868 890 ± 50 BP
    AD 1025 - AD 1120 (69.27%)
    AD 1015 - AD 1245 (95.52%).

One date (GU-2856) was derived from charcoal within a buried soil preserved beneath a putative turf bank or field wall. This turf bank appears to be part of a system that integrates with use of the rectangular structures. The second date (GU-2868) also comes from a buried soil profile.

Although no simple explanation can be given for this range of dates – partly because they do not result from full excavation – it is probable that they represent a series of earlier phases of site use. As such, these dates only serve as exemplars; they neither represent all periods of use nor describe the frequency of that use. Only a more ambitious dating programme from extensive archaeological excavation could resolve this issue. Nevertheless, these dates alone should serve to raise expectations of a medieval rural archaeology from which sites such as House 9 have evolved.

Artifacts: Pottery, Glass & Metalwork

The two main components of the artefactual assemblage were glazed pottery[9] and glass.[10] Five types of pottery fabric were identified: red earthenware, stoneware, white earthenware, bone china and coarse ware. In most cases the type of pottery was not chronologically distinctive but amongst the white earthenwares two distinctive pottery types were noted: Pearlware (3 vessels) and Pratt-type ware (6 vessels). The former probably date from the first half of the 19th century; the Pratt-type pottery was common between 1800 and 1820. There was no unequivocal evidence of 20th century manufacture.

From a total of 229 sherds, 45 vessels were recognised. However, almost all of these were recovered from topsoil. Only 8 vessels, represented by 8 sherds, were found within contexts that were unequivocally located in the sequence of construction or use. However, many of these contexts also contained sherds of vessels distributed throughout the stratigraphy. There are thus only 2 sherds (from Vessels 7 and 30) that are from unequivocally undisturbed contexts, and these both represent chronologically undiagnostic forms. Of the 12 vessels that were represented by more than one sherd, none came uniquely from construction or use deposits; all were represented by at least one sherd found within topsoil.

All of the glass assemblage was of a domestic nature with the majority of the sherds being bottle glass, mostly from wine bottles. Seven sherds were Crown glass, two of which were retrieved from later use or abandonment sediments and may indicate the one time presence of glazed furniture (such as cabinets) or windows within the building or within the vicinity. Examples of both the early and late 19th-century types were found throughout the stratigraphy:

GLASS
With Percentage of Each Type Retrieved from Topsoil (%)

18th C	Early 19th C	Mid 19th C	Late 19th C	Unknown	Total
1	37	32	7	6	85
0%	84%	81%	89%	0%	76%

The earliest piece was a folded foot from a wine glass, attributed loosely to the second half of the 18th century. It was discovered when the late, gable-end hearth was being dismantled and had been incorporated within the packing material behind the stone fire-back and the gable masonry.

A small assemblage of metallic items was also excavated from House 9. Most of this material was either uninformative slag or metal fragments. The only pieces worthy of comment were fragments of a large cast iron cauldron, which came from a late deposit on the interior of the building. This context was not easily interpretable but probably relates to the building after domestic use had ceased. It is extremely unlikely that this object decayed *in situ* and ought to be seen as evidence, along with much of the artifact assemblage, of dumping of refuse into the remains of House 9. Burt records an example of this practice amongst abandoned dwellings on the edge of towns.[11] The source of such material cannot be identified, but was presumably within the immediate area.

It is clear from the foregoing descriptions that most of this assemblage can be assigned to a period that largely spans the 19th century. Most of the assemblage was recovered from sediments that have been shown, by soil thin-section analysis, to have accumulated when the building was already in an advanced state of decay. It is therefore unlikely that much of the assemblage relates to the actual habitational use of the building. The correlation of the date of manufacture to date of deposition is also probably erroneous; there would have been a considerable time lag between manufacture, acquisition and disposal of artifacts. At best then, the artifacts indicate that the building was probably not occupied much before the late 18th century and that it had reached an advanced state of decay by half way through the 19th century.

Ecofacts: Charcoal & Grain

The source of the dated charcoal has already been discussed (see above). The charcoal from the interior deposits is generally less common than on prehistoric sites excavated at Lairg. Two locations were identified which had meaningful levels of charcoal within the deposits. One was the early, central hearth with the charcoal coming from the ash layer overlying the slabs. The second location was in the deposits that accumulated around the upslope end of the drain. While the former may have survived because the hearth was deliberately buried, it is possible that the latter deposits escaped much of the force of the internal floor erosion by being at the boundary between the byre and the domestic spaces.

Charred grain, identified as six-row hulled barley, oats and carbonised hazelnut shells were present as very minor components of internal sediments.[12] While these can be presumed to reflect aspects of local produce and diet, the assemblage is too small for any deeper analysis. The general lack of such materials on the site may reflect the nature of cereal processing, for example the use of a communal corn-drying kiln, the roasting of grain on the sheaf,[13] and the poor preservation of contemporary house-hold waste matter on the internal floor surface.

Historical and Archive Information

A wide range of sources have been searched for evidence of land tenure, land use and estate management. These include title deeds, legal processes, maps and estate plans, sheriff court and Court of Session records, Hearth Tax Records, Teind Commissioners Records and published works.[14]

There are place-name references to such early Christian sites as the island on Loch Shin (recorded as 'Ellan Murie', by Sir Robert Gordon in 1630 or 'Ylen Mulruy' in Pont's manuscript map of ca 1590 and probably synonymous with the chapel site of St. Maelrubha;[15] also to possible Pictish locations (eg Pitarxie) and to Norse settlement (Torroble, Arscaig). There are no secure references to the general locality of House 9 until the 16th century, when rental payments in kind are recorded from Lairg, Pitarxie and Shinness.[16] In 1738, the tenancy of Achiemor was separated from the farm of

Achinduich,[17] and for the next 100 years there is a fairly complete record of tenants for Achiemor:

1738	Robert Gordon[18]
1756	Robert Gray, tacksman farmer and drover[19]
1765	Robert Murray, sub-tenant to Robert Gray[20]
1776	Robert Murray in full tenancy after Gray's bankruptcy[21]
1787	after the death of Robert Murray, his widow, Katherine and son, Alexander were in possession[22]
1793	Alexander and his ?brother, John, as tenants with their mother living possibly as a cottar[23]
1807	Alexander and John's lease expired and they were removed, their mother retained her dwelling[24]
1808	Katherine evicted[25]
1812	Alexander MacDonald resident in Achumor [*sic*], working as servant or labourer on the Lairg Sheep Farm
1815	Alexander MacDonald may have moved to Achinduich, taking work as a shepherd[26]
1822	Achiemor in the possession of weavers[27]
1824	Achiemor again recorded as inhabited by weavers[28]

On the basis of these documents it seems improbable that extensive arable farming, which even throughout the previous hundred years probably had played only a secondary role to the cattle trade, continued at Achiemor after 1807. Maps of 1790[29] shows two clusters of buildings. The first perhaps comprised one small and six larger buildings clustered around a small enclosure. The second group lies to the south towards close to what appears to be a major march dyke. Abutting this dyke on its northern side is an enclosed area marked as 'arable lands'. It is possible that the latter area correlated to an area of broad rig recorded in aerial photography in 1991 and mapped on the ground in 1994.

INTERPRETATION

The Archaeological Evidence

The archaeological reconstruction of House 9 depends on the interpretation of and extrapolation from three sets of data. The physical evidence from excavation has recovered the form of the surviving elements of the building and has identified various elements from a putative structural sequence. Post-excavation analyses, particularly of the artifact evidence and soil analysis, have provided evidence of the source material for the sediments, mode of deposition, post-depositional processes and the nature of, and in the case of the artifacts the probable chronology for, the integration of exotic inclusions within those sediments. Finally the historical and ethnographic records have provided a cultural framework that offers the rare possibility of amplifying the terse archaeological evidence. Although the result may seem credible, care must be taken to avoid confusing proximity with proof. The end result will only be an interpretation.

The excavated remains of House 9 show it to have been a narrow (between 4 m and than 3 m wide internally) elongate structure (maximum external length 24 m). Built slightly skew to the slope, there was nevertheless a fall in floor level of 1.7 m. The walls of the building were certainly made of turfs, obtained from somewhere close to but not actually in the immediate vicinity. The slight evidence for a supporting sub-structure, to what was in effect a turf cladding, could not have been interpreted as the vestigial remains of cruck-supported creel- or hurdle-work had the ethnographic evidence not been so persuasive. The excavators were obliged to interpret the site as a multi-period entity: there was good evidence for multiple positions for the downslope gable, the central hearth had become buried, the hearth location shifted and the axial drain was replaced. Coupled to this, the degree of internal erosion clearly evident throughout, but especially at the upslope end, indicated that occupation had been of considerable duration. This erosion had clearly been anticipated by the occupants, in part at least, as is shown by the provision of a laid-stone pavement approaching the doorway.

In excavation it was clear that this evidence for erosion was contradicted by the accumulated internal sediments. This contradiction was resolved by the presumption that sediment formation only occurred where and when erosion was diminished. One area where accumulation of sediments could have occurred in the course of normal occupation would have been at the margins and particularly if these were enforced by physical barriers. As noted above, one such area was detected at the point where the upslope zone, centred on the hearth and the downslope zone, centred on the axial drain, merged. Here, the form of the sediments were suggestive of a partition and the localised high charcoal content in the sediment emphasised the reduced level of erosion.

This late partition only emphasised a demarcation between the upper and lower portions of the building that appeared to have been part of the original design. The identification of the hearth with human habitation and the central drain with accommodation for livestock would have been archaeologically reasonable. The all pervasive ethnographically recorded model for such structures, with cattle arranged with the hind-quarters over the drain and the heads tethered to the wall, with the human occupants' eating and sleeping arrangements focused on a central floor hearth, corresponded well to the excavated physical remains.

One fragment of evidence intimates the rigidity and permanence of this architectural tradition. The external drain, which was discovered beneath the upper stones of the pavement, was laid with the effect of preventing water getting to the threshold. This small feature hints at a clear understanding of how the building would perform, how use would effect its fabric and how a certain standard of accommodation would be achieved and maintained.

Initially, the excavators interpreted the remains of the walls and gables as indicating a clear progression from a wholly turf construction to one of stone and turf. Analysis of the constituents of these sediments has shown the primary turf phase to be no more than the native turf of the site upon which the building was erected. It would thus seem implausible that the massive clay-bonded, stone upslope gable was a secondary feature, although the hearth attached to its inner face was clearly a very late addition. Such stone gables are not generally considered to have come into vogue prior to the mid-19th century[30] and its presence here clearly conflicts with most of the other date of use evidence.

In addition to the use of architectural typology as a basis for chronology, the possibilities of using radiocarbon dating and artifact typology were investigated. The radiocarbon result acquired in 1989 cannot be attributed to either the construction or use of the building; instead it provides a *terminus post quem* for the inclusion of the charcoal into the topsoil that eventually was transported onto the site as the turf for the walls. The artifact evidence, with its inherent dichotomy between the 'known' date of manufacture and its unknown date of disposal, only offers broad and crude chronological boundaries. The glass and the ceramic evidence point to the use of the building, in its later phases, not earlier than the mid-19th century. Even though the pottery contained types whose date of manufacture can be relatively precisely dated to the first quarter of the 19th century, it is virtually certain that the discard date lies somewhere within the second half of that century. Further caution must be exercised because it is by no means certain that the period which witnessed the accumulation of sediments within the building and the accumulation of broken glassware and pottery coincided with the main phase of site use. The presence of micro-flakes of what was probably an internal wall render within the internal deposits may indicate that the building was no longer being maintained.[31] The longevity of the occupation is further stressed by the stratigraphically late insertion of the gable end hearth.

Integrating the Historical Evidence

In contrast to the bulk of the archaeological evidence, but perhaps in agreement with the inference drawn from the extent of erosion, the historical evidence points to a primary phase of use being prior to 1807. Significantly, subsequent records for Achiemor (census, muster records etc) do identify non-agricultural tenants in the subsequent decades, although research has not yet penetrated the record later than 1830.

Not only does this structure well illustrate the difficulty of keying in the evidence for duration of use of the site with its dating evidence, but it also adds depth to the raw historical data. From 1765 until 1776, Robert Gray is recorded as the sub-tenant at Achumor [*sic*]. After 1776, he was paying rent directly to the estate and after his death in 1787, the possession passed to his sons until they were removed in 1807. Their mother was evicted in the following year. While it would be foolhardy to claim that House 9, or indeed any of the upstanding group of sites can be related to known tenants, this record does identify several points in time when events identified in the archaeological record (such as the shift in the hearth location) might have occurred. Given the long duration of the Murrays' combined tenancy (42 years) both the extant historical record and the archaeological record are shown to be woefully ill-equipped when attempting to reconstruct past ways of life. Miller's description of a house interior,[32] seen in the 1820s, serves to underline the weakness of the link between archaeological sediments and primary use:

> We entered the cottage and plunging down two feet or so, found ourselves upon the dunghill of the establishment, which in this part of the country usually occupied an ante-chamber, which corresponded to that occupied by cattle a few years earlier.

These quasi-ethnographic records drawn from the literature of travellers and analysts journeying in the Highlands in the 17th, 18th and 19th centuries have not been scrutinised by archaeologists. The tendency and temptation is to extract odd anecdotes as and when they fit the needs of the archaeological text. One reason for this approach is that systematic synthesis has not been undertaken and there is frequently no means of gauging variation in time and space. For instance, I.F. Grant, when discussing the over-wintering of cattle, observes that there was an 'old standing variation in the methods of housing cattle between the east and west'.[33] It is also difficult to assess the effect of economic and political changes. Did the heavy recruitment by Scottish, Scandinavian, French and latterly the British armies distort the Highland pattern(s) of land-use and architecture? Indeed was there a uniform pattern within the diverse landmass of the Highlands? Did political boundaries such as that between the Gordon earldom of Sutherland and its neighbours, or more subtle cultural boundaries such as that between the Protestant Mackays of Strathnaver (with their centuries old links to the Netherlands) and their various Catholic and later Jacobite neighbours,[33] impinge upon the traditions of land-use and settlement of the rural population? The absence of a systematic archaeological approach to such data must clearly urge circumspection in their use.

The historical context of the occupation of House 9 and of the use of the Achiemor enclosure coincides with what is portrayed as the final death-throes of the old order. The later half of the 18th century witnessed the protracted assault on the political and cultural bastions of Gaeldom, with the transformations of the economy, landscape, language and religious observance, all coupled to the judicial suppression of dissent.[34] Devine has listed four sources:[35, 36]

1. *changes to the economic structure*: the increase in rentals which accompanied the transformation of land tenure to a process of competitive bidding for leases. This process is linked to the changing circumstances of the social elites, characterised by the ambitions of the

land owners to metamorphose themselves from chieftains to courtiers, from Gaelic leaders to absentee gentlemen;

2. *changes to the settlement structure*: the alteration of the location and form of settlements from the communal townships of the *baile* to the single tenant farms;
3. *changes to the social structure*: two changes can be identified: the replacement of the delicate and graduated hierarchies of the *baile* with more uniform and increasingly Protestant and English-speaking communities, and secondly the disappearance of the middle order gentry (manifested in the tacksmen) and their replacement by alien ranchers and sheep farmers;
4. *changes to the locations of population*: this was expressed in the evictions that presaged the establishment of the great sheep farms.

The actual impact of these changes are witnessed in the first hand accounts from the period. Donald Macleod's descriptions of the burnings and ruthless evictions in Strathnaver, orchestrated by Patrick Sellar, are still redolent with the sense of loss and betrayal.[37] (See Gouriévidis, this volume).

In the archaeology of prehistoric Scotland, substantial changes in the material culture have been identified – for example, that which occurs after 2000 BC, with changes in burial practice, pottery design, settlement form and both domestic and ritual architecture. How such transformations relate to or reflect broader social changes is a matter of continuing debate, but it would be difficult to imagine a more profound change than that claimed for Highland Scotland during the 18th century AD.

A broader chronological view reveals that quantitatively similar changes were occurring at regular intervals throughout the post-medieval history of the Highlands, from the internecine fighting of the 14th century up through the upheavals and dislocations that accompanied the political, religious and military turmoil of the 17th century.[38] Over the last few decades, archaeological investigations of the ethnographic record have attempted to test the nature of the link between social change and material culture. Typical of such exercises has been the examination of one of the key elements of the archaeological record: architecture. Numerous studies have sought to investigate the subtle role that buildings play as metaphors for the dwellers' perceptions of their various environments: the economic, the spiritual and the social.[39] If such analyses are sustainable, then perhaps it is in the archaeology of the dwelling that transformations in the social circumstances ought to be most readily observable.

Local Landscape Change:
Pollen, Soil & Documentary Analysis

The history of landscape change, and in particular vegetation change, has been a primary interest within the Lairg project. The results of two studies of the pollen record[40] indicate that by about AD 1000 the vegetation had acquired much of its modern character. At the Allt na Fearna quarry, it has been possible to chart the slow decline in the extent of arable land whilst at the same time the use and management of pasture was becoming an increasingly prominent characteristic. Indeed, it has been suggested that the use of fire, possibly in muirburn, was so extensive that charcoal dust actually reduced the natural drainage of some areas of tilled ground to a point where arable agriculture could no longer be sustained.

Analysis of the soils buried by the main head-dyke in Achiemor also emphasises the role of pasture management. The enclosure wall (speculatively dated to the late 18th century on the basis of documentary records)[41] sealed a deep soil. Within this soil profile several distinct superimposed ground surfaces were identified, which represented periods of stable turf interspersed with phases of soil accumulation. The turf layers contained layers of organic material, including burnt peat, which may represent midden deposited as a manure.[42] In addition, charcoal in the same turf layers indicate deliberate firing of the vegetation, presumably as a management technique. Within the accumulated soil profile, soil thin-section analysis identified discrete turfy sods, again possibly representing a manure. The source of this material cannot be identified with any certainty but it is not inconceivable that they represent discarded building or roofing reused as a manure or mulch. The effect of this application of reused midden, was to produce a soil that was far deeper than the pre-existing soil in the area and, to judge from the frequency of microscopic faeces, was also much more biologically active than the earlier soils. The purpose is less certain, but one explanation is that the pasture was being intensively managed.

Landscape management at a variety of scales is detectable during this period. A map dated 1809[43] records within the enclosure of Achiemor, discrete areas of 'arable land' and 'corn land'; and the map is sufficiently accurate for the area of 'arable land' to be located with some confidence. Today, this forms an area of poorly drained pasture within which it is still possible to detect a pattern of slight, 5 m wide rigs. Excavation in 1994 showed these rigs had been constructed upon very poorly drained ground. The soils were heavy, stony and gleyed, and today, do not seem capable of rewarding the obvious investment of labour that went into creating the rigs. Given the documented growth and clearance of the settlement within Achiemor, it seems reasonable that short-lived phases of tillage affected areas marginal to settlement. Similarly, areas of better pasture were created by burning off the scrub and rank heather and/or by manuring. These areas, like the so-called 'arable land', are unlikely to have been extensive,[44] and their use does not seem to have been sustained over long periods of time.

On a larger scale, pollen evidence from Lairg suggests that woodland regenerated during the second millennium AD in some areas.[45] Documentary sources (estate records[46] and the 1809 survey) suggest that managed woodland was well-established and it is likely that the systematic investment in woodland accounted for the observed expansion in the pollen record.

The image thus created is of a highly controlled landscape within which a subtle dynamism wrought gradual changes in the nature and scale of arable and of local woodland. The frequency of more striking changes is difficult to ascertain because detection of the results is unusual; however such changes can be occasionally recognised. Recent excavations at Gruids, on the opposite side of the River Shin from House 9, have identified evidence on one such event. In a long transect, through what is today rough pasture, archaeologists have identified the truncated remains of levelled narrow rigs. Charcoal, sealed within one of the preserved furrows, has been radiocarbon dated to approximately AD 1400.[47] This deliberate flattening of rigs may represent one stage in a cycle of land-use, but equally it could record a dramatic re-organisation of the nature of the agriculture at this locality and possibly of the society that it sustained. The single, biggest change in the landscape around House 9 was two-fold in nature and occurred as a result of the alterations to the nature of the pasture in the last 200 years. With the decline in cattle has come an expansion in bracken, and with the rise to dominance of sheep has come the removal of regenerating deciduous woodland. Over the same span of years, northern Scotland has witnessed the steady encroachment into the pasture land by plantation forestry. This expansion of industrial forestry can be traced in the pollen record and remains the single largest landscape change in the last 1000 years.

CONCLUSION

House 9 lies at a point in Highland history beyond which the key archaeological clues to understanding sediment formation process, itself the primary focus of archaeological excavation, rapidly become in-decipherable.[48] It seems likely that in all but the most remarkable locations, the active biology and chemistry of Highland soils tend to limit archaeological observations to an extremely crude level. Thus, it is in sites like House 9 that the current techniques have to be refined and new developments made if this temporal barrier is to be breached.

One avenue of research offered by such sites relies on the detailed analysis of ethnographic and historical records to define the nature and duration of the diverse elements of the mosaic of activities within the site and its landscape. In most cases, the historical researcher has sought other goals and the points of contact between the historical and archaeological research are few and ill-conceived. There are a limited number of excavated sites available for comparison with House 9[49] and clear architectural differences even exist amongst contemporary structures in the Lairg area.[50] These limitations, and the wide formal variance, point to deficits in current archaeological and architectural investigations. Here then is the challenge, but with the virtual ubiquity of such sites throughout the Highlands of Scotland, Wales and Ireland, here also is a fertile field of endeavour.

Acknowledgement

House 9 was excavated in 1991 by a team of field workers, directed by Mr Graham Wilson, on behalf of the Lairg Project. This work was funded by Historic Scotland. Mr Jerry O'Sullivan prepared the draft report of the results to which have been added reports on the historical record undertaken by Dr Malcolm Bangor-Jones, on the soil analyses undertaken by Dr Stephen Carter and Dr Tim Acott, on the artefactual analyses undertaken by Mr Gordon Turnbull and on the macroplant analyses undertaken by Dr Tim Holden. Pollen analyses have been undertaken by Dr Richard Tipping and as part of a doctoral research project undertaken by Ms Melanie Smith. Extracts from these various reports have contributed to a large bulk of this text. The historical documentary evidence, and particularly the references, result from the diligent researches of Dr Malcolm Bangor-Jones.

The author also must acknowledge the many points of information and advice received from visitors to site, particularly Dr Bruce Walker and Mr Ross Noble and from the many interested and knowledgeable people from the Lairg area. I would also wish to pay tribute to the Scottish Society for Northern Studies for organising the conference at Bettyhill. It was both educational and very enjoyable.

Notes

1. McCullagh, R.P.J. & Tipping, R. (eds) *The Lairg Project 1988 - 1996: The Evolution of an Archaeological Landscape in Highland Scotland*. 1998.
2. Burt, E. *Letters from a Gentleman in the North of Scotland to his Friend in London*. vol 1. 1756: 58.
3. Illustrated London News. *A Skye cottage*. 1853.
4. Kemp, D.W. (ed) *Tours in Scotland 1747, 1750 1760 by Richard Pococke*. 1887: 116.
5. Miller, H. *My Schools and Schoolmasters*. 1854: 89.
6. eg Burt *ibid*. vol 2: 80.
7. *ibid*. 80.
8. Dalland, M. 'The radiocarbon dating programme', in McCullagh, R.P.J. & Tipping, T. (eds). 1998.
9. Turnbull, G. 'Medieval and Post-Medieval pottery', in McCullagh, R.P.J. & Tipping, T. (eds). 1998.
10. Turnbull, G. 'Post-Medieval glass', in McCullagh, R.P.J. & Tipping, T. (eds). 1998.
11. Burt *ibid*. vol 2: 80, 29.
12. Holden, T. 'Charred plant remains', in McCullagh, R.P.J. & Tipping, T. (eds). 1998.
13. eg Burt *ibid*. vol 2: 80, 270.
14. Bangor-Jones, M. 'Documentary evidence for the development of the present day settlement', in McCullagh, R.P.J. & Tipping, T. (eds). 1998.
15. Innes, E. *Origines Parochiales Scotiae*. 1855.
16. NLS Dep. 175 rentals.
17. NLS Dep. 313/3134 Rectified State.
18. NLS Dep. 313/3134.
19. NLS Dep. 313/1721, SRO GD153/49.
20. SRO SC9/7/21, SC9/7/26.
21. SRO SC9/7/21.
22. SRO SC9/7/37.
23. NLS Dep.313/2123.
24. SRO SC9/7/55.
25. SRO SC9/&/55.
26. SRO SC9/86/11 & 20.
27. HRA Sutherland 2/1/13 p.25.
28. SRO SC9/87/96.
29. SRO RHP11600.
30. pers. comm. B. Walker.
31. Carter, S. 'Palaeopedology', in McCullagh, R.P.J. & Tipping, T. (eds). 1998.
32. Miller *ibid*. 249.
33. Grant, I.F. *Highland Folk Ways*. 1961: 75.
34. cf. Grimble, I. *The World of Rob Donn*. 1979: 58-76.
35. Devine, T.M. *Clanship to Crofters' War. The social transformation of the Scottish Highlands*. 1994: 28.

36. Devine *ibid*. 32-34.
37. Grimble, I. *The Trial of Patrick Sellar*. 1962: 61, 68.
38. MacInnes, A.I. 'The impact of the Civil Wars and Interregnum: Political disruption and social change within Scottish Gaeldom', in Mitchison, R. & Roebuck, P. (eds) *Economy and Society in Scotland and Ireland 1500-1939*. 1988: 58-69.
39. Parker Pearson, M. & Richards, C. 'Architecture and order: spatial representation and archaeology' in Parker Pearson, M. & Richards, C. (eds) *Architecture & Order*. 1994: 38-72.
40. Smith, M. 'Holocene regional vegetation history of the Lairg area', in McCullagh, R.P.J. & Tipping, T. (eds). 1998.
41. '... Achimor was held by a succession of tacksman farmers, including the leading cattle drover in Sutherland from 1750 to 1776: NLS Dep. 313/1661, 1721, 1723-5, 3134 Rectified State; SRO GD153/49 ...', in M. Bangor Jones, *Report on History of settlement and land-use in the Achinduich area near Lairg*. Internal report to the Lairg Project, 1993: 6. Unpublished.
42. Carter, S. & Acott, T. *Lairg soil analysis. Report on the evidence for agriculture*. Internal report to the Lairg Project. 1994: 9. Unpublished.
43. SRO RHP11600, a map, dated 1809, of the proposed new road.
44. This same map describes almost 30% of Achimor as 'corn lands', but today much of this area is extremely poorly drained and it is doubtful whether much of this corn land actually produced crops on a regular basis.
45. Smith, M. *Holocene vegetation history of the Lairg area, N E Scotland*. Internal report to the Lairg Project. 1995: 23. Unpublished.
46. Appointment of a local wood keeper: NLS Dep 313/3129 Accompt Sir Tho: Calder 1744; Dep 313/1721-6 SRO SC9/7/11; a 1737 account of wood extraction from Achinduich: SRO SC9/7/4 Munro v Gray; and tenants' duties of wood carriage: SRO SC/9/7/8 Tack Sutherland in favour of Matheson.
47. Carter, S. 'Radiocarbon dates for the age of narrow cultivation', in *Tools and Tillage*. VII. pt 2-3. 1993-94: 83-91.
48. Carter, S. *Lairg soil analysis: Report on the characterisation and interpretation of man-made sediments*. Internal report to the Lairg Project. 1994: 18. Unpublished.
49. Fairhurst, H. 'The deserted settlement at Lix, West Perthshire', in *Proc Soc Antiq Scot*. 101. 1968-69:160-199; Fairhurst, H. 'Rosal: a deserted township in Strath Naver, Sutherland', in *Proc Soc Antiq Scot*. 100. 1967-68: 135-169; Stewart, J.H. & Stewart, M.B. 'A highland longhouse – Lianach, Balquidder, Perthshire', in *Proc Soc Antiq Scot*. 118. 1988: 301-318.
50. Ketteringham, L. 'Cruck-framed building Rhianbreck, Lairg, Sutherland', in *Vernacular Building*. 1992 vol 16: 21-25.

Harvesting near Bettyhill.

THE STRATHNAVER CLEARANCES IN MODERN SCOTTISH FICTION: HISTORY, LITERARY PERCEPTION & MEMORY

Laurence Gouriévidis

BACKGROUND

Of the many novels which have evoked the Clearances period, the most widely cited and analysed are those which could be labelled the 'Strathnaver novels'. *Butcher's Broom* by Neil M. Gunn (1934), *And the Cock Crew* by Fionn MacColla (published in 1945 but started a decade earlier) and *Consider the Lilies* by Iain Crichton Smith (1968) all use the evictions implemented in Strathnaver by the Sutherland Estate in 1814 as the factual reference of their narratives.

The shadow of the Sutherland clearances looms large in Clearances 'records', whether in terms of scale, extensiveness, swiftness or the density of writing that they provoked. From Strathnaver, hundreds of families were removed in various stages between 1807 and 1822 (see Bangor-Jones, this volume),[1] but the 1814 evictions in particular provide the writer of fiction with ample material for dramatisation. They are steeped in controversy, notably with allegations of violence fuelled by the trial for arson and culpable homicide of the factor, Patrick Sellar, and his subsequent acquittal in 1816. That the name of Patrick Sellar and the 'Year of the Burnings' now rank high in Clearances demonology owes much to the retrospective and searing denunciation of a local and often quoted witness, Donald Macleod, but also to the nature of the evidence collected in Sutherland by the Napier Commission.[2] Beyond such testimonies based on recollection, the human dimension has left but little trace in contemporary documents, so that 'the human details must perforce reside mainly in the historical or literary imagination'.[3]

As a process, the Clearances in historical narratives have been inserted in analyses of agrarian revolution or economic change;[4] if the concept of a revolution is now phased out,[5] the period of the Clearances is still one marking the transformation of the Highlands, be it in terms of class formation, land use, ecology, demography or culture. The semantics of historical discourse on the period are laden with expressions connoting change or new birth.[6] Whatever the nature of the object of the analysis or the theoretical framework favoured, the Clearances clearly belong to those phases of the history of a place regarded as formative. Of those events, the philosopher Paul Ricoeur, in a study of the inter-twining of history and fiction, says that:

they draw their specific significance from their power to foster or reinforce the sense of identity of a community, its narrative identity as well as the identity of its members. Those events generate feelings of considerable ethic intensity – in the register of fervent commemoration, or execration, indignation, lament, compassion or even call for forgiveness. The historian, as such, is supposed to refrain from those feelings ... .

Later on he turns to the power of fiction, which he sees as creating an illusion of 'being'. 'Fiction gives the horrified narrator eyes, eyes to see and weep'.[7]

Indignation and outrage were the prime movers for such 19th-century polemical writers as Donald MacLeod, David Stewart of Garth or Alexander Mackenzie[8] – feelings shared this century by the popular historians, John Prebble and Ian Grimble. The treatment of the latters' work alongside a mention of historical fiction – Gunn and Smith – in Eric Richards's historiographical survey, points towards the existence of a fuzzy area where the notional boundary between history and fiction becomes unstable. History can bear the traits of fiction in its elaboration, readers' appeal and impact. This interchangeable quality surfaced in 1934 in the review of Gunn's *Butcher's Broom* by Edwin Muir: 'all the part of the book which deals with the actual clearances is both historically exact and intensely moving'.[9] If F.R. Hart entitles his literary presentation of the three Strathnaver novels 'the tragedy of the Clearances',[10] 'historical imagination' has appropriated from literary tradition this referential category and the events which affected the Highlands in the 19th century have been defined as 'tragic' by some socio-economic historians, although in substance their work may well abstain from ethical judgment.[11] At those intermittent crossroads between fiction and history emerges the essence of the image of the Clearances in popular representations: a social tragedy and a moral scandal.[12]

The purpose of this study is to examine the three Strathnaver novels in their role as signifiers of aspects of Highland identity, and to bring to light the different facets which intermingle in what are considered fictional representations of the Clearances. Hence the study will leave aside discussions of the notion of historical novel or historicity of the novels' content, but will, on the one hand, give pride of place to the nature of the image of the Clearances reconstructed, and on the other, to the process of appropriation of the Clearances by novelists as a text which can be read and explained in different ways and with different aims.

THE IMAGE OF THE CLEARANCES IN LITERATURE

The Strathnaver clearances have much to offer a fictional writer, but none of these three novels can be reduced to straightforward accounts of the clearances in Sutherland; and in the label 'clearances novels' lies the danger of simplifying the authors' aims and ironing out the variety between the narratives.

In Gunn's words, 'there is little of the clearances in *Butcher's Broom.* The tragedy is the destruction of a way of life, and the book is more about what is destroyed.'[13] Hence, central to the novel is the changing life of the Riasgan – a small Highland township – and its community before, during and after the evictions. *And the Cock Crew* and *Consider the Lilies*, by contrast, both have smaller casts. *And the Cock Crew* explores the spiritual dilemma of a minister whose congregation is faced with the prospect of eviction – are the clearances the mark of divine judgment as his fellow ministers assert, or are they the mark of landlord oppression and tyranny? *Consider The Lilies* presents the psychological study of a religious old woman, Mrs Scott, about to be evicted by Patrick Sellar. If the clearances filter through the narrative by means of identifiable images for *And the Cock Crew* and *Consider the Lilies*, in *Butcher's Broom* they give the novel its narrative structure. But through those three novels echoes, with remarkable coherence, a string of clearances motifs which can be grouped in three categories: themes, thematic imagery and characters.

Themes

Defining both time and setting, life before the evictions is contrasted to a life of poverty and near starvation in resettlement areas; a sense of loss and decline pervades such evocations. Yet 'former days' are not simply idealised in frozen pictures of perfect bliss; the vulnerability of the Highlanders' conditions of living, at times verging on destitution, is not toned down. Hence the 'golden age' of the community is encapsulated in the security of a glen, the perennial nature of a life following nature's seasonal rhythms and the reassuring intimacy of a close-knit and cohesive social group – the very representation of an order, a society and a culture.

Made powerful by the evocation of an old order is the major theme of betrayal which runs through each narrative. The people are betrayed both by their former chief, whose wish it is to turn the land they occupy into more lucrative sheep-runs, and by their venal religious leaders who terrorise them into acceptance through threatening visions of hell-fire. Although the double betrayal epitomised by the collusion of church and estate leaders is present in each novel, it is paramount in *And the Cock Crew* where betrayal is also manifold; it has infiltrated the community through one of its members, Lachlan, and is at the heart of the moral predicament of the minister, Maighstir Sachairi.

What places these three novels squarely under the umbrella terms of 'clearances novels' is the threat of evictions hanging over the three stories and, for *Butcher's Broom* and *And the Cock Crew*, actual scenes of evictions inserted in the main story lines. Both Gunn and MacColla resorted to a similar range of lurid details – terror of those evicted, wanton cruelty and violence, drunkenness of the evicting parties – to conjure up visions of horror and apocalypse.[14]

Thematic Imagery

In the three novels, the theme of eviction is explicitly equated with destruction, and more concretely with the use of fire and the burning of houses. Fire and related images also function at another level of meaning as they interconnect with visions of hell and hell-fire, thereby imposing on the Clearances process and its agents a reading not only dramatic but also inherently condemnatory.

Uniformly in the three novels the 'evil' of the policy or its perpetrators is intimated. In *Butcher's Broom* it is all-pervasive, starting with the factor's name changed to 'Heller', and maintained through a network of motifs where sheep carry infernal connotations. *And the Cock Crew* has the factor, Byars, 'a devil's servant', on many occasions identified with satanic forces. The association with evil in *Consider the Lilies* also crystallises in the character of the factor-evictor Patrick Sellar, described in a Gaelic poem quoted to him as 'roasting in hell like a herring'.[15] Such religious images of hell achieve their full impact in *Butcher's Broom* and *And the Cock Crew*, in eviction scenes where flames and fire rage.

But underneath these symbolic parallels lies the ambivalence of religious motifs which are at the core of interpretations of the Clearances. It is ironically exploited by all three novelists, although to varying degrees. If evictions represent figuratively hell on earth, they are also presented in the mouths of those of the ministers who connived at the schemes as God's punishment on the inhabitants for their sins; factors therefore become the human expression of God's will, and any resistance to their acts and decisions is deemed sinful or even 'satanic'. Critical distance consistently saturates such dogmatic positions in the novels but, in *And the Cock Crew*, the ambivalence of the vision constitutes the kernel of the narrative, fully explored by the novelist who centres on the crisis tormenting the conscience of the truly dedicated Sachairi.

Sheep are another aspect of the imagery of the novels which offer a variety of associations. At a literal level in the context of the Strathnaver Clearances, sheep replace men in the glens and are the mark of a basic change in land exploitation. In its religious sense, the image provides another reading which is often inverted – explicitly in *Butcher's Broom* and more implicitly in *And the Cock Crew* and *Consider the Lilies* – thereby giving an ironic commentary on the process envisaged. The ministers act as guides to their human 'flock', yet by their frightening sermons, they have turned them into 'sheep' who meekly bow to the move imposed on them, and it is like 'sheep' that the inhabitants stream out of the glens to the coasts to make room for their animal counterparts. Underpinning the image is a scathing assessment of the force of Calvinism.

Finally, though distinctive in terms of characterisation and point of view, the three novels display a similar range of characters epitomising specific values and ideas. This aspect of the narrative brings to light one of the greatest difficulties faced by novelists who choose to tackle, even as a backdrop, an historical event such as the Clearances: how to 'realise comprehensiveness in time, place and culture and still manage the novelist's focus on individual lives and relationships'.[16] Of the three novels, *Butcher's Broom* is the only one to present a wide-angle view of the situation, including substantial segments focusing on the 'improvers' and their ethos – landlords and estate managers. The function and importance of the characters represented are always subordinated in the end to the thematic purpose of the novelist, and they are most eloquent when reduced to a single idea or dogmatic position.

Factors are amongst such characters. They are unanimously portrayed with extreme disparagement, verging in the case of *And the Cock Crew* on caricature. Responsible for the practicality of the evictions, they range from the calculating and devious Patrick Sellar in *Consider the Lilies*; through the more complex Heller who stands for improvement and materialism, but also wanton destruction in the eviction scene of *Butcher's Broom*; and on to the oversimplified Byars in *And the Cock Crew*, whose cruelty and hatred of the Gaels borders on sadism.

The same range of nuances applies to religious characters and to what could be best defined as 'clearances victims'. However secondary or underdeveloped ministers or elders may be, they personify the same idea: the repressive role of the church. This pervades all three novels and is not only demonstrated through the ministers' acting as the corrupt lackeys of estate management – with the obvious exception of MacColla's Sachairi – but most of all through the impact of their creed on Gaelic culture and spirit. Although 'clearances victims' are not always among the main characters, they are all depicted as powerless before the law, desperately trying to save their few possessions. Standing prominent amongst those victims are female figures, old women like Mrs Scott or Dark Mairi in *Butcher's Broom*. Other characters embody the distressing experience of expulsion and are recurring features in the novels;[17] the repetition of such illustrations of the worst human consequences of the evictions in Clearances writing, both contemporary and modern, have virtually created archetypes whose fictional representations both re-create and strengthen.

Images of the Clearances: Some Initial Conclusions

Such then is the texture of the representation of the Strathnaver Clearances in fiction. Several points may be stressed as a preliminary conclusion .

What heightens the significance and amplitude of the motifs outlined is their repetition and consistency – their unity. Such unity endows this vision with a symbolic weight which has turned the grim features of the Strathnaver evictions into 'clearances paradigms', frequently introduced as part of indictments on the process. And indeed, underpinning the three narratives is a common moral assessment of the policy – an indictment of its aims, implementation and results. Feelings of such 'ethic intensity' as described by

Paul Ricoeur suffuse and impel the narratives, and reviewers were quick to point them out, along with their impact. Of *Butcher's Broom*, it was said that parts of the novel were difficult to read 'simply because of the strength of the anger and indignation they develop [in the reader] at this terrible betrayal of the Highland people',[18] while *And the Cock Crew* aroused a 'feeling of profound pity bring[ing] out the tragedy and inhumanity of the clearances'.[19] The novels' emphasis is on a vision of the Sutherland Clearances as a piece of social engineering, stimulated by the attraction of quick profit and disregarding the painful human consequences that such a mass expulsion entailed. This approach meant that novelists engaged with some of the most contentious issues in the historiography of the events: namely the question of greed as the prime motive behind clearances, the brutality of the methods used during eviction – in particular the use of fire – and the process as a fall from a timeless peasant golden age.[20] In the end, analyses of causation pale into insignificance, and what is retained is the practical and human impact of the change.

Twentieth-century fiction around the Clearances no doubt helps to perpetuate such images, which the very process of re-telling also reinforces. These two characteristics – retrospection and reiteration – make 20th-century fiction a legitimising vehicle which contributes to shaping the narrative identity of the Highlands, and eventually bolsters the place of the Clearances as a central landmark in the region's chronology. Yet initially essential in constructing and sustaining the memory of the Clearances, were those contemporary accounts which form the constituting origins of later narratives. Looking at the sources consulted by novelists, a few loom large. Amongst those, Donald MacLeod's *Gloomy Memories* and Alexander Mackenzie's *History of the Highland Clearances* are the most obvious. Polemical in style and purpose,[21] their tone and standpoint percolate through the three Strathnaver novels, perhaps most obviously in *Consider the Lilies* where Donald MacLeod is a major character. Of course, the time of writing conditioned the range and type of material available to novelists, and in the 1930s, research on the period had not witnessed the development it was to see after the second World War. Studies of the Clearances by economic historians for instance were embryonic. In the preface to *Consider the Lilies*, Smith refers those of his readers interested in the historical background of the clearances to the work of Ian Grimble and John Prebble, while Gunn 'waded through every last word that the Sutherland had had written for him anent his burning ploy to make sure [he] even had his side of the story'.[22] In the end, no matter the range of material sifted, the authors' own predilections and priorities gave the narratives their particular emphases: a focus on the plight of the peasantry and a critique of improvers. The process of selecting sources itself is a telling indicator of the novelists' ideological position, but more eloquent still are the narratives themselves.

It is, therefore, essential to consider the use of the Clearances as part of wider discourses on the Highlands and their history, and to examine their insertion in 'commentaries' from the authors. This will bring to light the different values attached to, and the use made of, the process in the three narratives, and implies a study of each novel in relation to its cultural and socio-political context.

IDEOLOGY AND THE NOVELS

In terms of the novels' dialectical content, they all hinge on antithetical oppositions, epitomised by central characters or groups.

In *Butcher's Broom*, tradition and humanism are opposed to improvement or 'Progress', and are given material form by setting the Riasgan community against the improvers; in *And the Cock Crew* the theological vision of the Highland situation is defended by Maighstir Sachairi against Fearchar the poet's historico-political understanding. *Consider the Lilies* functions on several levels of opposition: on the one hand the Calvinistic dogmatism of Mrs Scott is contrasted to and conquered by Donald MacLeod's free thinking; on the other, whilst Patrick Sellar sees the clearances as one aspect of the inexorable movement of history and of the progress of civilisation, Donald MacLeod's main concern is for the human beings uprooted.

Butcher's Broom and *And the Cock Crew* were cited by Kurt Wittig in 1958 as illustrations of 'a new attitude towards the Clearances' approached 'as the buried root of contemporary Highland difficulties, and as the immediate cause of the crofting problem ... . History is here regarded as the matrix of the present.'[23] The crofting problem, or more widely the Highland problem, was no new concept; but long-standing social and economic malaise tightened its grip around the region in the late 1920s and 1930s, exacerbated by more widespread economic crisis. The situation of the Highlands became a focus of interest and research for economists, politicians and intellectuals alike. In 1938 the Hilleary Report was produced, two years after the establishment of the Scottish Economic Committee; it made a series of recommendations to boost the economy of the crofting areas and create employment. At about the same time, research on the Highland problem was carried out individually by the economist Adam Collier and the ecologist Frank Fraser Darling, in an attempt to assess the circumstances of the region and their origins, and to examine its future prospects.[24] The outcome of their work appeared in both cases in the early 1950s; Collier's *The Crofting Problem* was posthumously published in 1953, and Fraser Darling's *West Highland Survey* in 1955. Both set a high premium on cultural and human values, and on an anthropological approach to the Highland problem. Evaluating the Highland 'problem', Adam Collier asserts that it 'really arises out of a clash of social philosophies'[25] and Fraser Darling that it:

> has continued to deepen through periods of increasing differences between the simple social culture and primitive agriculture of the Highlands and Islands on the one hand, and the highly urbanised, commercial civilisation of the rest of Great Britain on the other.[26]

Considered from the angle of a dominant culture imposing its socio-economic values on a more confined, albeit deeply-rooted and resistant one, the Clearances come to represent the paradigmatic example of such cultural infiltration.

A similar note was struck by nationalist activists who commented on the Highlands in the inter-war years, although with a different agenda in mind.[27] Among them was Gunn, whose involvement in the nationalist movement peaked then.[28] He had joined the National Party of Scotland in 1929 at a mass meeting in Inverness, and had become a co-founder of the local branch. In 1932 he was elected to the National Council of the Party and this involvement with party administration was to last until 1942, when he decided to devote his time and effort to his literary career; his contribution to the nationalist ideal would, henceforth, be through his writings. In an article in 1939 he suggested a direct link between the plethora of inquiries examining Scottish conditions and 'the re-awakened interest in self-government'.[29]

Butcher's Broom

It would be a bold step, nonetheless, to leap from this type of statement and impose on *Butcher's Broom* a nationalist layer of meaning which the narrative might not sustain. What the novel does attempt to render and celebrate is a Gaelic spirit, culture and vision of the world which Gunn identifies with the Highlands: the Clearances are deplored as one link in the chain of cultural subjection which eroded such cultural integrity and strength. Extracts from articles written in the early 1930s may be read in parallel with, and shed light on the author's perception of the Highlands, the place of the Clearances in the region's history, as well as the conception of the novel. He defined the Clearances as:

> ... the era throughout the whole of the Highlands of the creation of the large sheep farm, and of the dispossession of the people, frequently by means so ruthless and brutal that they may not bear retelling easily, and always with a sorrow and hopelessness that finally broke the Gaelic spirit. What the disaster of 1745 and the penal enactments of 1747 began, the clearances finished.[30]

The cultural dimension is even more explicitly stated in an earlier article where he argues that 'the language, tradition and nurture of the Gael' were 'interfered with from outside'.[31] The idea of the outsiders' lack of empathy with a different way of life and values, of their pre-conceptions leading to the production of distorted and derogatory images – Gaels' laziness and squalor – is echoed in *Butcher's Broom*, which is constructed around the opposition of 'insider versus outsider'.

The sense of tragedy surrounding the little community of the Riasgan springs from the clash between two visions of the Highlands which the novelist chose to convey through changes in the focus of narration, letting the reader into the thoughts of a large number of characters. For instance, although Mr Heller's mental world is explored, not least when he meets the Staffords at their home in London, the author's sympathy clearly does not lie with the improvers; it emerges through ironic distance, or more explicitly through narratorial interventions taking the form of quasi-didactic sections where, for short interludes, the story gives precedence to ideological, political and philosophical 'commentaries'.[32] The clash between two mind-sets is exposed both at the level of the story itself and through the narrator's own words. How then is it defined?:

> For the cleavage between the desires of the people and the desires of the landlords was fundamental and could never be bridged. On the people's part there was love of the land ... (*Broom* p. 267)[33]

At the core of the cleavage is the value of land, since what prevails for the landlord is its financial value. The stark terms of this opposition, money versus love, conceal the socio-cultural significance of the land which the novel contains. 'Love of the land' for the Riasgan community is not limited to a strong sense of place; it encompasses traditional social structures revolving around loyalty and kinship – implicit agreements and beliefs which constitute the basis of their way of life and have shaped their perception of their environment and society.

More specifically, those conflicting perceptions are expressed through a series of antithetical expectations and notional points of reference which give rise to the acute sense of betrayal experienced by the dispossessed. For the Riasgan, 'the land and all it contains is the common heritage' (*Broom* p. 71), 'fought for, increased and held' by the clansmen (*Broom* p. 213), while for the Stafford family and the estate managers, their relationship to the land is envisaged in terms of single ownership. The semantics of 'possession' dominate their discourse, as does the word 'law'. But the law which governs the Riasgan – oral, based on trust and largely around military enrollment – is a non-existent concept in the improvers' legal world, where law is written. The legal justification of the evictions is, therefore, as alien to the Riasgan Highlanders as the inalienable rights they claim are to the improvers. As a result, the concept of poaching is not part of their mental structure: 'So ancient had been their gaming rights, that no new laws or restrictions in favour of landlord or lessee could ever convict them in their own minds of poaching' (*Broom* p. 66). Here, the element of time – or rather timelessness, where tradition defies the passing of time – is the axis of their communal references and at the same time legitimises their claim in their own eyes. 'Immemorial', 'age-old' or 'ancient' qualify indifferently traditional rights and activities, songs and stories or the Gaelic language – a common cultural heritage. It is also applied to the concept of race – Gaelic race. Notions of purity of race percolate through the novel, and are suggestive of some of the racial ideas associated with the Highlands by nationalist Celticists in the inter-war period.[34]

The Gaelic race, timelessness, sense of place and the notion of a golden age coalesce into the vision of a community in harmony with its environment and with a rich past and a 'proud history'. This picture is in no way one of 'primitivism'. Of the Countess, the tacksman and his wife say:

> ... And she's of our blood. She was brought up in the Lowlands and in England. She lives in England. They were at the court of France. She – she hasn't it in her.' (*Broom* p. 214)

Interesting undertones of the corrupting nature of the outside world are perceptible here – an outside 'civilised' world. 'It' is defined by opposition to both the Lowlands and England. It is constructed around the antithesis 'insider versus outsider' and connotes a sense of belonging. The reader, invited inside the Riasgan community, discovers a social group where cohesion, generosity, resilience, honesty and a rich oral tradition are all-pervasive qualities – a deeply humanistic people. Yet in the eyes of the estate managers, the people fit the assumptions of laziness, ignorance and sloth, all validating a need for change. The contrast thus created is extreme, and the improvers impose on the Gaels a reading which the narrative inherently refutes as it does the ideology of Improvement – or Progress.

As championed by Heller, 'Progress' encompasses more than purely agricultural aims; it also includes reforming the Gaels – their way of life, language and working habits – following values from the south. 'The greatness of the schemes' for Heller, lies in 'improving the estate and introducing civilisation into the Highlands; essentially a work of sanitation!' (*Broom* p. 302). 'Civilisation' and 'sanitation', in the eviction scene of Part Three, take the shape of frenzied destruction and inhumanity. The process of land rationalisation, spurred on by industrial transformation, urbanisation and the impact of the Napoleonic Wars – the economic rationale behind the Clearances – which Lord Stafford expounds, is similarly reduced to ruthless calculation and absence of human considerations. The narrative itself, therefore, produces its own reversal of the concept of 'civilisation'.

The ideology of improvement has disastrous consequences on the community's living conditions and, beyond material loss, it deals a damaging blow at the core of the community which, broken-spirited and its cohesion gone, drifts into depression and fatalism. The Riasgan is shown as annihilated by the distant forces of 'political power', mastered by the estate management and wielded at the level of 'much humbler affairs' (*Broom* p. 264-5). The novel contains an attack on those political forces which sanction such a culturally destructive process as the Clearances, and on those individuals and institutions which partake in the course of action.

> But while Mr Heller – and his name may be taken to represent (or shield) superiors and underlings – was driving on his clear-sighted course, the great bulk of his victims were dumb in the grip of their Church, their chief, and his law. (*Broom* p. 268)

Power in the narrative is, at one point in Heller's thoughts, identified with England, but the novel does not rail against English imperialism; what the author decries most of all is the cultural and human cost on small communities of the pressures of a remote power system.

In its assessment of the past, the novel stands as a commentary on the situation of the Highlands at the time of its writing, and as an analysis of the reasons for their condition. The topic was one to which Gunn kept returning in essays and articles, particularly in the 1930s, with descriptions of the depressed state of the Highland economy: depopulation, abandoned crofts, dying fishing villages. The novel mirrors the author's assessment of the role of tourism in the region – an economic prop which he fears might prove more harmful than redeeming:

> The Highlands, of course, may yet become a popular tourist playground dependent on tourists and nothing else. After sheep, deer; and after deer, tourists. It is the ascending order of our age of progress. For those who know the deep humanism of a past age, there will be regret at the gradual passing of the human stock that was bred of it.[35]

Gunn's fiction was also a means of exploring his contemporary Scotland – an aim which he shared with many Scottish writers of the Literary Renaissance such as Lewis Grassic Gibbon[36] or Fionn MacColla. Whereas in *Butcher's Broom*, Gunn's political views are muted, in *And the Cock Crew*, MacColla's ideological reading of the Clearances and of Scottish history are central to the novel.

And the Cock Crew

When *And the Cock Crew* was first published, MacColla was praised in a short review for 'introducing political argument into his tale without leaving the suggestion that it has been forced in.'[37] If the main thrust of the novel is an illustration or, more to the point, an indictment of the effects of Calvinism on the Gaels, their culture and spirit, the key which unlocks the author's political reading of the Clearances is to be found in chapter seven where Maighstir Sachairi confronts Fearchar, the poet, in a powerful ideological duel. The words of the poet project the nationalist colour of the author's own vision of Scotland's past, as what is to befall the community of Strath Meadhonach is, in Fearchar's interpretation, only one aspect of the much wider scheme of English imperialism. MacColla's autobiographical works offer as many clues to the author's own assessment of Scottish religious life, politics and culture as they bear fruit for an understanding of the religious and political lines developed in the novel.

The bulk of MacColla's writings reveal a man outspoken in his opinions and putting his eloquence and vigour of expression to the service and defence of his own convictions. His autobiography mirrors the strength of his religious and political commitment and beliefs. Born into a family of Plymouth Brethren, he rejected their creed and later on in life became a Roman Catholic. Fascinated by Gaelic culture, he taught himself Gaelic. He had bitter recollections of the many years he spent teaching in the Highlands and the Western Isles, abhorring a role which he describes as 'simply the de-Gaelicisation' and 'Anglicisation' of local Gaelic-speaking children.[38] 'To kill a culture ... in essence is what I was expected to do.'[39] He relentlessly launched caustic all-out attacks on such themes as the effects – past and present – of Scotland's loss of independence, the influence of the presentation of history in a people's self-perception and perception of their past, and the role of the reformation and the reformers – those 'cult-figures' or 'gnyaffs' of whom he says:

> ... if it had not been for them and their infernal 'work', Scotland would be a flourishing autonomous, culturally brilliant nation to-day.[40]

Those words encapsulate the nature of MacColla's highly individualistic brand of Scottish Nationalism. Calvinism here is equated with cultural destruction and eventual loss of independence.

In *And the Cock Crew*, the focus on the agonising self-questioning of Maighstir Sachairi eclipses polemical and pungent religious harangues found elsewhere in MacColla's fiction. Nevertheless, the author's religious views do filter through the characterisation of two ministers, Maighstir Iain and Maighstir Tormod, both frightening their congregations into submission in return for promises of land and manse, and most importantly through their and Maighstir Sachairi's position and power within those communities. Whatever their personal stand as regards evictions, what is made most significant is the effects of their role as guides not only for matters spiritual but practical and secular too – paramount in the context of impending expulsion. Hence the hub of MacColla's religious argument goes further than the controversial involvement of the Church at the time of the Clearances, and encompasses the much broader aspect of the nature of Calvinistic creed in the Highlands. The debilitating effect of Calvinistic teaching emerges in the people's attitudes to evictions, in the poet's own isolation and in the thoughts of Maighstir Sachairi. Underlying the carefully-constructed scenario is a contrast between life before the advent of Calvinistic doctrine – symbolised by the coming of Maighstir Sachairi twenty years previously and Fearchar's subsequent loss of status as leader – and the time of the narrative.

The opening chapter of the novel sets the tone, presenting a people totally 'defenceless' and fatalistic in the extreme. Their former strength and courage are repeatedly set against their god-fearing attitude, sapping their will. Meekness of spirit, passivity, but also annihilation of a rich folk culture are the attributes of this life-denying religion which, in the person of Maighstir Schairi, has deprived the community of its poet and also of its tradition of music, singing, dancing and story-telling. Calvinism in the novel, therefore, equates to cultural iconoclasm. Meanwhile, the Clearances themselves are seen as part and parcel of a process of assimilation and inserted into a political argument which finds its roots in MacColla's vision of Scotland and her past – his nationalism.

MacColla's tendency to use characters in some of his novels[41] as 'neither fully realised individuals nor representatives, but embodiments of ideas, attitudes or historical experiences [he] wishes to explore',[42] applies also to *And the Cock Crew* in the form of Byars and Fearchar; the factor is simply reduced to a quasi-genocidal hatred of the Gaels, while Fearchar provides the novel's political commentary and acts as the author's mouthpiece. When, in chapter seven, Maighstir Sachairi's strictly theological perspective of the impending events and their context is challenged by Fearchar, narratorial intervention dictates the framework in which the minister's vision is to be received by the reader.

> Maighstir Sachairi's mind by the direction given to it even in infancy, as well as by his later training and long discipline, was able to act only (as it were) on the vertical plane: he thought of '*God*,' and '*man*' or '*men*,' and understood events only as produced in the tensions between the divine and human wills; and not otherwise was he able to understand the world. Hence he was unable to think historically, for that is as it were horizontally; incapable from the very nature of his mind of recognising the validity of a view which might seek to explain events as the product of factors working out in a process that must be called historical. (*Cock Crew* pp. 127-8)

The minister's approach thus appears limited and shaped by his own background and education. This 'theological' mode of thought, explicitly presented as fettering, stands against the 'historical' mode of thought of the poet, whose guiding light is nationalist in nature. Here in a nutshell, MacColla's own perception of Scotland's – let alone the Highlands' – woes, comes to light; and many of the questions raised in his autobiography are echoed.

In his own personal quest, Scotland's fate is a cardinal feature.[43] Hence his autobiographical essay includes reflections on the power of language, of history, the process of learning and their influence on people's sense of self-definition, of belonging and ultimately of self-worth. Maighstir Sachairi's character, with his blinkered theological vision, prefigures MacColla's argument on the power of language and words in 'conditioning' minds and outlooks.[44] The argument stretches far beyond the pure linguistic plane centring on the erosion of Gaelic to incorporate the dimension of English hegemony, and is fully verbalised by Fearchar. In his long ideological address, the Clearances are the glaring sign of England's process of subjugation, pursuing her conquest with such insidious means as bribery, cultural domination and legal measures.

> And so at last she, the Enemy, understands that our nation is never to be conquered by armies and invasions. Now she is more subtle, for Cunning is her name. Now she comes with feigned friendship; and with lying promises and gold for our traitors she is able to obtain it, and our liberty is at an end! (*Cock Crew* p. 122)

Treachery and betrayal are, in the context of evictions, seen as crucial and such words are applied to landowners, yet the censure implied is somewhat deflected by the strength of the argument around the process of cultural hegemony. Landholders epitomise such a process; their alien up-bringing in terms of place, language and values, has equipped them with a warped vision of their land and people; they reproduce the pre-conceptions absorbed through their education and are ultimately transformed into vehicles of national subjection.

> There had begun to be amongst us those that were not altogether Albannaich for they had forgotten the language of the forefathers and taken on an English language, with English ways. Now a man who speaks English and is English in his ways will begin to feel like those whose language he speaks, and it is his own countrymen that will seem like foreigners to him, for their ways are strange and he does not understand their language. (*Cock Crew* p. 124)

Assisting the process is the English law which first sanctioned the proprietorial status of former chiefs, and then enabled them to impose their will: transform their estate and dispossess tenants.

Superimposed on this scheme of Anglicisation is a racial dimension much more explicit and strident than Gunn's in *Butcher's Broom*. Gaels are being assailed yet again by Saxons, and the Clearances are the latest mark of the assault. About Byars, it is said 'here is a pig of a saxon at his old play of harrying' (*Cock Crew* p. 67). These are words redolent of the racial discourse appropriated by the Celtic nationalist faction of the National Party of Scotland in the inter-war years, in particular, Ruaraidh Erskine of Mar who founded, edited and wrote for many publications and publicised a nationalism resting largely on the racial premise of the intrinsic disparities between Celts and Saxons.[45] C.M. Grieve – Hugh MacDiarmid – was also a vocal proponent of the same stand. The strength of their personal commitment to these ideas, and their high journalistic profile, must not however obscure the fact that their position was far from dominant within the party.[46] In fact, MacDiarmid was expelled from the NPS in 1932 for his involvement in the creation of Clan Albain – a neo-fascist and paramilitary organisation which seemingly envisaged a number of spectacular actions including land raiding on the Island of Rum.[47] Both the plans and ultimate intentions of this expedition are enveloped in a thick mist on which MacColla's autobiography sheds a very personal light, mainly illuminating his role as the main instigator in the conception and organisation of the Rum raid; he also dismisses Clan Albain as 'totally imaginary'. It is worth recalling that at that point – 1930 – MacColla was a member of the NPS, having joined in 1928 after a spell with the ILP. Disillusionment with Labour's gradual volte-face on Scottish self-government, following their 1924 election to office, had brought him to the ranks of the Nationalists. MacColla's aim with the raid on Rum was to attract the attention of the press and, thereby the public, to the 'realities of Scottish history' and 'to let the large world know about the Clearances, that long-continued genocidal episode'; politically, his objective was to compel Labour to take a stand in the Highlands leading to 'the end of the Sporting Estate system ...; the repopulation of the Highlands – and with a Gaelic population; the salvation of the language. In effect, the Clearances in reverse.'[48]

Could it be said then, with one critic, that *And the Cock Crew* is an example of 'powerful, aggressive polemics in which great historical wrongs are savoured as prelude to renewed conflict'?[49] To overlook the nationalist dimension which, in the interpretation offered, eclipses the responsibility of landlords, is unquestionably to deprive the novel of one of its fundamental components.

Consider the Lilies

For Neil Gunn and Fionn MacColla, Scottish nationalism was a political belief to which they were both committed, and which could find its way into their fiction and colour their vision of the situation of the Highlands. For Iain Crichton Smith, ideologies – be they political or religious – are the object of mistrust and frequent attacks in his work. Describing himself as a man 'not committed to any ideology', he repeatedly singles out Scottish Calvinism as 'an ideology that weakens the will'[50] in his critical, poetic or fictional exploration of the Highland and Island experience – often drawing on his own childhood on the island of Lewis. *Consider the Lilies* is consonant with this reading, as the book's probing of Mrs Scott's psyche reveals a mind strapped into the straightjacket of religious indoctrination. In its indictment of the effects of Calvinism on the Gaels, *Consider the Lilies* chimes with *And the Cock Crew* where Maighstir Sachairi's narrow, theological perspective of the world and events corresponds somewhat to Mrs Scott's stunted emotions, warped judgment and limited vision. Nowhere is her distorted perception made more obvious than in her initial assessment of Donald MacLeod:

> He was the sort of man Patrick Sellar would like, a man who wasn't interested in the church and spent most of his time in Edinburgh. In fact he might help Sellar to pull the church down. (*Lilies* p. 97)[51]

This diagnosis could not be further removed from the character of Donald MacLeod as subsequently revealed – a Donald MacLeod, active defender of the Highlanders' cause, whose related confrontation with Patrick Sellar not only contradicts Mrs Scott's feelings but conveys the author's commentary on the Clearances process and the conditions of the Highlands. Donald MacLeod then fulfills two functions; he is one of the main catalysts in Mrs Scott's mental evolution and he acts as the author's mouthpiece.

The reader is led inside Mrs Scott's uncompromising mental world as the narrative follows her meandering thoughts – streams of consciousness alternating reflections on her past life and her present situation – and follows her gradual conversion and re-appraisal of some of her values and loyalties. In the words of the author 'she was to be broken out of her ideology to see how she could cope as a human being'.[52] And indeed Mrs Scott's mental journey is the kernel of the narrative. Yet although Mrs Scott functions as the *central* consciousness, the thoughts of Patrick Sellar and most of all Donald MacLeod are also penetrated. Regarded as one of the novel's weaknesses in evaluations of the book that prioritise the personal angle to the detriment of the more public dimension,[53] these 'lapses' in the focus of narration signify the importance of the Clearances in the novel's thematics. More than a mere backdrop to Mrs Scott's study, they are a fundamental constituent of the narrative, and it is through the character of Donald MacLeod that analyses of the Clearances, their causes, effects and interpretations, filter through to the reader, largely by-passing Mrs Scott. The words of the author himself on the historical MacLeod and his presence in the narrative – in this essential paratext which the preface is[54] – confirm the significance of his function: 'he seems to have been a wholly admirable person, with a great concern for his people and desire to *speak out* and *tell the truth*.' [My emphasis]. These words convey the essential Donald MacLeod of the text, and since he is defined – beyond his atheism – through his views of the Highlanders, the Highlands and their fate, a closer look at his role and ideas is necessary.

The dialectics surrounding the Sutherland Clearances in the novel hinge upon an opposition between materialism and humanism, vividly expressed in the confrontation between Patrick Sellar and Donald MacLeod. The two mind-sets also reflect two antithetical visions of history and its making on the one hand; and on the other, the perception and power of past events. Iain Crichton Smith introduces a reflection on the past and its re-telling, whose point of reference is the Clearances. For the author, the values of materialism are to be blamed for the disintegration of community life.

> There is no question in my mind that a society which lives by materialistic values will be destroyed by them ... . That belief in materialism is closely connected with the destruction of community is also, I am sure, a fact, for materialism depends on individuals being set over against each other.[55]

In *Consider The Lilies*, MacLeod regards the evictions and the progress of the sheep – 'the destruction of the Highlands' (*Lilies* p. 140) – as the outcome of the cupidity and extravagance of a few landowners. At the same time, what pervades Patrick Sellar's improving discourse in defense of the process, is the notion of the ineluctability of change overriding concerns of human cost – 'the movement of the age', 'the progress of civilisation [which] demands sacrifice' (*Lilies* p. 142). In this inexorable process, Patrick Sellar happens to be the lucky agent. Questioned by MacLeod on human grounds, the ideological bases attributed to the Clearances are later obscured by the scene in which he and Loch are all schemes and deceit in order to extort Mrs Scott's betrayal of MacLeod. Of the ideological veneer of the policy, little remains by then.

But what will posterity preserve of the Clearances? The exchange which opposes Patrick Sellar to Donald Macleod presents a commentary on the making and use of historical landmarks: how and for what purpose would the

Clearances be committed to history? How will the events and their main actors be immortalised? Patrick Sellar attaches little importance to the poetical propensities of the Highlanders and the force of their accounts, thereby reproducing the improvers' prejudice against the Highlands' cultural and linguistic patrimony and specificity.[56] Nevertheless, artistic creation produces abiding images, later becoming fixed in popular memory and the source of further retrospective artistic work. Such is Smith's point when, with a statement which sounds both prophetic and anachronistic but which is, in fact, based on the author's own experience and use of hindsight, he has Donald MacLeod warning Patrick Sellar about the image poets have and will popularise of him – Patrick Sellar in hell.

> You see, Mr Sellar, you will become a legend. You have become a legend. Are you flattered? Is that perhaps what you wanted? You talk about the future. Yes, true enough, you too will have a future. Children will sing in the streets in different countries, countries you will never visit. They may even recite poems about you in the schools. Yes, your name will be on people's lips. (*Lilies* p. 144)

The transition from 'agent of evictions' to 'legend' encapsulates art's power of mythic amplification; historical events and their actors find themselves elevated to the status of heroes or – more to the point in the case of Patrick Sellar – anti-heroes. The novel itself is testimony to this magnifying power of art – in this case fiction. Here, reality and the vision of reality created by art confront each other; and central to this opposition is the notion of truth. The exchange between the two men is indeed saturated by an underlying reference to 'truth'. The motivations behind MacLeod's writings are his feelings of 'anger' and his urge 'to tell the truth of what is happening' (*Lilies* pp. 133, 141), to which Sellar retorts: 'Don't you know that the day has come when the truth is what we care to make it?' (*Lilies* p. 142). Sellar's view of the process in which he partakes is one of cynical manipulation, which MacLeod tries to puncture. This vision of the construction of events, of history and of the memorialisation of past figures and acts, including here orally-transmitted poems and songs, is suggestive of the divergent representations which have made the Clearances one of the most controversial episodes in Scottish, let alone Highland history.

CONCLUSION

Commenting on a commemorative procession in 1884 which took one of the survivors of its clearance, Grizzel Claggan, back to Strathnaver, Eric Richards underlines the influence of individual memories in nourishing 'the passion associated with the Clearances' – a passion which he sees perpetuated by the fictional narratives set against the period. 'The imaginative evocation of the common people and their times may be juxtaposed with the emerging contemporary record.'[57] This points towards two important aspects of the role of early fictional writing on the Clearances which pre-dates the emergence of a 'people's history'. Little had emerged about the life of the crofters affected by evictions in the histories written in the first half of the 20th century, beyond the acrimonious words penned by Tom Johnston.[58] Such literary production filled an historiographical silence and stands as the reflection of the 'memory of the Clearances'.

In this respect, the nature of the image of the Clearances presented in the three novels is significant. A thematic consistency which gives pride of place to cultural arguments is striking. At the same time, its inflection and colour changed with the ideological and philosophical priorities of each of the novelists considered, at times projecting the political climate in which the author evolved. In this sense, the representations of the Clearances are shaped by the environment of each of the authors concerned; the individual and the collective coalesce. Although the core of the representation remains unaltered from the 1930s to the late 1960s, its interpretation produces different tunes. In the words of Raphael Samuel, 'memory is inherently revisionist and never more chameleon than when it appears to stay the same.'[59] Most of all, memory is now regarded as a crucial element in collective identity.[60]

The importance of the three Strathnaver novels lies in their being transmitters of a memory of the Clearances – a memory encapsulated in the Strathnaver evictions and saturated with moral outrage and condemnation. Their recurrent fictionalisation in the 20th century reinforces the memory of the Clearances as a formative event having shaped a country – let alone a region. It has also become fixed in eloquent 'sites of memory':[61] commemorations and Scottish anthologies. In 1986 the Crofters' Act was celebrated in a commemorative exhibition,[62] a process echoed in the growing number of monuments built to commemorate events and figureheads of the Crofters' War.[63] More telling still are the anthologies.[64] Through a selection of literary texts written by Scots and outsiders alike, these anthologies seek to capture the essence of a place, 'to represent the foundations of Scottish reality'.[65]

In this atomisation of Scotland through its past, its landscape and people, many voices are heard; but the Clearances are one of the constant features. Here are found repeated in even more emphatic terms the themes, motifs and feelings which form the fabric of their popular image.

Notes

1. Richards, E. *A History of the Highland Clearances*. 2 vols. London. 1982-85. i. chaps. 10 & 11; Bangor-Jones, M. 'The Strathnaver Clearances', in *North Sutherland Studies*. (Scottish Vernacular Buildings Working Group). Glasgow. 1987: 23-37.
2. MacLeod, D. *Gloomy Memories in the Highlands of Scotland*, initially published as a series of letters in the Edinburgh *Weekly Chronicle*. 1841; also reprinted in Mackenzie, A. *History of the Highland Clearances*. Inverness. 1883; *Evidence taken by Her Majesty's Commissioners of Inquiry into the Condition of the Crofters and Cottars in the Highlands and Islands of Scotland*, 4 vols. Edinburgh. 1884, see in particular the evidence collected at Bettyhill on 24 & 25 July. ii. 1883: 1594-1662.

3.   Richards *op. cit.* 307.
4.   See the histories published in the first half of this century, eg Brown, P.H. *History of Scotland to the Present Time.* 3 vols. Cambridge. 1911. iii; Mackinnon, J. *The Social and Industrial History of Scotland.* London. 1921; Mackenzie, A.M. *Scotland in Modern Times, 1720-1939.* Edinburgh. 1941.
5.   For studies of the period since the second World War, see in particular Gray, M. *The Highland Economy, 1750-1850.* Edinburgh. 1957; Grimble, I. *The Trial of Patrick Sellar.* London. 1962; Prebble, J. *The Highland Clearances.* London. 1963; Bumsted, J.M. *The People's Clearances, 1770-1815.* Edinburgh. 1982; Hunter, J. *The Making of the Crofting Community.* Edinburgh. 1976; Richards, E. *A History of the Highland Clearances.* 2 vols. London. 1982-85: (i) *Agrarian Transformation and the Evictions 1746-1886*, (ii) *Emigration, Protest, Reasons*; Devine, T.M. *The Great Highland Famine.* Edinburgh. 1988; Withers, C.W.J. *Gaelic Scotland.* London. 1988; Devine, T.M. *Clanship to Crofters' War.* Manchester. 1994.
6.   For instance: Hunter, J. *The Making of the Crofting Community*; Withers, C.W.J. *Gaelic Scotland;The Transformation of a Culure Region*; Devine, T.M. *Clanship to Crofters' War*; or perhaps more strikingly the chapter heading 'A Society in travail' in Gray, M. *The Highland Economy 1750-1850.*
7.   My translation of Paul Ricoeur, *Temps et récit.* 3 vols. (Editions du Seuil, Paris). iii. *Le temps raconté.* 1983-85: 272, 274.
8.   See 2 above; David Stewart of Garth *Sketches of the Character, Manners, and Present State of the Highlanders of Scotland.* 2 vols. Edinburgh. 1822.
9.   *The Listener.* 14 November 1934: 840.
10.   Hart, F.R. *The Scottish Novel.* Harvard. 1978. chap. 15.
11.   See eg Gray *op. cit.* 86, 89; Richards *op.cit.* ii: 139.
12.   Gouriévidis, L. *The Image of the Highland Clearances, c.1880-1990.* (Univ. of St Andrews Ph.D thesis). Unpublished. 1993.
13.   Hart F.R. & Pick, J.B. *Neil MGunn: A Highland Life.* Edinburgh. 1985: 103.
14.   Here Donald MacLeod's account provided the details.
15.   This vision of Sellar is confirmed by the knowledge that previously Iain Crichton Smith had written a Gaelic play about Patrick Sellar's trial – in hell.
16.   Hart, F.R. *The Scottish Novel.* 1978: 328.
17.   The old bed-ridden woman rushed out of her house on a blanket on fire, the young woman who gives birth to a still-born baby and also characters driven to insanity are repeated example, taken from Donald MacLeod's account.
18.   *Scots Magazine.* vol. XXII, no 2. December 1934.
19.   *The Scotsman.* 13 December 1945.
20.   Mitchison, R. 'The Clearances', in D. Daiches (ed), *A Companion to Scottish Culture.* London. 1981: 69.
21.   For an assessment of their aims and effects, see James Hunter's introduction to his *The Making of the Crofting Community.* Edinburgh. 1976.
22.   N.M. Gunn to Agnes Mure Mackenzie 15 December 1946, NLS. MS 9222; for details of the sources consulted see also: Hart F.R. & Pick, J.B. *Neil M. Gunn. A Highland Life.* 1985: 104; Gunn, N.M. 'Caithness and Sutherland', in A. McCleery (ed), *Landscape and Light. Essays by Neil M. Gunn.* Aberdeen. 1987: 31.
23.   Wittig, K. *The Scottish Tradition in Literature.* Edinburgh. 1978 ed: 324.
24.   Collier was assistant secretary of the Scottish Economic Committee and helped with the preparation of its report, *The Highlands and Islands of Scotland: A Review of the Economic Conditions with Recommendations for Improvement*, (Chairman E.L. Hilleary). Edinburgh. 1938.
25.   Collier, A. *The Crofting Problem*, Cambridge. 1953: 4.
26.   Darling, F.F. *West Highland Survey.* Oxford. 1955. preface.
27.   Gouriévidis *op. cit.* Part iii. chap. ii & chap. iv, 4.1 & 4.2.
28.   N.M. Gunn was instrumental in bringing the National Party of Scotland and the Scottish Party together to form the Scottish National Party in 1934. See Brand, J. *The National Movement in Scotland.* London. 1978: 102 & chap. 12; Finlay, R.J. *Independent and Free.* Edinburgh. 1994. chap. 3; Hart F.R. &Pick, JB. *op. cit.* chap. 8.
29.   Gunn, N.M. ' ... And then Rebuild it', in McLeery A.(ed), *Landscape and Light.* 1939: 155.
30.   Gunn, N.M. 'Caithness and Sutherland', in *Landscape and Light.* 1935: 31.
31.   Gunn, N.M. 'The Gael Will Come Again', in *Landscape and Light.* 1931: 167-8.
32.   Gérard Genette has shown the importance of the analysis of the changes in the focus of narration and the role of the narrator in his *Figures iii*, a study of Marcel Proust's *À la recherche du temps perdu.* (Collection Poétique, Editions du Seuil, Paris). 1972.

33. All quotations from the 1987 edition by Souvenir Press.
34. This point will be developed below with Fionn MacColla's novel which is explicitly nationalistic in tone and nature.
35. Gunn, N.M. 'Caithness and Sutherland', in *Landscape and Light*. 1935: 34. See also '"Gentlemen – The Tourist!": The New Highland Toast', in *The Scots Magazine*. vol. XXVI. 1936-7. Also worthy of note is Gunn's later involvement in the Commission of Enquiry into Crofting Conditions set up in 1951 – the Taylor Commission – whose report came out in 1954; see Gouriévidis *op. cit.* Part iii. chap. iv: 282-302.
36. Gifford, D. *Neil M. Gunn and Lewis Grassic Gibbon*. Edinburgh. 1983: 147-9.
37. *The Scots Magazine*. Vol. XLIV. no 4. January 1946.
38. MacColla, F. *Ro Fhada Mar So A Tha Mi. Too Long in this Condition*. Caithness. 1975: 72.
39. MacColla, F. 'Mein Bumpf', in D. Morrison (ed), *Essays on Fionn MacColla*. Caithness. 1973: 27.
40. MacColla, F. *Ro Fhada ...* . 1975: 41.
41. In particular in *At the Sign of the Clenched Fist*. 1967.
42. Murray, I. 'Fionn MacColla: Pilgrim of Independence', in *Leopard Magazine*. March 1980. no 57.
43. MacColla, F. *Ro Fhada ...* . 1975: 3.
44. *Ibid.* 27, 99.
45. Gouriévidis *op. cit.* 248-251.
46. Finlay, R.J. 'Nationalism, Race, Religion and the Irish Question in Inter-war Scotland', in *The Innes Review*. vol. XLII. no 1. 1991: 46-67.
47. Marr, A. *The Battle for Scotland*. 1992: 75-84; Finlay, R.J. *Independent and Free*. chap. 3.
48. MacColla, F. *Ro Fhada ...* .1975: 88-95.
49. Reilly, P. 'Catholics and Scottish Literature 1878-1978', in *The Innes Review*. 29. 1978: 193.
50. Smith, I.C. 'Real People in a Real Place', in *Towards the Human*. Edinburgh. 1986: 53, 58.
51. All quotations from the 1981 edition, Pergamon Press.
52. Quoted in the preface to the 1987 edition of the novel, p. viii.
53. See Alan Massie's review of the novel in *The Scotsman*. 9 March 1986.
54. See Genette, G. *Seuils* (Editions du Seuil, Paris). 1987: 182-218.
55. Smith, I.C. 'Real People ... '. 1986: 56.
56. See Withers, C.W.J. *Gaelic Scotland. The Transformation of a Culture Region*, for a study of this particular aspect.
57. Richards, E. *A History of the Highland Clearances*. i. London. 1982: 359-60.
58. Johnston, T. *The History of the Working Classes in Scotland*. Glasgow. 1920. On this point see Price, R. *Neil M. Gunn. The Fabulous Matter of Fact*. Edinburgh. 1991. chap. 3.
59. Samuel, R. *Theatres of Memory*. London. 1994. preface p x.
60. Le Goff, J. *Histoire et Mémoire*. Paris. 1988.
61. Nora, P. (ed) *Les Lieux de Mémoire*. 7 vols. Paris. 1984-92.
62. A book edited by MacLean, M. & Carrell, C. *As An Fhearann. From the Land*, was published in 1986, following the exhibition; in it, the Act is commemorated as the end to a century of 'population clearance, forced evictions, and emigration under duress'. p 5.
63. On the more recent cairns designed by Will MacLean and erected in Lewis, see eg Duncan Macmillan's article in *The Scotsman*. 20 May 1996.
64. Eg Lindsay, M. *Scotland An Anthology*. London. 1974; Bruce, G. & Rennie, F. *The Land out there: A Scottish Land Anthology*. Aberdeen. 1991; Dunn, D. *Scotland An Anthology*. London. 1991.
65. Dunn, D. *Scotland An Anthology*. 1991: 9.

SOUTERRAINS IN SUTHERLAND

Alex. Morrison

BACKGROUND

The terminology of these sites has varied considerably over the past 150 years, with labels such as *Pict's house*, *eirde house*, *earth-house* (RCAHMS *Sutherland Inventory* 1911), *weem* and *leabidh fholaich* being used at different times, and mostly suggesting a dwelling or refuge function. Some of this has been discussed by Brothwell (1977. 179), who avoided the word *souterrain* as:

> ... a more cautious term – covering as it does an underground passage, tunnel, subway structure – but does not imply any expanded or terminal 'living' or 'storage' area which some seem to show, and it is difficult to determine how much of some structures was originally underground.

Most recent writers on the subject appear to be well aware of the limitations involved in the use of the word 'souterrain', and of the implications for living, storage and even possible 'ritual' functions of the surviving remains. Despite the lack of evidence, in some cases, as to whether the structures were completely or partially underground, the word 'souterrain' will be retained here, and will be used to refer to structures of 'typical' souterrain shape – to passages, more or less curved; and to underground chambers which might not be passages but which seem, in some examples, to have good evidence of being attached to surface structures.

The number of structures under this heading [Fig. 10.1] is not large for the size of the area involved, nor is the information available consistent in quantity and quality. Not all structures recorded in the 1911 Royal Commission *Inventory* and later sources are undoubted souterrains, and some of the sites listed here have a question mark against them as an indicator of incomplete information. Some sites are listed from hearsay reports, others have disappeared or perhaps been destroyed – for example, the site at Deanside, Tongue (no. 7 on the present list), which was 'washed away in a flood' (Horsburgh 1868. 276).

In some cases a 'depression' in the ground has been accepted as evidence of an underground structure. The dimensions listed for some can, therefore, be only indications. However, enough is known to allow some discussion and comparison, particularly in the light of more recent excavations, avoiding, for the present, too many firm conclusions. It can also be argued that such structures should not be discussed as separate entities but rather as part of the overall settlement complex. This would indeed be the ideal situation and some attempt will be made here to review evidence for possibly

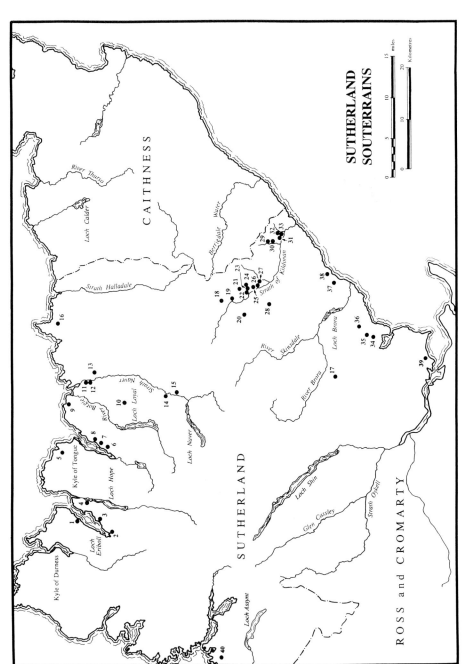

Fig. 10.1   Distribution map of Sutherland souterrains. Numbers refer to the souterrains listed in Fig. 10.2.

linked surface structures, but it should be remembered that, by the very nature of their subterranean construction and survival, as against the destructive activities which have occurred on the surface, many have no evidence of associated structures at all.

DISTRIBUTION

Of the 40 certain and probable Sutherland souterrains listed, 29 (72%) lie between sea level and 107 m, and 10 (26%) lie between 120 m and 200 m [Fig. 10.1; 10.2]. The vast majority of the sites, therefore, lie in the zone of greatest archaeological destruction, and they have mostly been discovered by man's activities, agricultural or otherwise. The Fouhlin souterrain (no. 2) is the lowest-lying site at around 6 m above sea level. A single site, on Beinn a'Bhragie at Golspie (no. 36), lies at a height of about 350 m, near the monument to the first Duke of Sutherland. It is listed as a souterrain by the Royal Commission (1911) and the description is in keeping with many others of known souterrains, but an Ordnance Survey field worker (NMRS Archive) noted 'the situation on a steep, exposed hillside would be unusual for a structure of this type'. It is unusual only because of its extreme height above sea level, but it serves as a reminder that souterrain sites, and thus settlements, may be located higher than 200 m in Sutherland. It is likely that more of these structures await discovery, and that in remote areas with land of little modern value, many will never be discovered. We are thus mapping survival and fortuitous discovery, and the 'real' distribution of souterrains and its significance are likely to remain elusive.

The distribution is fairly scattered, apart from what might be considered a concentration in the Strath of Kildonan – 16 souterrains (or 40% of the total) lying between 61 m and 183 m above sea level in this region. This is again an example of a zone of discovery/destruction: a strath, quite narrow in places, broadening out elsewhere, with water supply, routeway, accessible tributary glens and soil suitable enough to have been used for settlement and farming since prehistoric times.

SHAPE, SIZE & STRUCTURE

Early descriptions of souterrains can be deceptive as to depth and surviving length, since many were examined without any attempt at excavation, and sometimes the first description was recorded long after discovery. As James Horsburgh (1868. 276) noted of the site at Ribigill, Tongue (no. 6) in 1867: ' ... it had often been opened before'.

The RCAHMS *Sutherland Inventory* (1911. xxxi-xxxiii) defined three types of souterrain:

LIST OF SUTHERLAND SOUTERRAINS

No. on Location Map [Fig. 10.1]	Grid Ref.	Height OD	Length	Width	Height	Surface Structures
1. Portnancon, Durness	NC 428 613	24m	7.7m	0.71-1.7m	0.9-1.4m	X
2. Fouhlin, Durness	NC 404 541	6m	21.9m	0.6-1.2m	1.07-1.58m	X
3. Eriboll, Durness	NC 433 563	76m	12+m	0.6-1.1m	1.2-1.4m	
4. Loch Hope, Durness	NC 469 590	46m	c.20m	-	-	X
5. Achintyhalavin, Tongue (?)	NC 566 643	30m	-	-	-	
6. Ribigill, Tongue	NC 582 545	30m	-	-	-	
7. Deanside, Tongue (?)	NC 591 557	12m	-	-	-	
8. Kirkiboll, Tongue	NC 59 57	61m	7.6+m	0.76-1.2m	-	
9. Skerray Mains, Tongue (?)	NC 660 631	15m	-	-	-	
10. Cracknie, Farr	NC 665 509	168m	12.8+m	0.6-1.82m	1.3-1.47m	?
11. Achnabourin, Farr	NC 709 585	15m	c.16.5m	c.2.7m	-	
12. Achnabourin, Farr	NC 710 582	18m	c.13.4m	-	-	
13. Skelpick Burn, Farr	NC 728 563	76m	c.2.3m	-	-	X
14. Syre, Farr (?)	NC 692 440	51m	12+m	-	-	
15. Rosal, Strathnaver, Farr	NC 689 417	98m	12.8m	0.6-1.06m	0.84-1.45m	?
16. Strathy, Farr	NC 836 651	15m	-	-	-	
17. Cnoc Achadh na h-Uaighe, Rogart	NC 717 075	198m	c.l2m	2.5-3.0m	-	X
18. Creag nan Caorach, Kildonan (?)	NC 86 31	183m	-	-	-	X
19. Kinbrace Hill, Kildonan	NC 86 29	137m	c.7.6m	1.2m	1.67m	X
20. Loch Ascaig, Kildonan	NC 845 253	137m	c.14m	-	-	?
21. Allt Bad Ra'fin, Kildonan	NC 900 265	128m	-	1.2m	-	X
22. Suisgill I, Kildonan	NC 892 251	82m	7.3+m	0.76-0.91m	-	
23. Suisgill II, Kildonan	NC 898 251	82m	3.6+m	0.95-1.45m	1.3m	

No. on Location Map [Fig. 10.1]	Grid Ref.	Height OD	Length	Width	Height	Surface Structures
24. Suisgill III, Kildonan	NC 897 251	82m	4.5+m	0.6+m	1.4m	?
25. Ach an Fhionn-fhuaraidh, Kildonan	NC 904 240	152m	c.l0m	-	-	X
26. Achinnearin, Kildonan	NC 903 232	122m	12.2m	0.71-1.37m	0.81-1.88m	?
27. Kildonan Burn, Kildonan	NC 91 22	122m	7.9m	3.4m	(chamber)	X
28. Tuarie Burn, Kildonan	NC 825 204	183m	-	-	-	X
29. Allt Cille Pheadair, Kildonan	NC 993 193	91m	-	-	-	X
30. Allt Cille Pheadair, Kildonan	NC 992 190	91m	9.6m	0.6-1.2m	0.71-1.37m	X
31. Salscraggie Lodge, Kildonan	NC 999 183	61m	6.7m	0.6-1.06m	0.71-1.57m	
32. Caen Burn, Kildonan	NC 011 184	91m	7.9m	0.83-1.06m	1.2-1.47m	X
33. Caen Burn, Kildonan (?)	NC 0l 18	61m	-	-	-	X
34. Kirkton, Golspie	NC 797 987	40m	11.28m	1.3m	1.8m	
35. Silver Rock, Golspie (?)	NC 80 99	107m	-	-	-	
36. Beinn a'Bhragie, Golspie	NC 814 009	351m	c.12.2m	1.2m	1.5m	
37. Clyne Milton, Clyne (?)	NC 912 068	30m	-	-	1.67m	
38. Kintradwell, Loth	NC 919 077	46m	-	-	-	?
39. Cyderhall, Dornoch	NH 753 883	17m	7.2+m	1.7m	1.5m+	X
40. Gleann Leireag, Assynt (?)	NC 153 312	c.60m	c.11m	0.80-0.90m	0.6-1.0m	

Fig. 10.2 List of Sutherland Souterrains.

    X   Evidence of associated surface structures

    ?   Possibility of associated surface structures

First, those having access from one end only, measuring 20' to 40' or thereby in length, with no definite chamber attached other than that produced by a slight expansion at the end, curving in their course inwards more or less to the right, with a width along the gallery of from 2'6" to 3', and a slightly greater width towards the inner end.

... Those of the second variety differ conspicuously from the first by having an opening at both ends and definitely formed chambers. There are but two examples, viz. one at Kirkton [no. 34 on the present list; Fig.10.3E] and the other at Kintradwell [no. 38 on the present list; Fig. 10.3I].

... The examples which form the third variety resemble the so-called 'pit-dwellings'. They have been oval chambers with their sides built and only partially sunk in the ground. Three of these are noted, but as all are roofless, few details are obtainable regarding them without excavation. One by the Kildonan Burn [no. 27 on the present list; Fig. 10.4B] is connected with a hut circle, while that situated by the Silver Rock near The Mound [no. 35 on the present list] and the other close to the broch of Carrol show no remains of a related structure adjoining them.

The Sutherland souterrains vary in size if not greatly in shape [Figs. 10.3-10.5]. Wainwright (1953. 225-6) suggested that they had a similarity in shape and plan with the souterrains of Angus, and:

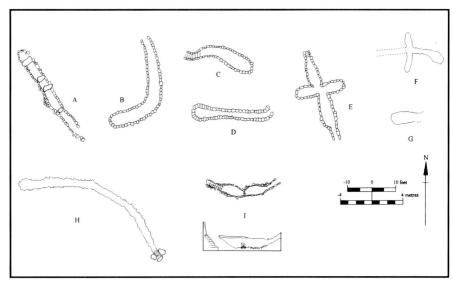

Fig. 10.3   Sutherland souterrain plans.
   A: Rosal, Strathnaver   F: Suisgill III
   B: Achinnearin   G: Suisgill II
   C: Salscraggie Lodge   H: Fouhlin, Loch Eriboll
   D: Eriboll   I: Kintradwell
   E: Kirkton, Golspie

... the fact that they are all essentially passages, as distinct from chambers, sets them apart from the structures of the northern isles.

... Perhaps the Sutherland souterrains of this kind were normally adjuncts to surface structures, in which case they would have more in common with the souterrains attached to Hebridean wheel-houses than with the souterrains of Angus. The latter ... were not subsidiary to any other structure.

The excavations at Newmill (Watkins 1980b) and the greater numbers and forms of souterrains now identified by aerial photography in 'Southern Pictland' (Maxwell 1987), suggest that simple comparisons based on size and shape can no longer serve to distinguish the Sutherland structures from those of Angus. Nor can the Angus souterrains any longer be assumed to be generally independent of surface structures, or to be specifically intended for sheltering animals.

The majority of Sutherland souterrains so far discovered are indeed 'essentially passages', but there are a few exceptions. The descriptions of a

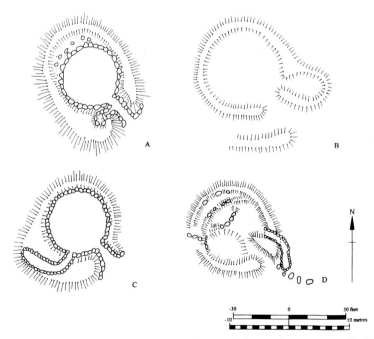

Fig. 10.4   Souterrains or possible souterrains attached to surface structures in the Strath of Kildonan. The numbers in brackets refer to the site numbers in the RCAHMS *Sutherland Inventory* (1911), from which the plans were taken.

> A: Allt Cille Pheadair (No. 327)
> B: Creag Druim nan Rath, Kildonan Burn (No. 344)
> C: Allt Cille Pheadair (No. 328)
> D: Caen Burn (No. 318)

couple of the sites in the Strath of Kildonan indicate something like an underground oval chamber approached through, and buried under, the wall of a hut – emphasising the essential association of the surface and subterranean structures. At the site on Creag Druim nan Rath, Kildonan (no. 27) [Fig. 10.4B], the roof covering has disappeared, leaving the oval outline of the underground chamber beneath the foundation of the hut circle wall. The souterrain listed as Suisgill III (no. 24), excavated by Gordon Barclay in 1980, is cruciform-shaped [Fig. 10.3F], and it is possible that Suisgill II (no. 23) [Fig. 10.3G] could also be of this form (Barclay 1985, 194). In their cruciform shape they resemble the site at Kirkton, near Golspie (no. 34) [Fig. 10.3E], but that structure has two entrances and door checks resembling those on brochs and some duns. Barclay (*loc. cit.*) has suggested that Suisgill III should be dated to the mid-first millennium BC. If this is accurate, then it might be argued that the cruciform-shaped sites are an earlier form than the simple passages, but much more excavation and dating evidence is needed.

Another exception in shape is the site at Kintradwell (no. 38) [Fig. 10.3I], which was originally described as '... two chambers, separated by a low division wall, each having an entrance from the outside at its extremity' (RCAHMS 1911, no. 469). The plan (from Joass 1864) shows that there was a definite entrance with steps down into the passage, but the opposite end, according to Joass, was simply an 'opening'. The dividing wall was only 0.6 m high and did not completely block access from one part of the passage to the other. Unless a more formal entrance had been destroyed before Joass's visit to the site, the eastern opening might be regarded as a later means of access to what could have originally been a single-entry structure.

The Fouhlin souterrain, Durness (no. 2) [Fig. 10.3H] has a western, lower entrance with four steps down into the passage (Morrison & Reid 1964, 1965: report forthcoming). This entrance and the steps are at the rounded, slightly expanded, end of the souterrain passage. In many of Sutherland's single-entrance souterrains this is the shape of the inner, closed end of the passage – the 'pear-shaped expansion'. It could be suggested that this western entrance is a secondary construction inserted into the 'dead end' of a pre-existing single-entrance souterrain – perhaps found necessary because of the unusual length of the passage, or because of an extension of that passage – but there is no definite proof of this. The actual entrance gap is very narrow, only 0.58 m wide. It is flanked by two large, upright orthostatic stones which play no part in supporting the last roofing slab. These orthostats are surrounded by very well-constructed dry-stone walling which continues the walls of the passage out into the open and above the top of the last slab of the roof. Despite its smallness and narrowness, this western opening is a true entrance with steps and vertical 'doorway'. By comparison, the south-eastern, upslope entrance looks much more like a 'trapdoor' leading down through the floor of a house, but this was perhaps the original and 'proper' entrance. Three large slabs around the opening are very like paving on the floor of a surface structure or dwelling, and there were traces of the ruined wall of a possible hut circle running just beyond the edge of the opening, so that it could be suggested that the entrance to the souterrain passage at this end was through the floor of a hut. This would not be unusual, considering the number of souterrains known to be connected with the walls of hut circles in the Strath of Kildonan [Fig. 10.4] and elsewhere. The 'steps' leading down from this end, to the passage below, are quite unlike those at the western end. They consist of thin slabs, almost flagstones, projecting from the end of the souterrain passage, with a gap under each slab, more resembling a ladder than a stairway. The Fouhlin structure thus had two entrances, one of which might have been a later addition. There are relatively straight-passaged souterrains such as Eriboll (no. 3), Rosal (no. 15) and Beinn a'Bhragie (no. 36), but the majority of the passage forms are curved. The curving might have been related to the nature of the surface structures with which the souterrains were associated. Some appear to curve around the periphery of a hut wall, as, for instance, at Allt Cille Pheadair, Kildonan (no. 30) [Fig. 10.4C] or perhaps at Caen Burn, Kildonan (no. 32) [Fig. 10.4D].

Only 27 out of the 40 sites recorded here have information on length. Allowing for truncated passages, the range of lengths among these 26 runs from 2.3 m (surviving) at Skelpick Burn, Farr (no. 13) to 21.9 m at Fouhlin, Durness (no. 2), the Fouhlin structure being the longest so far discovered in the county. Bearing in mind the incompleteness of some of the information, there is a clustering of lengths around 6-8 m (7 sites) and 11-14 m (11 sites). Internal widths (again where information is available, in 20 cases) range from 0.6 m to 3.4 m, but the 0.6 m width is for the narrowest part of eg Rosal (no. 15) which widens to 1.06 m in places, and the 3.4 m width is for the widest surviving part (the rounded 'end chamber') of the Kildonan Burn souterrain (no. 27). Even fewer (17 sites) have surviving evidence of internal height, ranging from 0.71 m (lowest part of Allt Cille Pheadair, Kildonan (no. 30) and Salscraggie Lodge, Kildonan (no. 31)) to 1.88 m (highest part of Achinnearin, Kildonan (no. 26)).

The component parts of most Sutherland souterrains would appear to be:
* the trench
* the stone-built walls of the passage lining the trench, with any steps leading out
* the roofing.

At Fouhlin (no. 2) [Fig. 10.3H] the trench was dug into fluvio-glacial material, and the line of the original cutting could be seen in profile in the face of some of the sections excavated. The ochreous, compacted fluvio-glacial material had been excavated by the souterrain-builders to form a trench about 2.1 m deep and 2.1 - 2.4 m wide (the trench for the souterrain passage at Cyderhall, Dornoch (no. 39) was 2.25 m wide).

The dry-stone walling along the sides of the trench is fairly typical of souterrain construction, having large basal stones supporting several courses of smaller stones. Building material was available from the surrounding hill slopes, which are strewn with glacial boulders. Since the majority of the boulders used are rounded rather than slabby, a fair amount of selection must have been necessary in order to produce a stable wall, and wedging or pinning stones had been jammed or hammered into the gaps between the larger stones to improve stability (cf. Watkins 1980b. 169-170).

The roofing slabs are of irregular shape but they fit closely enough to leave only small gaps in the roof. The roof and wall tops had been packed with stones to increase stability and to seal any gaps. The largest and heaviest roofing slabs, up to 2.4 m in length and 0.3 m thick, are at the western end, and this is also where the passage expands into the rounded 'end chamber' shape. The problem of roofing the passage with slabs, which in some places were rather shorter than desirable, was overcome by having two courses of large flat stones at the top of the wall projecting slightly in a crude form of corbelling and weighted at their outside edges with boulders. This device enabled the builders to construct a passage wider than would otherwise have been possible with the available slabs. In general, the information for the roofing of Sutherland souterrains, while incomplete, indicates that stone slabs were used on most sites. But for reasons varying from the absence of suitable building material to the requirements of function, some appear to have had other forms of roofing. At Rosal (no. 15) [Fig. 10.3A], Corcoran, despite the presence of three roofing slabs *in situ*, noted the general absence of stones of passage-roofing proportions in the vicinity and suggested partial roofing with timber (1968. 115):

> In souterrains roofed entirely by stone slabs, the side walls are usually given a slightly inward batter so that the weight of the roof gives stability to the walls. At Rosal the walls were given a slightly backward batter, and so retain their stability without the weight of roofing stone.

At Cyderhall, Dornoch (no. 39) [Fig. 10.5] the surviving length of souterrain passage had four opposite pairs of post holes, which appeared to be primary features, along the inner face of the passage wall, three pairs 0.8 - 0.9 m apart transversely and the fourth pair only 0.45 m apart, possibly representing the end or entrance to the passage (Pollock 1992. 152-153, illus 2-4). On Pollock's plans, a 'gully', running off to the west and interpreted as being associated with the round house, looks remarkably like the surviving stretch of souterrain in form, including the pairs of post holes along the sides of the structure, but without the stone lining. There might have been a continuous structure here, considering how much of the site had been cut away, and the excavator does state that the gully had 'some similarities to the souterrain'. It would admittedly produce a structure with a highly unusual 'kink' to the line of its passage. The presence of posts close to the wall of the souterrain might have been to revet the wall itself and/or support a roof where the stone walls were perhaps not stable enough, because of the sandy gravel matrix, to support the roof on their own. The space between each post along the wall-face seems rather wide to offer much support to the wall, unless the posts were also supporting horizontal timbers against the wall face. No stone slabs long enough to bridge the passage were found during the excavation, so a timber roof seems likely. Watkins (1980b. 195-196) reached similar conclusions about the very much wider souterrain at Newmill, Perthshire, where slabs up to 5 m in length would have been necessary. At Cyderhall and Newmill, the excavators see no problems in the construction of a timber roof by groups who were well experienced in the use of wood in the building of surface round houses.

ASSOCIATION WITH SURFACE STRUCTURES

As listed, there are only 15 sites with evidence for surface structures associated with the souterrains, 38% of the total. This rises to 54% if the sites where there is possible evidence are included. Much of the surviving evidence shows souterrain entrances opening from the inner face of the wall and down through the floor of a hut circle. Portnancon (no. 1) is noted as having been entered from what was originally the south-east arc of a hut circle. Loch Hope (no. 4) was entered probably from under a 'lintel slab' on the south side of the interior of a hut circle. At Skelpick Burn (no. 13) the wall of a hut circle was expanded to incorporate the souterrain, and at Cnoc Achadh na h-Uaighe, Rogart (no. 17) the souterrain was attached to one of three hut circles. The greatest quantity of evidence for entrance from surface habitations comes from the sites in the Strath of Kildonan (nos. 18, 19, 21, 25, 27, 28, 29, 30, 32, 33), and at Cyderhall, Dornoch (no. 39) the souterrain was associated with a possible round house.

During the excavation of the Fouhlin site (no. 2), traces of surface structures were detected. Some of these appear to have been built across the line of the roof of the souterrain, but they were fragmentary and not easy to follow. What seemed to be parts of the foundations of hut-circle walls petered out before much of the circumference could be determined, and in places the stones were missing altogether. Examination of the remains of what might have been a surface hut foundation above the south-eastern entrance revealed parts of querns. A matching lower quern stone for one of these was found on the floor of the souterrain passage just at the bottom of the steps of this south-eastern entrance, supporting the suggestion that, at this end at least and at one stage of its use, the souterrain could have been entered through the floor of a surface building. At Cyderhall (no. 39), a possible round house above the souterrain [Fig. 10.5] had a sunken floor, which may have been deliberately hollowed out to allow easier access to the underground structure.

It seems now logical to suggest that no souterrain existed in total isolation and, where not directly connected to one, some may have been positioned within reach of several habitations. This could have been the case at Rosal (no. 15), where Corcoran (1968. 117) noted that the souterrain's floor area of about 9 square metres would perhaps have been more than needed for storage of a year's supply of foodstuffs for a single family unit. At Fouhlin (no. 2), the sheer length of the souterrain would have provided

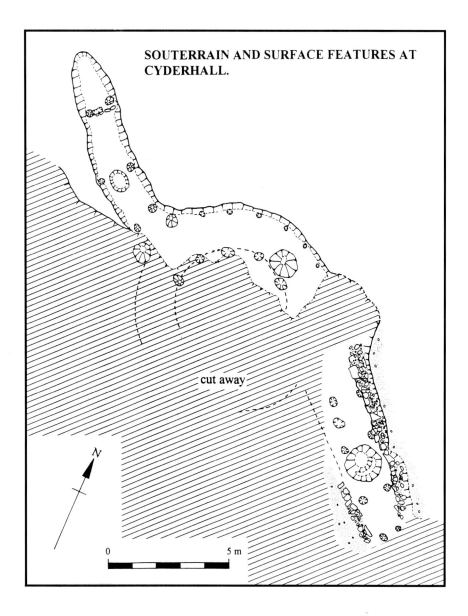

Fig. 10.5 Souterrain and surface features at Cyderhall. After Pollock (1992): illustrations 2, 3 & 4.

space for storage for a number of families, and the double entrance might have been an adaptation towards allowing access from different surface structures or by different users. The question of size and space for storage is thus bedevilled by the problem of access. Even two 'end-entrances' would not bring within easy reach materials stored in the middle of a souterrain the length of Fouhlin. There is still a possibility that some structures had roofs not below, but flush with the ground surface, and that occasional (or regular) removal of roofing slabs was necessary to get at the contents. This would also remove such structures from consideration as 'places of refuge'.

FUNCTION, CONTENTS & DATING

> There are 3 subterraneous passages, or tumuli, in this parish, which, it is said, lead from one cairn, under the bed of the river of Helmsdale, to another on the opposite side. They are covered at the top with large flags, above a trench of 3 feet broad, and 5 or 6 feet high [0.9 m x 1.5-1.8 m]. From their construction and direction, they seem to have been places of retreat for the inhabitants, with their effects and cattle, from the pursuit of invading enemies, in troublesome times; or sally ports, for facilitating their escape from a victorious enemy.

Thus Donald Sage, minister in Kildonan parish, described three of the souterrains in the Strath of Kildonan, in the *Old Statistical Account* of 1791. The 'cairns' from which the 'subterraneous passages' lead were no doubt the ruinous remains of hut circles or round houses such as those at Caen Burn [Fig. 10.4D] or Allt Cille Pheadair [Fig.10.4C], with which souterrain passages are connected. The theory that these structures were places of refuge was current for a long period of time. In one of the earliest descriptions, Martin Martin (1716. 154) writing of the island of Skye, stated: 'There are several little stone Houses, built underground, call'd Earth-houses, which serv'd to hide a few People and their goods in time of War.' Describing the *eirde house* at Eriboll [Fig. 10.3D], Arthur Mitchell (1866) noted that other underground structures in the district were known as *leabidh fholaich* ('hiding beds'). Wainwright (1963. 14) dismissed the 'refuge' theory, noting the impossibility of defending such a structure from the inside and particularly that their location would not be unknown to a potential attacker. It would also be unlikely if, as suggested above, the roofing were visible on the surface. The Sutherland sites are even less likely, on account of their narrowness and lower roofing, to have offered safe refuge in times of trouble. By contrast, many of the Irish souterrains, with their elaborate air vents, angled passages, hidden chambers, drop holes and 'creeps', seem to be constructed for defence or protection rather than storage (Warner 1979).

The 1911 RCAHMS *Sutherland Inventory* (1911. xxxii-xxxiii) casts doubt on the possible use of the structures as dwellings or 'sleeping-chambers' because:

... the extreme narrowness of the first variety [see above] and the small dimensions of the expansions at the inner end, together with the lack of air and light, make them very unsuitable places for human habitation.

[As hiding- places they were too conspicuous] ... notably in the hut circle by the Cille Pheadair Burn ... with its huge covering bank, or in that of the third variety by the Kildonan Burn ... which must have displayed a marked elevation close to the entrance of the hut circle. Situated as some of these are, opening out of conspicuous hut circles, presumably the daily abodes of the people, they do not seem to answer to the requirements of a secure retreat.

But the writer did note the checks and constrictions in the passages at Cracknie and Caen Burn and that '... much food refuse, as well as other signs of occupation, were discovered in both examples'. No mention of food remains is to be found in the descriptions of these sites in the *Inventory* (nos. 220, 318) or elsewhere, and in this respect they seem to have been confused with Kirkton (no. 34) and Kintradwell (no. 38), which had checks, constrictions and food refuse in the form of animal bones and shells of limpet and periwinkle. For some sites, storage was not ruled out: '... if these galleries were used as granaries, the presence of querns, as in that at Salscraggie, is easily understood'.

As far as the Scottish souterrains are concerned, and despite arguments of dampness and difficulty of easy access, the storage function has most support at the present time. Other suggestions have been smoking or curing places for fish or meat, and sunken dairy compartments. The Cyderhall souterrain (no. 39) had a pit, 1.5 m deep and 1.5 m in diameter, dug into the floor. 'This would have made access up and down the interior of the souterrain very difficult, unless it was covered over by planking, and the purpose of such a unique feature is not clear, unless it was simply to create an extra volume of storage space.' (Pollock 1992. 153). Traces of hemp and cultivated flax were recovered from the souterrain floor, suggesting either storage of these crops or the presence of hemp or linen sacks. Other uses are hinted at by the presence of evidence for faecal material on the floor. Storage of grain in the souterrain is regarded as unlikely – there was a grain pit in the floor of the associated round house, with the main evidence being for six-row barley but also traces of emmer wheat and oats, and possibly spelt and rye.

P-R. Giot, in a discussion of Armorican souterrains (1960), discussed the difficult problems posed by interpretation of their use. Many had been found completely empty, yielding little information. If some had been used as grain stores, traces of organic material might be expected. Earlier interpretations included suggestions that they had been burial places, with slight traces of ash and burned bone (of indeterminate nature) seeming to indicate cremation burials. This was opposed by the argument that these underground structures were meant to be used primarily by the living, although this would not rule out the possibility of their later use as burial sites or even deliberate backfilling by subsequent users of the site. 'Le fait que le boyau ou les puits d'entrée de tant de souterrains était soigneusement obturé peut aussi avoir une signification analogue, plutôt qu' une raison de sécurité, pour éviter des accidents ou le comblement par dégradation' (Giot 1960. 60).

'The careful excavation of the souterrain of Kervénarc'hant in Pleyber-Christ [Brittany] showed clearly that pottery sherds, bone debris, charcoal, burnt stones and earth were mixed together in successive levels and ... thus this souterrain had been deliberately blocked with a variety of debris from neighbouring dwellings' (Giot *loc. cit.*). From this it was concluded that souterrains were complementary to dwellings.

In a later account, Giot (1971. 158) noted:

> Most often the chambers and tunnels contain absolutely nothing left from their period of occupation, and all that one finds come from this fill. And, in the more rare occasions when there are some objects in the occupation layer, it is possible to ascertain that there are sherds of more recent pottery types amongst the material of this fill.

The interpretation here appears to be of an original storage function, always associated with a surface structure. After normal use the passage, or at least its entrance area, becomes a dump for rubbish, in the process acquiring materials of a period or of periods much later than that of the souterrain's original use. This is reminiscent of the re-use of grain pits as rubbish dumps in some Iron Age settlement sites. A reasonable conclusion would be that of Christie (1979. 210): 'The function of souterrains still eludes us, if indeed there ever was one overall function applicable to the whole group of monuments under this heading, which seems unlikely'.

The infilling of souterrains could have taken place for a variety of reasons, and the above-mentioned evidence suggests that some sites were dumping places for rubbish from the surface settlement, obviously at some time after the original function of the passage had been superseded. At Cyderhall, the excavator has proposed that the deliberate infilling of the passage there might be related to some of these structures having 'a significance beyond the purely utilitarian for their Iron Age builders' (Pollock 1992. 159). The site at Northwaterbridge, Kincardineshire (Small, Cottam & Dunbar 1974) appears to have been back-filled before the structure was completed, perhaps because of the unstable nature of the material into which the trench had been dug.

The reference to burials is interesting, since there are reports of human remains being discovered in association with souterrains. Among the Sutherland souterrains, a human arm bone was recovered during the clearing-out of the passage of the structure at Salscraggie Lodge in the Strath of Kildonan (no. 31) [Fig. 10.3C]; two 'urns' or vessels of clay which 'crumbled away' were said to have been found in the souterrain at Skerray Mains, Torrisdail, Tongue (no. 9), and Stuart (1868) refers to portions of an urn with chevron ornament in relief and bits of charred wood being found when an *eirde house* on the bank of the Helmsdale River at Torrish was cleared out. The 'urns' could have been domestic pottery, and charred wood is no guarantee of cremation, but there are other instances of human remains being found in Scottish souterrains.

The major question is *when* the material came into the souterrain passage – whether during the 'normal' initial use of the structure, or in a later secondary phase or phases when perhaps the initial function had been forgotten and the passage had acquired another, possibly quite different, purpose. A bronze spiral finger ring and a bronze spherical object '... showing numerous small hammer-marks', were said to have been found in the souterrain at Eriboll (no. 3) (Mitchell 1866). A small ring of shale about 2.5 cm in diameter and a fragment of another were recovered from the site at Kirkton, Golspie (no. 34) and 'much food refuse lay on the floor' (RCAHMS 1911). At Salscraggie Lodge (no. 31), apart from the human arm bone, parts of two rotary querns and a saddle quern were recovered from the interior of the souterrain; it was noted that the querns were found around the entrance but the human arm bone was not.

At Kintradwell, Joass, in what can only be described as a cursory examination of the souterrain there, discovered a low dividing wall, not unlike the 'creeps' in some Irish souterrains. Built into this wall was a large block of stone which bore on one perpendicular face scratches which Joass likened to 'early Scandinavian letters'. The stone was subsequently lost before proper analysis could be carried out, but the marks shown on Joass's sketch of the stone do not resemble 'runes' so much as accidental scratches. Even if they had been runes, this can only be seen as further evidence that many of these passages could have been open at a late date, that structural alterations might have been made for functions quite different from those of the original building, and that finds in the passage do not necessarily date the primary use of the structure. Joass (1864) also noted '... numerous shells of the limpet and periwinkle, with animal bones, and portions of very hard black peat', suggestive of midden remains (no. 38) [Fig. 10.3I].

Shell midden material in the passage at Fouhlin (no. 2), including mussel and oyster shells, was part of what may have been a much larger concentration on the surface. It is possible here, too, that a roofing slab of the souterrain might have been deliberately removed in order to dispose of some of the surface accumulation, at a time when the souterrain itself was no longer serving its original purpose. There are two areas where roofing slabs are missing. One is where modern clearance for house foundations broke through the roof of the souterrain; there is no shell midden beneath this. The other gap is immediately above the concentration of midden material in the passage. There is no midden material at the bottom of the 'steps' at the south-eastern entrance to the souterrain passage; the shelly mixture begins about 2.4 m along the passage from this end. This suggests that, if the rubbish were deliberately dumped in the passage through a gap made in the roof, the true entrance was already obscured or blocked. It also means that any objects under the midden material in the passage (eg there were discrete patches of rust in the floor at this point) pre-date the intrusion of that material. They too may have been dumped, but they may also belong to the period of original use of the souterrain.

At the time of the discovery of the Fouhlin souterrain, a small pair of bronze toilet shears was discovered projecting from between the wall stones near the roof and just beyond the collapsed roofing slab (*Proc. Soc. Antiq. Scot.* vol 94. 1960-61. 327). The shears are unique in Scotland, if not in the British Isles, and comparisons of form and decoration have been made with bucket handles from Traprain Law and Dowalton Loch, Kirkcudbright, the Benwell torc and the Newstead tankard holdfast (McGregor 1976. no 277). Again, the completely unstratified location can indicate only deposition at some period, probably early, in the souterrain's use. Excavation of the surface structure connected with the south-eastern entrance to the souterrain uncovered a bead of greenish glass with a yellow enamel spiral running through it. This type has been classified by Margaret Guido (1978. 85-87, Fig. 33/2) as a North Scottish spiral-decorated bead, possibly derived from, but later than, the Meare spiral beads. These Scottish beads were presumably made in the early 1st century AD or shortly before. It is impossible to say accurately when they ceased to be produced, but it may have been in the late 1st century AD. Some may have survived until the late 2nd century, but probably not later. This unfortunately does not tell us when the bead arrived at Fouhlin, although the discovery of the matching quern stone at the bottom of the south-eastern steps indicates that souterrain passage and hut circle floor were connected at some point.

At Cyderhall (no. 39), calibrated radiocarbon dates show occupation of the site somewhere between 400 and 200 BC or earlier, the souterrain contemporary with at least one phase in the use of the surface structure. At Dalladies, Kincardineshire (Watkins 1980a), a number of ditch features associated with round houses had characteristics (timber or dry-stone wall lining) which the excavator sees as being related to souterrains; some of these show evidence of having been deliberately filled in. The time-range for occupation of the site, based on several calibrated radiocarbon dates, is from the 3rd century BC to the beginning of the 7th century AD. At Newmill, Perthshire, a souterrain of the Angus type was excavated and radiocarbon dates (uncalibrated) were obtained for the souterrain itself: 55 ± 90bc, ad 40 ± 70 and ad 195 ± 55 (Watkins 1980b). The latter date (charcoal from the souterrain infill) is presumed to date the destruction or deliberate filling-in of the structure. There were also dates for the adjacent house: ad 40 ± 55, ad 60 ± 55 and ad 85 ± 60, demonstrating the contemporaneity of the structures. But:

> ... the adjacent house continued at least for a while, and the site was apparently still in use in the ninth century. The present indications, imprecise and insufficient as they may be, seem to point to the abandonment of souterrain use by or soon after the third century (Watkins 1984. 78).

Alcock, in considering the Angus souterrains, has no doubts of their proto-Pictish and Pictish attribution, and in the case of sites beyond the Angus/Fife region, suggests a main period of use in the early first millennium AD (Alcock 1980. 68-69).

The Cyderhall radiocarbon determinations suggest a 3rd century AD date for the end of souterrain use there also, but the overall secure dating evidence is minimal and we are still a long way from a firm chronology for the building and original use of souterrains; some might have been built much later than the dates suggested here. These, and other tantalising scraps of evidence raise many important questions:

* What had the function of these deliberately infilled structures been?
* Had the function ended or was it continued elsewhere, on the surface, using other structures or methods?
* Was the infilling simply for purposes of safety or hygiene, or perhaps for some ritual associated with a hitherto unrecognised function?

The investigation of the hut-circle site and the dates obtained at Kilphedir, in the Strath of Kildonan (Fairhurst & Taylor 1971), may be mentioned here as generally relevant to chronology. The range of radiocarbon dates (uncalibrated) for two phases of the occupation of the site show a 5th/4th century bc early phase and a 3rd century bc/1st century ad later phase. The later phase dates are from the massive-walled, expanded-entrance Hut V, which Fairhurst & Taylor (1971. 92-93) compared with other hut circles which have souterrain structures attached – at Kilphedir (nos. 29-30) and Caen Burn (no. 32) in the vicinity, and at Kildonan (no. 27).

CONCLUSIONS

From the foregoing, it will be appreciated that many souterrains contain and preserve evidence for a succession of developments and changes on the surface, and perhaps in the functions of the structures themselves. Some of these developments obviously occurred after the souterrain's 'original' function had ceased, and when it may have become a receptacle for some of the rubbish of the surface settlement or have been re-used for a totally different function, possibly even by groups unconnected with the original builders. The study is complex, and although storage has been proposed as a reasonable interpretation, it does not have unqualified approval. Even the incomplete evidence for the group discussed here indicates differences of usage and, as Patricia Christie noted (1978. 332), in referring to Cornish *fogous* '... each monument has its unique qualities and, like all man-made structures, certainly in prehistory, no two are quite alike'.

Chronology, particularly dates of construction and primary use, is still tenuous, and can obviously not be based on material discovered in the passage or in the floors of surface structures, directly connected or not. There is thus a need for excavation under and behind the stone wall linings of souterrain passages in all future excavations, and in known sites where there has been no major disturbance of these elements.

The evidence from about half of the known Sutherland souterrains suggests that they were connected or associated with surface structures, and careful examination or excavation of the areas immediately surrounding some of the other sites listed might reveal similar evidence. If we can demonstrate that most or all souterrains were constructed as important adjuncts of surface structures, then we may be closer to answering the question of their functions and to using them as a true indication of settlement distribution.

> Now I believe the Troglodytes of old,
> Whereof Herodotus and Strabo told;
> Since everywhere about these parts, in holes
> Cunicular men I find, and humane moles.
> (Brown 1673, quoted in *Antiquity* 1938)

Acknowledgement

I am grateful to Lorraine McEwan, Department of Archaeology, University of Glasgow, for drawing the distribution map and plans, and to the National Monuments Record of Scotland for allowing me to check my list against theirs.

References

Alcock, L. 'Populi bestiales Pictorum feroci animo: a survey of Pictish settlement archaeology', in W.S. Hanson & L.J.F. Keppie (eds) *Roman Frontier Studies 1979* (Papers presented at the 12th International Congress of Roman Frontier Studies). B.A.R. (Int. Ser.) 71. 1980: 61-95.

Anderson, J. 'Notes on the structure, distribution and contents of the brochs, with special reference to the question of their Celtic or Norwegian origin', in *Proc. Soc. Antiq. Scot.* 12. 1876-78: 314-355.

Anderson, J. *Scotland in Pagan Times – The Iron Age.* 1883.

Anon. 'Underground dwellings in Central Europe', in *Antiquity* 12. 1938: 359-361.

Barclay, G. 'Newmill and the souterrains of Southern Pictland', in *Proc. Soc. Antiq. Scot.* 110. 1980: 20-208.

Barclay, G. 'Excavations at Upper Suisgill, Sutherland', in *Proc. Soc. Antiq. Scot.* 115, 1985: 159-198.

Brothwell, D. 'On a mycoform stone structure in Orkney, and its relevance to possible further interpretations of so-called souterrains', in *Bull. Inst. Archaeol. Univ. London* 14. 1977: 179-190.

Brown, E. *A Brief Account of Some Travels in Hungaria.* 1673.

Buxton, R.J. 'The earth-house at Portnancon, Sutherland', in *Proc. Soc. Antiq. Scot.* 69. 1934-35: 431-433.

Childe, V.G. *The Prehistory of Scotland.* 1935.

Christie, P.M. 'The excavation of an Iron Age souterrain and settlement at Carn Euny, Sancreed, Cornwall', in *Proc. Prehist. Soc.* 44. 1978: 309-433.

Christie, P.M. 'Cornish souterrains in the light of recent research', in *Bull. Inst. Archaeol. Univ. London* 16. 1979: 187-214.

Corcoran, J.X.W.P. 'The souterrain at Rosal, Strath Naver', in *Proc. Soc. Antiq. Scot.* 100. 1967-68: 114-118.

Curle, A.O. 'On the examination of two hut circles in the Strath of Kildonan, Sutherlandshire, one of which has an earth house annexe', in *Proc. Soc. Antiq. Scot.* 45. 1910-11: 18-26.

Fairbairn, A. 'Account of the discovery of a cinerary urn with other relics, near Marchhouse, Muirkirk, and the Excavation of an Earth-house at Yardhouses, Carnwath', in *Proc. Soc. Antiq. Scot.* 58. 1923-24: 333-343.

Fairhurst, H. & Taylor, D.B. 'A hut-circle settlement at Kilphedir, Sutherland', in *Proc. Soc. Antiq. Scot.* 103. 1970-71: 65-99.

Friell, J.G.P. & Watson, W.G. *Pictish Studies: Settlement, Burial and Art in Dark Age Northern Britain*. B.A.R. 125. Oxford. 1984.

Goudie, G. 'An Underground Gallery recently Discovered on the Island of Tiree: with a note of another in the same island, from a Plan of Sir Henry Dryden', in *Proc. Soc. Antiq. Scot.* 51. 1916-17: 100-108.

Giot, P-R. 'Les souterrains armoricains de l'age du fer', in *Annales de Bretagne* 67. 1960: 45-65.

Giot, P-R. 'Hill settlements, souterrains and the chronology of the Iron Age in Brittany', in D. Hill & M. Jesson (eds)*The Iron Age and its Hill-forts* (University of Southampton Monograph Series No. 1). 1971: 155-159.

Guido, M. 'The Glass Beads of the Prehistoric and Roman Periods in Britain and Ireland', in *Soc. Antiq. London, Research Report No. 35*. 1978.

Henderson, I. *The Picts*. 1967.

Home, D.M. 'Account of a subterranean building found near Broom-house, the property of Colonel Logan Home, in the parish of Edrom, Berwickshire', in *Proc. Soc. Antiq. Scot.* 8. 1868-1870: 20-28.

Horsburgh, J. 'Notes of cromlechs, duns, hut circles, chambered cairns, and other remains, in the county of Sutherland', in *Proc. Soc. Antiq. Scot.* 7. 1866-68: 271-279.

Hutcheson, A. 'Early underground buildings in Scotland', in *Proc. Trans. Dundee Naturalists' Soc.* 1 (ii). 1913-15: 33-51.

Joass, J. 'Two days diggings in Sutherland', in *Proc. Soc. Antiq. Scot.* 5. 1862-64: 242-247.

Kendrick, J. 'Excavations at Douglasmuir, 1979-80', in D.W. Harding (ed) *Later Prehistoric Settlement in South-East Scotland*. 1982: 136-140.

Macgregor, M. *Early Celtic Art in North Britain*. 1976.

MacRitchie, D. *The Underground Life*. 1892.

MacRitchie, D. 'Earth-houses and their occupants', in *Proc. Soc. Antiq. Scot.* 51. 1916-17: 178-197.

Martin, M. *A Description of the Western Islands of Scotland*. 1716 (2nd edition).

Mathieson, J. 'Earth-house or galleried building near Durness, Sutherland', in *Proc. Soc. Antiq. Scot.* 59. 1924-25: 221-223.

Maxwell, G.S. 'Settlement in Southern Pictland: a new overview', in A. Small (ed) *The Picts: a New Look at Old Problems*. Dundee. 1987: 31-44.

Mitchell, A. 'Eirde house at Eriboll, in the parish of Durness, Sutherlandshire', in *Proc. Soc. Antiq. Scot.* 6. 1864-66: 249-250.

Mitchell, A. 'On some remarkable discoveries of rude stone implements in Shetland', in *Proc. Soc. Antiq. Scot.* 7. 1866-68: 118-122.

Morrison, A. & Reid, R.W.K. 'Fouhlin earth house', in *Discovery and Excavation in Scotland*. 1964: 51.

Morrison, A. & Reid, R.W.K. 'Fouhlin earth house', in *Discovery and Excavation in Scotland*. 1965: 39.

Munro, R. *Prehistoric Scotland*. 1899,

Pennant, T. *A Tour in Scotland*. 1774. 3rd edition, Warrington.

Pollock, R. 'Cyderhall Farm (Dornoch parish)', in *Discovery and Excavation in Scotland*. 1988: 17.

Pollock, R. 'The excavation of a souterrain and roundhouse at Cyderhall, Sutherland', in *Proc. Soc. Antiq. Scot.* 122. 1992: 149-160.

RCAHMS. *Inventory of the Historical Monuments in Sutherland*. 1911.

Ritchie, A. 'The archaeology of the Picts: some current problems', in J.G.P Friell & W.G. Watson (eds) *Pictish Studies*. B.A.R. 125. Oxford. 1984: 1-6.

Scott, L. 'Gallo-British colonies. The aisled round-house culture in the north', in *Proc. Prehist. Soc.* 14. 1948: 46-125.

Small, A., Cottam, M.B. & Dunbar, J.G. 'Souterrain and later structures at Northwaterbridge, Kincardineshire', in *Proc. Soc. Antiq. Scot.* 105. 1972-74: 293-296.

Stevenson, R.B.K. 'Metal-work and some other objects in Scotland and their cultural affinities', in A.L.F. Rivet (ed) *The Iron Age in Northern Britain*. 1966: 17-44.

Stuart, J. 'Report ... of a fund left by the late Mr. A. Henry Rhind, for excavating early remains', in *Proc. Soc. Antiq. Scot.* 7. 1866-68: 289-307.

Tait, L. 'Notes on the shell-mounds, hut-circles, and kist-vaens of Sutherland', in *Proc. Soc. Antiq. Scot.* 7. 1866-68: 525-532.

Thomas, C. 'Souterrains in the Irish Sea Province: a note', in C. Thomas (ed) *The Iron Age in the Irish Sea Province*. CBA. Research Report No. 9. 1972: 75-78.

Wainwright, F.T. 'Souterrains in Scotland', in *Antiquity*. 27. 1953: 219-232.

Wainwright, F.T. 'Houses and graves', in F.T. Wainwright (ed) *The Problem of the Picts.* 1955: 87-96.

Wainwright, F.T. *The Souterrains of Southern Pictland.* 1963.

Warner, R. 'The Irish souterrains and their background.', in H. Crawford (ed) *Subterranean Britain.* 1979: 100-144.

Watkins, T. 'Excavations of an Iron Age open settlement at Dalladies, Kincardineshire', in *Proc. Soc. Antiq. Scot.* 110. 1978-80: 122-164.

Watkins, T. 'Excavation of a settlement and souterrain at Newmill, near Bankfoot, Perthshire', in *Proc. Soc. Antiq. Scot.* 110. 1978-80: 165-208.

Watkins, T. 'Where were the Picts? An essay in settlement archaeology', in J.G.P. Friell & W.G. Watson (eds) *Pictish Studies.* B.A.R. 125. 1984: 63-86.

Welfare, H. 'The southern souterrains', in R. Miket & C. Burgess (eds) *Between and Beyond the Walls.* 1984: 305-323.

Welsh, T.C. 'Glen Leirag – structure', in *Discovery and Excavation in Scotland.* 1971: 46.

Wilson, D. *The Archaeology and Prehistoric Annals of Scotland.* 1851.

PALAEO-ENVIRONMENTAL HISTORY OF THE STRATHNAVER AREA OF SUTHERLAND: 0-12,000 BP

Jacqueline P. Huntley

INTRODUCTION

The area under discussion, although centred upon Strathnaver in Sutherland, includes material from both the east and west coasts of northern Scotland. The vegetation of the whole area of the extreme north of Scotland today relates to the physiognomy of the land [Fig. 11.1], and consists of three broad categories. Inland there are extensive tracts of heathland and moorland on essentially upland blanket peat; on the coast are nutrient-rich shell loams used for cultivation and grazing; and on the sides of some more sheltered valleys, a generally stunted birch woodland has developed. There is considerably more agriculture in the east, in Caithness, where the extensive flat land on the Caithness flags is particularly suitable for cultivation.

From the wide and varied archaeological sites and monuments present throughout the region, it is clear that people have been living here for many millennia. This paper seeks to discuss the different landscapes in which people have found themselves since the last Ice-Age, and to look at how their economies have been adapted to suit a particular environment.

That the plant communities seen today have developed as a result of both changing climate and human impact can be demonstrated using the techniques of pollen and macrofossil analyses. Pollen is produced by all plants as part of the reproductive process, and the pollen grains consist of complex proteins which are highly resistant to decay under anaerobic conditions. Thus, if they fall into a lake or on to the surface of a bog, they will be incorporated into the sediments and be preserved. In time these sediments build up, thus preserving the pollen evidence in the form of 'time capsules'. By taking a series of samples from different depths within these deposits, and identifying and analysing the pollen grains within them, a picture may be built up of the changing vegetation through time. It is fortunate that many plants produce pollen which can be identified to at least genus, if not species, although this is not true in all cases. A similar situation can occur with macrofossils such as fruits, seeds, leaves and even flowers. With the use of radiocarbon dating of the sediments or, indeed, individual seeds, 'real time' can be assigned to those sediments. The changes in composition of pollen types can then be discussed in years and related to, for example, archaeological sites with their typological dating.

Many plants have specific requirements for growth in terms of soil and climate, and many have climatic limits beyond which they will not grow. If

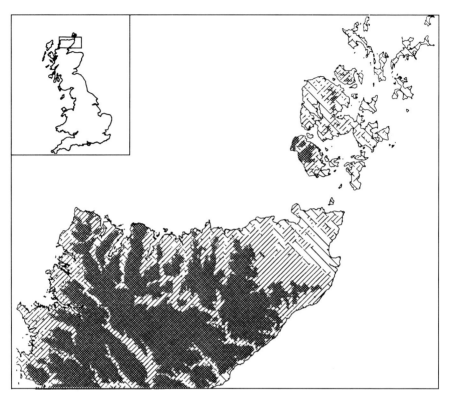

Fig. 11.1 Topography of northern Scotland: 0-50 m, 50-150 m and >150m OD shaded.

these are known from modern ecological work, as for example for *Tilia cordata* (Pigott & Huntley 1981), and assuming that they have not changed for the individual taxa over the millennia, then some inference of the climate may be gained by looking at the pollen spectra from specific deposits (eg Huntley & Prentice 1988). Inevitably, people also have had an effect upon the vegetation, and the traditional method of evaluating this in a pollen diagram has been to look at the so-called 'cultivation indicators' (Turner 1964; Behre 1981). These, however, include taxa growing naturally on coastal ground, such as shingle and sandy places, and therefore are not always reliable where such communities naturally occur, for example as at Freswick Bay, Caithness (Huntley 1995). Conclusive evidence of human impact includes the presence of cereal pollen grains, but unfortunately these rarely travel far from the site of growth/processing and therefore only occur in very low numbers in most pollen diagrams – which are generally prepared from peats/lake deposits at some distance from cultivated ground. Where the two are in close proximity, useful interpretations may be offered (Huntley *op. cit.*).

As has been mentioned, independent dating of the pollen-bearing sediments is important and radiocarbon is, perhaps, the most familiar. A relatively new method which is relevant to the northern Scottish material is that of tephrochronology – identifying tephra or volcanic ash layers in deposits, characterising their mineral composition and relating that to known volcanoes and dates of eruptions. For example, Hekla, on Iceland, produces such characteristic tephra that its ash has been identified in deposits from Altnabreac in Caithness (Dugmore 1989; Dugmore et al. 1992).

One of the interpretative problems with pollen is that of dispersal – by nature the grains are generally small and light and easily blown by the wind; wind pollination, therefore, is an important mechanism in the reproductive cycle of many taxa. Thus pollen grains may be found in a deposit, but the plants which produced those grains may be many miles away and from different plant communities altogether. By looking at macrofossils this problem can be alleviated somewhat, in that they are generally larger and fall close to the parent plant. In addition, material may be present on excavated archaeological sites that can be definitely attributed to human activity – cereal grains for instance.

These, then, are some of the lines of evidence used to reconstruct past vegetation and landuse. The following section applies those available to a discussion based upon the Strathnaver area.

THE EVIDENCE

Pollen diagrams are available for a series of sites in northern Scotland, from the east to the west coasts [Fig. 11.2]. Most have been used for the interpretation of vegetation generally rather than related to specific archaeological sites, although the Hill of Harley site in Caithness is an exception (Huntley 1995). Not all of the diagrams have independent dating associated with them, the authors rather infer dating from other, local, dated diagrams.

For each dated diagram, pollen values of selected taxa were extrapolated at 1,000 year intervals, calculated assuming a uniform sedimentation rate between radiocarbon dates. The cereal pollen curve was always used when present. Data for *Plantago lanceolata* (ribwort plantain), *P. major/media* (other plantains), *Chenopodiaceae* (oraches and fat hen), *Compositae* (daisy family), *Rumex acetosella* (sheep's sorrel), *R. acetosa* (sorrel), *Polygonum spp.* (knotweeds) and *Pteridium* (bracken) were defined as representing agriculture, although interpreted with caution (see above). The summary curve of trees/shrubs/herbs was used in the broad discussion of vegetational changes.

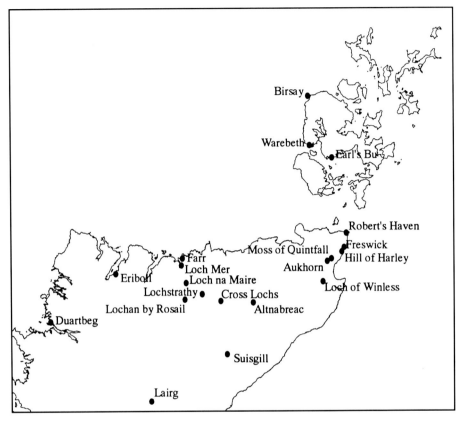

Fig. 11.2   Palynological and macrofossil sites in northern Scotland.

GENERAL DISCUSSION

Late-Glacial & Early Post-Glacial Vegetation (12,000-10,000 Years Ago)

The area was deglaciated by ca 12,500 years ago (Sissons 1974), although there was a further cold period ca 10,300 years ago during the Loch Lomond re-advance. Pollen evidence from two sites – Loch of Winless (Peglar 1979) and Sionascaig (Pennington 1972) – indicates a tundra-like vegetation; a predominantly treeless landscape with patches of *Salix* and *Juniperus* scrub. Interestingly, many of the taxa extracted as cultivation indicators are present throughout this period, although they simply indicate an open vegetation at this time. They reiterate the difficulties in interpretation of pollen data.

Holocene (10,000 Years Ago - Present)

Pollen & Charcoal

Essentially, the north-west was dominated by birch followed by birch-hazel woodland (Birks 1977) by ca 8,000 years ago. It is during this general period that several diagrams present peaks in charcoal fragments. These may reflect either natural fires, or fires started by humans in order either to clear ground for use or to drive animals towards a hunting trap.

Cross Lochs, Caithness (Charman 1992) has evidence of initial fire clearance of birch woodland at 7,500 BP. Subsequent to this, although increased values of *Sphagnum* spores indicate wetter conditions, further peaks in charcoal do occur and this would suggest human influence. There are, however, no clear indications of human activity. The difficulty here is envisaging what might indicate human activity, other than cereal pollen (eg Edwards, in Birks *et al.* 1988; Edwards & Ralston 1984). There is no evidence for early cultivation of cereals. Archaeological evidence is largely restricted to coastal sites which produce secure evidence for Mesolithic people (Edwards, in Bonsall 1990) and where marine resources of shellfish were exploited. However, remains of reindeer carcasses from the Inchnadamph Caves, dated to 8,300 BP, indicate that hunting parties travelled inland and on to the hills to procure meat. (For a review of the status of reindeer in Scotland, see Clutton-Brock & MacGregor 1988).

Throughout the mid-Holocene there was a general expansion in values of alder. This is a tree of wet ground, and would imply that the climate was becoming wetter; increased values of *Sphagnum* spores at several sites reinforce this. *Alnus* expanded in the west at places such as Eriboll (Birks 1977) and in the east at Loch of Winless (Peglar 1979) some 6,500 years or so ago, although birch-hazel woodland remained dominant in the central part at Loch Mer and Lochan by Rosail (Gear 1989). The alder expansion was then followed by steady deforestation, with the development of bog from 5,000 years ago. Values for sedge pollen and associated herbs rise drastically as a result.

This late-Holocene period is the one during which agricultural indicators appear in most dated diagrams for the region. *Plantago lanceolata* appears about 4,000 years ago at Sionascaig (Pennington 1972), Loch Mer (Gear 1989) and Hill of Harley, but not until about 3,000 years ago at Loch of Winless (Peglar 1979). Although plantain pollen grains become constant in occurrence at these time, their values always remain very low; *Chenopodiaceae* grains, also possibly representing agricultural clearances, appear at about same time, although occurrences remain sporadic. Cereal pollen is first recorded at ca 2,700 years ago at both Loch Mer and Loch of Winless. Individual cereal (barley-type) grains were recorded at Hill of Harley from about 5,000 years ago, with a continuous curve from about 2,000 to 1,200 years ago.

The pollen evidence thus shows essentially natural modifications due to changing climatic and edaphic conditions, from woodland to moorland, through the early and middle Holocene, with human effects showing for certain only in the last 5,000 years.

Macrofossils: Seeds, Fruits, Cereal Chaff Remains

Although pollen analytical work can give indications of the vegetation at both broad and narrow scales (ie regional and local to the sampled sites), it is appropriate macrofossils that can be directly tied to human activity. For example, evidence of diet has been obtained through studying fruits and seeds from several sites on Orkney, as at Warebeth Broch, Stromness (Bell & Dickson 1989), Brough of Birsay (Donaldson & Nye 1989) and Earl's Bu at Orphir (Huntley (a) *in prep.*).

At Warebeth, Dickson identified barley and linseed fragments from a coprolite, and suggested that they had been cooked for a long time, probably simmering with meat. Dating of a cattle bone from this site indicated an Iron Age occupation. Brough of Birsay and Earl's Bu produced large numbers of burnt hulled barley and oat grains, as well as linseed. Both of these sites are broadly Norse to early Medieval. On the Scottish mainland, very few sites in the north have been sampled for carbonised or, indeed, other plant remains. Freswick Links (Huntley 1992, 1995) produced large numbers of hulled barley and oats, and a small amount of wheat and flax. The material was dated from the Pictish to early Medieval periods, but there were no significant differences in the proportions of grain between these times. Pollen analytical work was also carried out near to this site and demonstrated little evidence for the cultivation of cereals, other than a small peak of barley-type pollen dated to the Pictish period. It was suggested that limited cultivation had taken place at the earlier periods of occupation, but that the site was served mainly by trading with other areas during the Norse period. Macrofossil analysis of material from Robert's Haven (Huntley (b) *in prep.*) is producing similar evidence.

Flax seeds have been reported from a number of sites on the Orkney Islands, and it has been suggested that these seeds do, in fact, represent local cultivation (Bond & Hunter 1987). Such a crop could have been used for production of fibre (linen) or oil (linseed), or indeed both.

There is very limited evidence for legumes – Celtic bean and pea – but this may be under-represented since these crops do not require contact with fire at any stage of processing, unlike many cereals which need to be dried before storing.

The earlier site at Suisgill, Helmsdale – dated from early to mid first millennium BC – produced predominantly naked 6-row barley, a little hulled 6-row oats and hexaploid wheat (van der Veen, in Barclay 1985). Little or no chaff, the straw or ear fragments, were recovered and she therefore considered that the site was possibly a consumer site, although the sampling was not extensive and this could have led to biased results. Pollen data from nearby suggest an essentially open birch-pine woodland with heathland. Cultivation in small fields may not, therefore, be represented in the pollen record.

For the medieval and later periods there may be documentary evidence – for example of the clearances – but, to the author's knowledge, no palynological nor macrobotanical work has been carried out upon material from these periods with the express intention of looking at human impact upon the landscape.

SUMMARY

After the retreat of the ice, most of the area of northern Scotland was covered by a tundra-like vegetation consisting of an essentially treeless landscape, perhaps with small patches of juniper and willow scrub developing with time.

Archaeological evidence for Mesolithic activity is restricted largely to coastal sites where marine resources of shellfish were exploited and with parties moving inland to hunt the larger mammals. There is no evidence for early cultivation of cereals. As the climate became warmer, birch and hazel scrub woodland developed, as did pine woodland in suitable places. In the central and eastern part of the region the pine woodland was a short-lived episode, with the trees declining for edaphic (probably climatically-induced) reasons since there seems to have been a general increase in wetness – possibly as a result, at least in part, of ash clouds. Peats developed over much of the area, and these were too wet and too acidic to cultivate. The coastal strips, therefore, were further exploited. The soils derived from glacial drift and coastal sands were most suitable for cultivating cereals and other crops, as well as for pasturage; and the people remained close to the sea for fishing.

It is interesting that Loch Mer, Loch of Winless and Hill of Harley are the only sites with cereal pollen. This is considered a genuine lack of cereal pollen and not an artefact of either choice of pollen site (being too far from the cereal pollen source) or interest of analyst (not separating cereal pollen from other *Gramineae* types). These two sites reinforce the notion that the east of the region, and the northern coastal strip, remained best suited for arable cultivation. The hills remained primarily as hunting grounds. Finally, in modern times, there were massive clearances of agricultural communities from inland areas in order that sheep could be raised on the hills and, as a consequence, people were restricted even more to the coast.

People have exploited the landscape as and when they could, but the area has always been marginal with respect to cereals. To study the landscape and people in more detail requires that archaeologists and palaeobotanists work more closely together, as at Freswick and Lairg (McCullagh & Tipping 1998). Such work is producing a framework for the east of northern Scotland, but the west remains enigmatic. In addition to the two disciplines working together, fine spatial and temporal resolution palynological work is essential to fine-tune what are, at the moment, simply broad hints as to changing agricultural practices.

References

Barclay, G.J. 'Excavations at Upper Suisgill, Sutherland', in *Proc. Soc. Antiq. Scot.* 115. 1985: 159-198.

Behre, K-E. 'The interpretation of anthropogenic indicators in pollen diagram', in *Pollen et Spores* 23. 1981: 225-245.

Bell, B. & Dickson, C. 'Excavations at Warebeth (Stromness Cemetery) Broch, Orkney', in *Proc. Soc. Antiq. Scot.* 119. 1989: 101-131.

Birks, H.H. 'Studies in the vegetational history of Scotland. III. A radiocarbon-dated pollen diagram from Loch Maree, Ross and Cromarty', in *New Phytol.* 71. 1972: 731 et seq.

Birks, H.J.B. 'Flandrian forest history of Scotland: a preliminary synthesis', in F.W. Shotton (ed) *British Quaternary Studies Recent Advances.* Oxford. 1977.

Birks, H.J.B. 'Long-term ecological change in the uplands', in M.B. Usher & D.B.A. Thompson (eds) *Ecological change in the Uplands.* Special publication 7. B.E.S. Oxford. 1988.

Bond, J.M. & Hunter, J.R. 'Flax-growing in Orkney from the Norse period to the 18th century', in *Proc. Soc. Antiq. Scot.* 117. 1987:175-181.

Charman, D.J. 'Blanket mire formation at the Cross Lochs, Sutherland, northern Scotland', in *Boreas* 21. 1982: 53-72.

Clutton-Brock, J. & MacGregor, A. 'An end to medieval reindeer in Scotland', in *Proc. Soc. Antiq. Scot.* 118. 1988: 23-35.

Donaldson, A.M. & Nye, S., in C.D. Morris (ed) *The Birsay Bay Project Volume 1: Coastal sites beside the Brough Road, Birsay, Orkney Excavations 1976-1982.* University of Durham, Department of Archaeology. Monograph series number 1. 1989.

Dugmore, A.J. 'Icelandic volcanic ash in Scotland', in *Scottish Geographical Magazine* 105 (3). 1989: 168-172.

Dugmore, A.J., Newton, A.J. & Sugden, D.E. 'Geochemical stability of fine-grained silicic Holocene tephra in Iceland and Scotland', in *Journal of Quaternary Science* 7 (2). 1992: 173-183.

Durno, S.E. 'Certain aspects of the vegetational history in north-east Scotland', in *Scottish Geographical Magazine* 73 (3). 1957: 176-184.

Durno, S.E. 'Pollen analysis of peat deposits in eastern Sutherland and Caithness', in *Scottish Geographical Magazine* 74. 1958: 127 et seq.

Edwards, J. 'The hunter-gatherer/agricultural transition and the pollen record in the British Isles', in H.H. Birks, H.J.B. Birks, P.E. Kaland & D Moe (eds) *The Cultural Landscape – Past, Present and Future.* Oxford. 1988: 225-266.

Edwards, K.J. & Ralston, I. 'Postglacial hunter-gatherers and vegetational history in Scotland', in *Proc. Soc. Antiq. Scot.* 114. 1984: 15-34.

Gear A.J. *Holocene vegetation history and the palaeoecology of Pinus sylvestris in northern Scotland.* Unpublished PhD thesis, University of Durham. 1989.

Huntley, B. & Prentice I.C. 'July temperature in Europe from pollen data, 6000 years before present', in *Science* 241. 1988: 687-690.

Huntley, J.P. 'Carbonised plant remains', in C.D. Morris & D.J. Rackham (eds) *Excavations at Freswick Links, Caithness, 1980-1982*: 1992: 76-84; 'Environmental column samples from the cliff-side', in C.D. Morris & D.J. Rackham (eds) *Norse and later settlement and subsistence in the North Atlantic.* Dept of Archaeology, University of Glasgow. 1992: 43-102.

Huntley, J.P. 'Section 1.3: Pollen analytical investigations' pp 8-16; 'Section 11.7: Carbonised plant remains' pp 220-224; fiche 8 C9-E4, in C.D. Morris, C.E. Batey & D.J. Rackham (eds) *Freswick Links, Caithness: excavation and survey of a Norse settlement in Caithness.* Inverness/New York. NABO/Allan Sutton. 1995.

Huntley, J.P. (in prep. a) *Carbonised plant remains from Earl's Bu, Orphir, Orkney.* Unpublished Archive Report.

Huntley, J.P. (in prep. b) *Carbonised plant remains from Robert's Haven.* Unpublished Archive Report.

McCullagh, R.P.J. & Tipping, R. *The Lairg Project 1988-1996. The Evolution of an Archaeological Landscape in Northern Scotland.* Scottish Trust for Archaeological Research Monograph no. 3. Edinburgh 1998.

Moar, N.T. 'A radiocarbon dated pollen diagram from north-west Scotland', in *New Phytol.* 68. 1969: 201-208.

Morris, C.D. (ed) *The Birsay Bay Project Volume 1: Coastal sites beside the Brough Road, Birsay, Orkney Excavations 1976-1982.* University of Durham, Department of Archaeology. Monograph series number 1. 1989.

Peglar, S.M. 'A radiocarbon-dated pollen diagram from Loch of Winless, Caithness, north-east Scotland', in *New Phytol.* 82. 1979: 245-263.

Pennington, W., Haworth, E.Y., Bonny, A.P. & Lishman, J.P. 'Lake sediments in northern Scotland', in *Phil. Trans. Roy. Soc.* B. 264. 1972: 191-294.

Pigott, C.D. & Huntley, J.P. 'Factors controlling the distribution of *Tilia cordata* at the northern limits of its geographical range. III. Nature and causes of seed sterility', in *New Phytol.* 87. 1981: 817-839.

Robinson, D. 'Investigations into the Aukhorn peat mounds, Keiss, Caithness: pollen, plant macrofossil and charcoal analyses', in *New Phytol.* 106. 1987: 185-200.

Shotton, F.W. *British Quaternary Studies: Recent Advances.* Oxford. 1977.

Sissons, J.B. 'The Quaternary in Scotland: a review', in *Scot. J. Geol.* 10(4). 1974: 311-337.

Turner, J. 'The anthropogenic factor in vegetation history', in *New Phytol.* 63. 1964: 73-89.

Illustrations

Cover   Harvesting seaweed in Loch Laxford, 1973 (John Baldwin)
p. vi   Bettyhill crofts and Torrisdale Bay, ca 1930 (RCAHMS).
p. viii   Crofts at Achina at the mouth of the River Naver, ca 1930 (RCAHMS).
p. x   Map of Sutherland Parishes (Douglas Lawson, adapted).
p. xii   Broch at Baile Mhargaite, Invernaver. Sketches by J. Horsburgh, 1867 (RCAHMS).
p. xiii   Pictish stones at Sandside, 1991 (T.E. Gray) and Golspie, 1987 (RCAHMS).
p. xiv   Pictish cross-slabs at Reay and Clachan, Bettyhill, 1991 (T.E. Gray).
p. xiv   Cross-slabs from Grumbeg, Strathnaver, 1991 (T.E. Gray).
p. xviii   Harbour at Port Skerra, Melvich, 1974 (John Hume).
p. xviii   Lime kilns at Ard Neackie, Loch Eriboll, 1983 (RCAHMS).
p. xix   Steading at Tongue Mains, 1974 (John Hume).
p. xix   Pulpit in Farr Church, Bettyhill, 1985 (Joanna Close-Brooks).
p. 100   Harbour at Port Vasgo, Melness, 1974 (John Hume).
p. 142   Durness, ca 1886. Erskine Beveridge (RCAHMS).
p. 194   Harvesting near Bettyhill (Jim A. Johnston).
p. 236   Peat-cutting in north Sutherland (Jim A. Johnston).
p. 246   Mechanised peat-cutting, northern Sutherland (Jim A. Johnston).
Cover   Tarbet, with the portage across to Loch Laxford, 1973 (John Baldwin)

CONTRIBUTORS

JOHN R. BALDWIN, formerly an educational adviser with Lothian Region, has research interests in Scottish material culture and now tutors part-time for the Centre for Continuing Education, University of Edinburgh.

MALCOLM BANGOR-JONES, a policy officer attached to Historic Scotland in Edinburgh, researches into estate and family papers relating to northern Scotland.

COLLEEN BATEY is Curator of Archaeology, Glasgow Museums, and has particular interests in the Scandinavian period.

ELIZABETH BEATON, formerly Assistant Inspector in northern Scotland for Historic Scotland, lives in Moray and maintains interests in rural and coastal buildings.

MARY BEITH, a freelance writer living in Melness, Sutherland, researches widely into Highland medical and domestic traditions.

BARBARA E. CRAWFORD is Lecturer in Medieval History, University of St Andrews, with major research interests in Scandinavian Scotland.

LAURENCE GOURIÉVIDIS, a former lecturer in Scottish History, University of St Andrews, now lectures in British History at the University of Clermont Ferrand II, France.

ROBERT GOURLAY was archaeologist for the former Highland Regional Council, Inverness.

JACQUELINE P. HUNTLEY, North-East Regional Adviser in Archaeological Science for English Heritage, is based in the Department of Archaeology, University of Durham.

DOROTHY M. LOW is an archaeologist working with The Highland Council, Inverness.

R.P.J. MCCULLAGH, formerly Senior Field Archaeologist with AOC (Scotland) Ltd., is now an Inspector of Ancient Monuments with Historic Scotland, Edinburgh.

ALEX. MORRISON is Senior Research Fellow in the Department of Archaeology, University of Glasgow.

W.P.L. THOMSON, formerly Rector of Kirkwall Grammar School, lives on Burray and continues to research widely into Orcadian history.

DOREEN WAUGH, Assistant Headteacher at The Mary Erskine School, Edinburgh, is a place-name specialist with particular interests in Norse names.

THE SCOTTISH SOCIETY FOR NORTHERN STUDIES
is a Scottish-based group having much in common with the Viking Society for Northern Research. It was founded in 1968 to explore the inter-relationships between the Scandinavian, Celtic and Scottish cultures, and provides a forum in Scotland for specialists and enthusiasts of many disciplines to pursue their common 'northern' interests. Through its seminars, conferences and publications, the Scottish Society for Northern Studies seeks to encourage further exploration and research, locally throughout Scotland and beyond.

PUBLICATIONS
1. *Scandinavian Shetland: An Ongoing Tradition?* 1978.
   (ISBN 0 9505994 0 9)   (out-of-print)
2. *Caithness: A Cultural Crossroads.* 1982.
   (ISBN 0 9505994 1 7)   (out-of-print)
3. *The Scandinavians in Cumbria.* 1985.
   (ISBN 0 9505994 2 5)   (out-of-print)
4. *Firthlands of Ross and Sutherland.* 1986.
   (ISBN 0 9505994 4 1)
5. *Galloway: Land and Lordship.* 1991.
   (ISBN 0 9505994 6 8)
6. *Moray: Province and People.* 1993.
   (ISBN 0 9505994 7 6)
7. *Peoples and Settlement in North-West Ross.* 1994.
   (ISBN 0 9505994 8 4)
8. *Shetland's Northern Links: Language and History.* 1996.
   (ISBN 0 9505994 9 2)
9. *The Province of Strathnaver.* 2000.
   (ISBN 0 9535226 0 1)

FORTHCOMING
10. Orkney

Contributions to the Manx Conference appeared in *Man and Environment in the Isle of Man* (BAR British Series 54. 1978. 2 vols.)
(ISBN 0 86054 034 0)

The Society also publishes a regular journal, *Northern Studies.*
(ISSN 0305 506X)

FURTHER INFORMATION, and details of membership of the Scottish Society for Northern Studies, may be obtained from:
   The Scottish Society for Northern Studies
   c/o School of Scottish Studies
   University of Edinburgh
   27 George Square
   Edinburgh EH8 9LD   Scotland